THE DZOGCHEN PRIMER

The
Dzogchen Primer

Embracing the Spiritual Path
According to the Great Perfection

Compiled and edited by
MARCIA BINDER SCHMIDT

Introductory teachings by
CHÖKYI NYIMA RINPOCHE
and
DRUBWANG TSOKNYI RINPOCHE

SHAMBHALA
Boston & London
2002

SHAMBHALA PUBLICATIONS, INC.
Horticultural Hall
300 Massachusetts Avenue
Boston, Massachusetts 02115
www.shambhala.com

9   8   7   6   5   4   3   2   1

First Edition
Printed in the United States of America

⊚ This edition is printed on acid-free paper that meets the
American National Standards Institute z39.48 Standard.
Distributed in the United States by Random House, Inc.,
and in Canada by Random House of Canada Ltd

Library of Congress Cataloging-in-Publication Data
Schmidt, Marcia Binder.
The Dzogchen primer: an anthology of writings by masters of
the great perfection: foreword, introductory teachings by
Chèokyi Nyima Rinpoche and Drubwang Tsoknyi Rinpoche /
compiled and edited by Marcia Binder Schmidt.—1st ed.
p.   cm.
Includes bibliographical references.
ISBN 1-57062-829-7 (alk. paper)
1. Rdzogs-chen (Räniçn-ma-pa)   I. Title.
BQ7662.4 .S34   2002
294.3'420423—dc21
2002004532

*Not only the Dharma should be Dzogchen;
the individual should be Dzogchen as well.*

—KYABJE TRULSHIG RINPOCHE

CONTENTS

PREFACE

The Dzogchen Primer offers a joyful way to access the traditional principles of Tibetan Buddhism. It is a guidebook on how to study, contemplate, and meditate in a supportive environment abundant in rich material and practices. Here is a definitive map showing where practitioners of this path are going and how to get there. *The Primer* includes the basics for proper understanding and practice—a source anyone on this path can turn to for guidance.

These days there is a strong interest in the Vajrayana, especially the Dzogchen and Mahamudra teachings. As Tulku Urgyen Rinpoche says, "During this age, the Vajrayana teachings blaze like the flames of a wildfire. Just as the flames of negative emotions flare up, so do the teachings. During the Age of Strife, it seems as though people are seldom amiable; rather, they are always trying to outdo one another. This fundamental competitiveness has given rise to the name Age of Strife. But this is exactly the reason that Vajrayana is so applicable to the present era. The stronger and more forceful the disturbing emotions are, the greater the potential for recognizing our original wakefulness. Thus, the vast amount of conflict in the world today is precisely why the Vajrayana teachings will spread like wildfire."[1]

The Primer provides a much-needed corrective to the many misconceptions and wrong views being promoted about Dzogchen—and there are many. One of the most serious obstacles that can confront practitioners is the entertainment of wrong views. Unless we study, we will not know how to differentiate between what is correct and what is incorrect. Study does not have to mean the extensive program of a Tibetan *shedra*. Here, study is presented in the *kusulu* fashion, the style of a simple meditator.

"The causal and resultant vehicles—Hinayana, Mahayana, and

Vajrayana—differ in what they regard as path. In particular, to actually apply Vajrayana in practice, there are three different approaches: taking the ground as path, taking the path as path, and taking the fruition as path. These three approaches can be understood by using the analogy of a gardener or farmer. Taking the ground or cause as path is like tilling soil and sowing seeds. Taking the path as path is like weeding, watering, fertilizing, and coaxing crops forth. Taking the fruition as path is the attitude of simply picking the ripened fruit or the fully bloomed flowers. To do this, to take the complete result, the state of enlightenment itself, as the path, is the approach of Dzogchen. This summarizes the intent of the Great Perfection."[2]

So, here we are, practitioners in the Age of Strife, replete with inner and outer conflicts, who are described further as being extremely sharp but extremely lazy. It is only natural that we, materialistic seekers of objects of high quality, would be drawn to the pinnacle of vehicles. Lacking in diligence, we are attracted to what is the least complex and most unelaborated.

Unfortunately, gaining the right understanding is not that easy. It is extremely important not to oversimplify and lose sight of the true meaning. Although Padmasambhava gave us these custom-made teachings, designated for our particular times and temperament (the beauty of Hidden Treasures), we need the proper conditions to connect with them. These include the presence of a fully realized teacher and qualified lineage holder, as well as our own circumstances of being born at the right time and place with the right frame of mind.

The right frame of mind means that we trust and appreciate the teachings and the teachers and have devotion and pure perception. Likewise, it is fundamental that we aspire to put these teachings into practice for the benefit of the countless other less fortunate beings of the dark age who lack the opportunity to meet the teachers and the teachings. The Dharma needs to be practiced. Teachings—no matter how high or lofty—have little value for the individual who does not apply them.

As Sogyal Rinpoche states, "Whichever way the training is tailored, from the traditional point of view, there must be a solid grounding in the basic Dharma teaching. The main points, the heart of the teaching, must be instilled in the student's mind so that he or she will never forget them. For example: refraining from harm, the crux of the Fundamental Vehicle; developing Good Heart, the essence of the Mahayana; and pure perception, the heart of the Vajrayana."[3]

The Dzogchen Primer offers a way to acquire the correct grounding

as well as the confidence that we can continue on the path to enlightenment. Not only do we need to study; we need to integrate the teachings
into our beings. This integration is twofold. It is important not to separate the spiritual, or absolute truth, from our ordinary mundane experiences, or relative truth. We need to bring all circumstances onto the path
and maintain our dharmic perspective as much as possible. Also, it is
crucial to be truly convinced that we can eventually benefit beings and
reach accomplishment. Unless we gain certainty in our own inherent
nature, we might not trust that we can reach realization. Like enlightened beings, we embody the basic material for buddhahood, the buddha
nature. We need to cut the net of doubts that surrounds us. Yes, we are
in a compromised state now; we are obscured, but this is only temporary. We can purify our obscurations through the various practices.
These teachings show us how to unfold the view "from the top" while
ascending the path from below. *The Primer* thus allows readers to share
in this profound approach at any point on the Vajrayana path. All the
pieces in this book are pith instructions from qualified masters.

The *Primer* draws on the teachings of some of the greatest masters
of Dzogchen and Mahamudra (see the list of contributors at the end of
the book). In particular, Tulku Urgyen Rinpoche and his sons Chökyi
Nyima Rinpoche and Tsoknyi Rinpoche have a distinctive teaching style
in common, widely known for its unique directness in introducing students to the nature of mind in a way that allows immediate experience.

As mentioned briefly earlier, traditionally in Tibetan Buddhism there
are two main approaches, the analytical approach of a scholar and the
resting practice of a simple meditator, a kusulu. Through either of these,
or through a combination, it is possible to establish with certainty the
natural state of all things. The ultimate result of the scholarly approach
is to go *beyond* analysis. So, depending on our temperament, we will be
drawn to one style or the other.

To quote Chökyi Nyima Rinpoche:

There are some people who can trust a master and be introduced
to the natural state without using any lengthy explanations. They
do not need to establish the meaning through reasoning or through
quotes from scriptures. Maybe they are not interested; maybe they
"have no need." It is possible for them to understand simply and
directly. There are other people for whom that is not enough. Then
it is necessary to use quotes from the scriptures and intelligent reasoning to establish certainty in the view.

According to the analytical meditation, everything is examined, until the scholar has run out of analysis. That is the point of arriving at the understanding of the true view, intellectually. After that, he still needs to receive the blessings of a qualified master and to receive the pointing-out instruction from such a master.[4]

What this book emphasizes is a combination of these two approaches. The buddhas' words are not valid and correct merely because we are Buddhists and accept them on blind faith. They are true because they describe the nature of how things are, whether we are Buddhists or not. One vital way that that truth can be logically arrived at is through reasoning and study. Moreover, after studying the teachings, we blend them into our being by applying them in practice. Then through our own personal experience we come to know that there is no contradiction in what we have learned and what we have assimilated and understood. From another angle, study clears away doubts and uncertainties that may arise in our practice. In short, we combine the three perfect measures of the words of the Buddha and the great masters with our own individual intelligence. This is absolutely crucial for the skeptical Western mind.

My own experience is different from that of most people living in the West. I have spent over twenty years living closely with realized teachers and extraordinary practitioners in Nepal. With my own eyes, I have seen the value of the tradition borne out by the result that practice and study can bring. Even gifted individuals, like recognized reincarnations of enlightened masters, still undergo years of study and training. The result of this discipline is the many great younger teachers we can meet these days. But this fruition can be seen not only in *tulku*s, who we might believe begin with a higher potential than ordinary beings. I have watched many other practitioners nurtured by this tradition go on to develop into impressive individuals who benefit whomever they encounter.

When it comes to practice itself, the approach is to unfurl the view from the top like a canopy and ascend with the conduct from the bottom. "Conduct" here refers to the various applications of the methods of Vajrayana, used as the ladder to climb to the top. Here is Tulku Urgyen Rinpoche's explanation of this style—his own style, in fact:

According to the traditional method of Tibetan Buddhism, the student begins practice with the four or five times 100,000 preliminaries in the proper, correct manner. Then he or she proceeds on to the yidam practice with its development stage, recitation, and completion stage. After that, the student is introduced to the true view of

Mahamudra and Dzogchen. The sequence is conventionally laid out in this order: first you remove what obscures you; next, you suffuse your being with blessings; finally, you are introduced to the natural face of awareness.

These days, however, disciples do not have so much time! Also, masters do not seem to stay in one place and teach continuously. The view and the conduct need to be adapted to the time and circumstances. In the world now, there is a growing appreciation of and interest in Buddhism. This is because people are more educated, more intelligent. When masters and disciples do not have a lot of time to spend together, there is no opportunity to go through the whole sequence of instructions. I usually also give the whole set of teachings in completeness, all at once.

This approach, of giving the essence at the beginning and then later teaching *ngöndro*, development stage, mantra recitation, and completion stage, can be compared to opening the door all the way from the start. When you open the door, the daylight penetrates all the way in so, while standing at the door, you can see to the innermost part of the shrine room.

Honestly, if one has received the teachings on mind essence and then practices the preliminaries while remembering to recognize the nature of mind, it multiplies the effect tremendously. It is taught that to practice with a pure attitude multiplies the effect 100 times, while to practice with pure samadhi multiplies the effect 100,000 times. Combine the preliminaries with the recognition of mind essence and your practice will be tremendously effective.

You could also practice the preliminaries with simply a good and sincere attitude, and this alone will definitely purify your negative karma. But a good attitude in itself does not suffice as the true path to enlightenment. If you embrace these practices with the correct view of recognizing mind essence, however, the preliminaries become the actual path to enlightenment. If you have a painting of a candle, can it somehow generate light in the room? Wouldn't it be better to have the actual candle flame spreading light? There is only one way to be free from the threefold concepts, and that is to recognize the true view. I do not feel there is anything inappropriate in giving the pointing-out instruction to people. They can practice the preliminaries afterwards. It is perfectly fine.[5]

In particular, *The Dzogchen Primer* begins with instilling confidence in ourselves. We can attain buddhahood because we already possess the potential, the buddha nature, which is the powerful starting point addressed in part 2. But how do we know from the outset that buddha nature is intrinsic to our being? As Tsoknyi Rinpoche has said, "It is substantiated without us ever having to be told, without us having to be indoctrinated, influenced, or conditioned to the idea that we have buddha nature, the capacity for enlightenment. That is because everyone has the spontaneous quality sometimes, of being free in one's state of mind, of being insightful, bright, clear, wide open, which doesn't come from anywhere, other than within ourselves. These are all proofs that we have the ability to be fully free, awakened or a buddha and is why we can be enlightened."[6] Moreover, that we feel love, kindness and compassion, and the wish to be a spiritual person are all additional indications of buddha nature. Accepting the potential and revealing the methods to recognize and stabilize that recognition was Tulku Urgyen Rinpoche's way. It is also the basis for the arrangement of great texts such as *The Light of Wisdom* and *The Jewel Ornament of Liberation*.

The fruition is present at the time of the ground, only it is not yet actualized. All the various practices offered in part 3, Integration, are done to unify ground and fruition. There is no separate path, nothing else to blend with, nothing other than this.

To reiterate, *The Primer* combines study and practice from the approach of both the simple meditator and the simple scholar. Stylistically, it unfolds this according to the teaching method of Tulku Urgyen Rinpoche and the two above-mentioned texts. Practically, it includes pieces that support this tradition and are simple, direct, profound, and easy to comprehend.

The idea for *The Dzogchen Primer* originated after many years of organizing seminars as well as translating and sitting in on private interviews with qualified masters. Being familiar with my fellow students' recurring questions, problems, and misunderstandings, I decided to devise a study and practice program that was easy to undertake and comprehend and that closely followed the teaching method of my teacher, Tulku Urgyen Rinpoche. This uncomplicated plan for study and practice is tailored for working Sangha who might not be able to commit to a time-consuming study program but still want to delve into the Dzogchen teachings. This first volume, *The Dzogchen Primer*, covers material for the first year of the program, based on *The Light of Wisdom*, *The Jewel Ornament of Liberation*, and, in the style of Tulku Urgyen Rinpoche, the Four Dharmas of Gampopa, a complete path for enlightenment within itself.

The first of the Four Dharmas, "How to turn one's mind toward Dharma practice," includes the *four mind-changings*. "How to ensure that one's Dharma practice becomes the path" embodies teachings on the preliminary practices. "How to make the path clarify confusion" contains teachings on development stage, recitation, and completion stage. Finally, "How to let confusion dawn as wisdom" comprises teachings on how to gain certainty, realization of the natural state by means of the three great views of Dzogchen, *Mahamudra,* and *Madhyamika.*

This volume encompasses the first of the Four Dharmas and part of the second. The two subsequent volumes will continue from the second Dharma through to the end of the fourth Dharma. The material and program connected to them include advice for deity practice and conceptual and nonconceptual meditation, among other things.

The Dzogchen Primer can be used by beginning students as well as longtime practitioners who serve as teachers at their local Dharma centers. These facilitators can use it as a veritable textbook for their students, an accessible sourcebook. Newer students will be able to find, in a single source, a complete outline of the entire path as well as in-depth explanations of each part of that path, along with ways to apply these teachings to their own practice. The facilitator guidelines at the end of the book provide an outline for further reading to support group discussions of chapters. The book adapts the presentation of the Dzogchen path for the modern student, while using traditional principles; among key topics, for example, are renunciation, compassion, devotion, and recognizing mind nature.

Moreover, *The Primer* can serve as a support for students who do not have a teacher or a center close by, to help them carry on in the right direction. It provides background material to use for inspiration and encouragement. However, a book can never substitute for meeting genuine, realized lineage masters of the Dzogchen and Mahamudra traditions. It is crucial that students include in their programs time to participate in important teachings and retreats with such masters.

To conclude, I would like to quote Sogyal Rinpoche once more: "The future of humanity is linked to the accessibility of spiritual teachings like the Buddha Dharma. This, I think, by any analysis, is clear, and it is the practicality and ingenuity of the West that can make the Dharma more accessible. There is an almost desperate hunger and need, in countries like America, for spiritual vision. I feel that the Buddha Dharma can play a great part in answering this need for all kinds of people, and in building a spiritual culture here in the West."[7]

MARCIA BINDER SCHMIDT
Nagi Gompa

ACKNOWLEDGMENTS

Sincere gratitude goes to Chökyi Nyima Rinpoche, who gave essential points to adhere to, and to Drubwang Tsoknyi Rinpoche, who helped chart the course from the beginning and conscientiously examined the manuscript to prevent any mistakes. Moreover, many thanks to my husband, Erik Pema Kunsang, the translator of many of these pieces, who coached on difficult points as well as supplied needed material, and to Stephen Goodman, who infused this project with his remarkable enthusiasm. Special mention must go to Michael Tweed, who transcribed and edited the two introductions, looked over the manuscript, and gave many helpful suggestions. Of course, this book would not have come into being without the skillful staff at Shambhala Publications.

May this work be a contributing cause for the many hidden Dzogchen yogis in the West to advance further on the path, to reach accomplishment, and to benefit countless beings!

THE DZOGCHEN PRIMER

PART ONE

INTRODUCTORY TEACHINGS

INTRODUCTION

Chökyi Nyima Rinpoche

One of our main tasks as human beings is to seek and to discover what is real and true. We must use intelligence as our main tool and sound reason as the verifier. That is all we have at this point. However, as we go about deepening our understanding, we still carry one problem with us: this mind that reasons so intelligently is still basically confused. Therefore, every "insight" is saturated by confusion. I am sorry to say it so bluntly, but human understanding is confused. It is not unmistaken wisdom, and it is not authentic until complete enlightenment. Can we admit that we are not yet enlightened?

The awakened state of a buddha is one of perceiving clearly, distinctly, and completely the nature of things and all that exists. It is a wisdom that knows things as they are without confusion, without distortion. This is why we ordinary human beings cannnot avoid seeking support in the words and teachings of a buddha.

These days we find a variety of religions, belief systems, and schools of thought; I am not sure why this is, but I believe that it is an expression of people's individual karma and past inclinations. Most spiritual people regard the Buddha as a wise teacher and proponent of peace. Some place the Buddha on the same level as the founder of their own religion, some lower. It is natural to feel that "my philosophy, my religion, is the truest. The words our founder spoke are the most sublime, the clearest picture of reality." It is human nature to believe that what we have is the best. Often, because of such belief, people tend to regard everyone else's view or spiritual path as dead wrong and leading them astray. So, as we find ourselves in this diverse global society there is no point, when addressing the public, to begin by saying, "Our Buddha, and only our Buddha, is right and true!"

To be honest, the self-supporting trait of human nature is nothing new; it has always been like this. That is why the tradition of Buddhist studies has always placed emphasis on testing the validity of the Buddha's words and the statements of later masters by means of intelligent reasoning. The intellect uses logic to create a reliable support.

In recent centuries, there has been an ascendancy in philosophical views that emphasize material reality; these include modern science. Inventiveness, in terms of products and technologies, is glorified. Similarly, we see that new ways of thinking that distance themselves from the past have become popular and are applauded. Contemporary society seems to be fascinated with novelty. Anyone who can come up with something new that has never been seen before—a new perspective, a new way of thinking—automatically becomes the founding father of a new "religion." Isn't it true that schoolchildren are taught that Albert Einstein was a fabulous genius, the founder of a new way?

Today we see a heightened interest in the Buddha's teachings throughout the world; there is a lot of contact between people of various backgrounds and the traditional teachings of the Buddha. It is my impression that Westerners who are new to Buddhism often feel more comfortable with a teacher who is well versed in psychology or science—even one who has only a cursory understanding of what the Buddha taught—than with a well-educated Buddhist master. This is understandable considering their upbringing.

Someone who teaches Buddhism while downplaying the Buddha and what he taught is received with open arms and tends to become quite popular, respected and regarded as an authority. Also, for instance, someone who expediently says, "Bowing down is useless" receives immediate applause. "There is no need to do *ngöndro*, the preliminary practices. It's just a Tibetan cultural artifact"—louder applause. It is human nature to prefer ease and dislike hardship, and catering to this attitude will always be popular. Those who want to adapt their teachings to people's weaknesses and brand it "Buddhism" will likely become popular leaders of a new movement. New followers will exclaim, "Your style is so free and open—I like it!"

I cannot, at present, say whether this is good or evil; it is merely an observation. Just the same, if you are concerned with a Buddhism of authentic value, I would suggest that we give center stage to the Buddha surrounded by the great masters of the lineage, the learned and accomplished masters of India and Tibet. Actually, I consider this of vital importance for the future of the Dharma.

I know that the new is often preferred over the old. This is reflected in the fact that publishing books on Buddhism that present translations of the words of former masters is not regarded as that praiseworthy. Rather, if one of you were to rewrite a classic treatise in your own words or make a comparative study to show conflict or harmony between scholars, such a book would be regarded as special.

My main point is that the original words of the Buddha are very important.

In relation to the above, it is a fact that Marcia and Erik Schmidt have worked with me for many years, and we have deep affection for one another. They have often repeated that my teaching style is suitable for our time and should be published in one book after another. Of course, I try my best, but in my heart I feel that translating original scriptures is far more vital for the transmission of the Dharma to the West. I would prefer studies to be anchored in the authoritative works of the great masters. They are and should remain the common ground for all Buddhist teachings.

If Dharma studies become centered upon one single living person such as myself, there is a danger that people will intermingle the teachings with their own personal likes and dislikes—some people like me, some hate me, some trust me, others don't. Even during Nagarjuna's time, a climate of debate and counter-arguments prevailed in India, and some Buddhists accused him of distorting the Buddha's words. The same thing happened to Padmasambhava. That is why we should give the original words of the Buddha special emphasis.

In the framework for Buddhist studies found in this book, the first main point concerns our basic material, our basic ground—our buddha nature. I feel it is important that we gain some comprehension of this point. Next is the path stage, our present situation that proceeds from the occurrence of confusion. What does this confusion consist of? How is it perpetuated? What is being confused and how? How sound is the tendency to maintain a duality of perceiver and perceived? How do we fool ourselves into believing in a self? How does this confusion trigger karmic actions, emotions, and further tendencies? These are important topics, and we must admit that we are confused. We are in the middle of a chain reaction that has already begun. We cannot cleverly step around it and feign purity and enlightenment. We are already confused; that is our present situation. The next step is to understand that our situation is not irreparable. The tendency to confuse does not have to be repeated forever.

One of the essential points in Buddhism is that confusion is only a temporary event and not our basic nature. Therefore, confusion can dissolve, be cleared up, and cease. This is where Buddhist practice comes in, because the general methods and the extraordinary Vajrayana instructions are the practical tools for dissolving the tendencies of confusion.

At this point, the question often comes up whether a beginner can find his or her own way by reading a few books and doing a little sitting practice. I am sorry to say that the confused mind is not its own solution. Some support is necessary. We usually refer to this support as refuge: the Triple Gem, the Three Precious Ones—Buddha, Dharma, and Sangha.

In our immediate experience the most effective support is the Dharma, because when we hear a truly valid statement and method, think it over until it is clear, and then put it to use, its validity is proven by its clearing up our otherwise mistaken and bewildered state. Without our doing this, the confusion would have continued its own habit.

Because the teachings and their authentic value are a reality in their minds, we receive the Dharma from the present holders of the living lineage. Someone who has realized the end of confusion can genuinely represent the Buddha's lineage, and such an ambassador is called Sangha. The advice that he or she imparts is the Dharma, and the source of such valuable instruction is the Buddha. This is why the Three Jewels are called precious. The reason for this is experiential and not merely a belief. Belief is tenuous and often blind.

If mere belief is the common denominator to spirituality, then anything goes. Isn't it true that every religion regards its particular system of beliefs as extremely important? I doubt there is any exception in this regard. But most often there is a point where reason is abandoned, where you are no longer encouraged or allowed to ask why, or there is simply no answer:

"The divine principle created everything."

"Why?"

"It is the teaching, and so it is my belief."

Often faith involves pleasing either a universal or an individual god: "God is supreme. I am inferior. If I please God, with my love and loyalty, he will protect me and save me. This is my main task—faith alone will save me. Why? Because the power to save is in his hands, not in mine. I must respect him and not make him upset. If I do it well, then at some point he will transport me to a safe place." I am not rejecting people's holding of beliefs. I am just saying that such belief does not withstand much intelligent scrutiny.

Interestingly enough, faith is also regarded as vital in the practice tradition of Buddhism, but the defining quality of Buddhist faith is radically different. It is referred to as "trust through knowing the reason." How does one know the reason? We know it by applying the pith instructions. When we do so, the actual experience of nonduality gives rise to trust in the teaching that provides for this experience. In this way, we can be free from even the slightest doubt. Such trust is due to knowing the reason, namely that applying the Dharma liberates confusion. The Sangha introduces us to this fact, and the Buddha is the source. Hence, the Three Jewels are interconnected with our own practice. We *can* have true trust.

Trust and pure perception are two essentials in Vajrayana practice, and when brought vividly alive in our personal experience, they open a door to direct recognition of the original wakefulness that is the nature of emptiness.

In the general teachings of the Buddha, devotion can often be understood as admiration and a fondness for understanding. The more sincerely interested a practitioner is in realizing the empty nature of personal identity and of the identity of things, the closer he or she comes to realizing it. While in Vajrayana devotion is regarded as one thought among all other thoughts, it is the most potent, the most effective. In this sense it is equal to another type of thought state, that of compassion. These two are considered the most noble and most powerful. It is their immense power and goodness that succeeds in interrupting all other kinds of thoughts, especially the unwholesome types.

The pith instructions and spiritual songs always emphasize an intensity of devotion and sincerity, which is not often found in the philosophical textbooks. An overwhelming and almost unbearably pure state of compassion or devotional yearning strips the mind bare of conceptual veils so that awareness is revealed in its most naked state. Please understand the vital importance of devotion and compassion—and in Vajrayana, especially that of devotion.

If you have already found and accepted a Vajrayana master, then this of course implies that you try to regard whatever he or she says or does as pure. Not only the master but also your fellow practitioners—whatever they do or say you must try to appreciate with a certain purity. The general teachings do not speak much about pure perception, and I understand that it could be a problematic issue. However, the training in pure perception is, in itself, extremely effective for fast progress. It is a swift path.

Let me summarize the essential point of the sacred Dharma. Weariness and renunciation are essentials, as are loving-kindness and compassion, as well as trust and devotion. When these three aspects conjoin in a practitioner, he or she can readily recognize and realize the view of emptiness. If something is amiss with these three, it is difficult to realize the view. Without weariness one doesn't feel the need to practice; lacking love and compassion is like trying to fly without wings or walk without legs. Without trust and devotion—I'm sorry to say this so bluntly—one cannot comprehend the profound teachings of Vajrayana at all. Renunciation here should be the renunciation of ego-clinging, not just of some filthy place. Love and compassion should be not just for friends and family but for everyone, without bounds. To have these, we need to train ourselves.

A synonym for Vajrayana is Secret Mantra. "Secret" refers to the fact that its own nature is a secret to the confused mind. The fact that accomplishment can be reached within a couple of years or within this very lifetime is entirely connected to realizing this nature of mind, and this requires trust and devotion.

The importance of trust and devotion is not so clearly stated in the Buddha's general teachings for good reason: it is hard to accept. Dear reader, isn't it true that most people would not accept this? Isn't it true that if beginners were told, "Obey every word this Buddhist master tells you and see everything he does as perfect," then their immediate reaction would be to say, "It's a cult!" And yes, it definitely looks like it, at first glance anyway. This is certainly a difficult issue.

Let us not limit pure perception to the master, however. A Vajrayana practitioner should regard his or her vajra siblings with the same respect and purity. This principle does not apply only to our vajra siblings; we should regard every sentient being that way and all phenomena as well. A Vajrayana practitioner should repeatedly train in seeing everything that could possibly appear and exist as having the nature of the three kayas. The great mandala of appearance and existence as the manifest ground—that is the pivotal point of inner Vajrayana, no matter from which angle you approach it.

These three principles—weariness and renunciation, loving-kindness and compassion, and trust and devotion—allow you to quickly experience the highest, noblest view. This is my earnest conviction. Dharma studies separated from those three may enable you to speak eloquently on the Buddhist view, but, honestly, when has mere talk ever been able to transform the mind? Talk is cheap. You can teach a parrot to say "*tongnyi*" (emptiness), "*kadag*" (primordial purity), or "*lhündrub*" (spontaneous presence).

I would like to add that progress on the Buddhist path does not require far-reaching study and reflection. Rather than gather information, it is much more important to take the topics personally as one goes along and apply them to oneself. It does not necessarily follow that extensive studying leads to renunciation of ego-clinging. There is no guarantee that being learned also means being compassionate, nor does it necessarily follow that one has deep trust and compassion. Sometimes it does happen that vast learning hinders progress, so I would like to emphasize that we pay special attention to the proper method of studying the Dharma.

Here is how *not* to approach it: Do not use Buddhist information to fuel your ego and sharpen your intellect in order to find faults only in others. The tendency to attack, believing that the opponent is other than oneself, inflates a certain type of pride that makes it very difficult to open up and tame one's mind. Isn't this obvious?

When you study the Dharma, please do so with a willingness to admit, "I do have some faults. They are mine and I am also the one who needs to change them." Once we face ourselves with this type of sincerity, the door is wide open to genuine progress by quickly taming our own minds.

I know it is human nature to think, "I am flawless; the others are wrong!" We have the tendency to always place the blame and point away from ourselves. If we maintain such an attitude while studying the sublime statements of the Buddha, of course we can learn the words, but we then tend to use them to embellish and inflate our pride and look down on others. One may also begin to criticize everyone but oneself. This often happens to those who have done some study.

In short, the way to use this study book is to integrate the topics with your own personal experience. The guideline is always this: we need to tame and soften our own minds. Otherwise, the Dharma does not work. Mere talk does not help, no matter how impressive. I tried to encapsulate this in a poem once:

Studying the Buddha's words and the treatises
Removes your triple faults and makes you gentle and peaceful.
By reflecting, you feel sure of liberation from the depths of your
    heart.

By meditating, you experience self-existing wakefulness from
within.
Therefore, persevere in learning, reflection, and meditation.

The real benefit of studying the Buddha's teachings and the statements
of enlightened masters is to be inspired to change the way we think,
speak, and behave, which will make us more civil, gentle, and peaceful.
When we thoroughly investigate the value of the meaning presented, it
becomes obvious that we *can* become free—each and every one of us.
This confidence is achieved through understanding, and understanding
is a result of thinking the teachings over. We do not need to let the
teachings remain as mere words or ideas; we can put them to use in our
own experience. This is how the buddha nature can be revealed, since it
is already present in every one of us. That is why I encourage you to
study, reflect on, and personally apply the teachings.

Let me phrase this differently. If you want to have the certainty that
Dharma practice will liberate you and others, it is necessary both to
study and to reflect: What is it that obscures our basic nature? Why do
we lose track of it and get bewildered? Well, yes! It is due to this habitual
clinging to duality. If this is so, how do we dissolve dualistic clinging?
Well, yes! We need to train in being free of clinging to duality. When
this attitude, which maintains duality, is allowed to not be formed, to
disappear, to dissolve, to vanish—what is left? What remains is given
the name "nondual wakefulness." Well, yes! This is the freedom from
duality; this is how to be free. Now it is clear! Liberation is to be free
from clinging to an ego. Liberation is to be free from fixating on solid
reality! This is how we can gain some genuine certainty, even without
having to go through detailed studies.

For many people, liberation from samsara is imagined to be a place
far away; this is true for many religions. "When I get to paradise, the
buddhafields, then I will be free! I will pray to God or the Buddha, purify
myself, create merit, and please the gods, and they will take care of me.
They will magically transport me to that pure land." This may well be a
popular belief, but the true Buddhist liberation is to be free of the two
obscurations. For that, wouldn't it be better to understand what the two
obscurations are? They are the emotional and cognitive obscurations. As
Nagarjuna taught, stinginess and the like are the emotional obscuration;
and thoughts that conceptualize the three notions—subject, object, and
action—are the cognitive obscuration. All you need is a good explanation
to understand and identify them in yourself. Of the two, unless and until

you manage to dissolve the tendency to conceptualize the three notions, there is no true freedom from deluded experience.

When someone has recognized and is able to sustain the true Dzogchen view of primordial purity, then all aspects of practice are automatically included within it. The realization of the view is the ultimate refuge; it is also the ultimate *bodhichitta* as well as the true dedication and perfect aspiration. In other words, everything is included within that one state. If it is authentic, such a person can just sit without doing any conventional practice whatsoever. Other people may think, "He's not doing his chants, refuge and bodhichitta." But the fact is that such a master is actually practicing the perfect refuge and bodhichitta in completeness. This is an extraordinary and incredibly special quality, and, of course, its actuality is hard to grasp.

Let me make one thing clear: in order to dissolve this tendency to conceptualize the three notions, unless and until you recognize and become able to sustain the continuity of original wakefulness that does not conceptualize the three notions, deluded experience will not end, nor will it vanish. Whether this is said bluntly or sweetly, whether or not you do a lot of purifying of bad karma and gathering of merit, you always have to return to this central point. Any practice that lacks this vital point will, of course, reduce the intensity of confusion. Every noble intention, every altruistic frame of mind, will undeniably loosen up the rigidity of confusion and weaken the clinging to things as being real and permanent, but not permanently and not completely. The only sure way is to train in thought-free wakefulness. Isn't this obvious? This is what we need. It is the most important point of all.

INTRODUCTION

Drubwang Tsoknyi Rinpoche

Let's take it as a given that you are one of those people who have set their mind on becoming a buddha. You have heard that one can attain enlightenment, and you want to attain it as well. So, how does one go about doing so? How do we make ourselves capable of being buddhas?

There is one particular approach that emphasizes pithy instructions and simple methods, as was the way of Tulku Urgyen Rinpoche. Nowadays, people believe that there is such a style of using just a few quotations from scriptures and primarily focusing on simplicity. This may very well be true, but if we look into the fine details we see that Tulku Urgyen Rinpoche's approach is based on the traditional Dzogchen teachings.

Tulku Urgyen Rinpoche's style of teaching was entirely based on this traditional foundation, and it is here that he invited individual practitioners to embrace the traditional Dzogchen instructions and to progress along the path to becoming a buddha. *The Dzogchen Primer* is an attempt to formulate Tulku Urgyen Rinpoche's unique style into a study and practice book. This is the aspiration I was presented with, and I am delighted to add my good wishes. However, I would like to make clear that in his teachings, Tulku Urgyen used a path that is outlined in the *Lamrim Yeshe Nyingpo,* which is published in English as *The Light of Wisdom* (Rangjung Yeshe Publications) one that gives a very clear-cut way of proceeding. That was the basis he used. It is for this very reason that I am happy to see that Marcia Binder Schmidt has tried her best to select teachings that cover the same instructions in the same sequence as *The Light of Wisdom.*

There is another traditional text that is much loved and well used, namely, *The Jewel Ornament of Liberation.* In this book Gampopa, the great lord of the Dharma, begins by stating, "I will write this for the benefit of both myself and others, using the words of my guru, the great yogi Milarepa, as a basis." Gampopa then begins the teachings with this sentence: "Generally speaking, all phenomena are included within two: samsara and nirvana." This means that all phenomena, no matter what we may experience, belong to either samsara or nirvana. Gampopa continues, "That which we call samsara is, by nature, emptiness." But so is nirvana. If samsara and nirvana are both empty by nature, it would appear there is no difference. What is the difference? "Samsara's form is one of confusion, and its characteristic is such that it is experienced as painful." This is the point when you have to wake up, look around, and begin to wonder, "What is this all about? What is my life? What is the very nature of aware experience?" You should begin to admit and accept that your life is one of confusion, that in fact your way of experiencing is the way of samsara, and it is painful. That is when you gain the sincere wish to be free.

Now, what is nirvana? We can hear long stories and lengthy explanations about the enlightened qualities, but let's begin with this simple definition: nirvana means having transcended suffering. Gampopa says that its nature is emptiness. He also states, "Its form is one in which all confusion is exhausted and has vanished. Its characteristic is to be free of each and every type of suffering."

Now comes one of the main questions, which is raised by Gampopa himself: "So, who gets bewildered into this state of samsaric confusion?" Whom are we talking about when we use the word *samsara?* Gampopa answers his own question: "It is the sentient beings of the three realms who get bewildered."

Why does this happen? "What is the basis for this bewilderment?" he asks. "They are bewildered about emptiness," he replies.

Gampopa continues to question, "What causes them to be bewildered?" He replies, "The great ignorance bewilders them." "How do they get bewildered? They get bewildered into the experiences of the six classes of sentient beings."

Gampopa raises and answers more questions: "What is the analogy for this bewilderment? They get bewildered just like in sleep and dreams. How long have they been bewildered? They have been bewildered since beginningless samsara. What is wrong with being bewildered? It is to experience nothing but suffering. When is this bewilderment cleared up?" When does the confusion dawn as wisdom? Gampopa replies, "It is cleared up the moment you attain unexcelled enlightenment."

And here is the last statement: "If you think that this bewilderment will clear up by itself, then samsara is famed as being endless."

Gampopa concludes his opening to *The Jewel Ornament* with this summary: "Consequently, the way of samsara is one of bewilderment, has immense suffering, lasts interminably, and does not become free by itself. Therefore, from this very day forth, you must strive the best you can to attain unexcelled enlightenment."[8]

Here we have Gampopa's basic view on why to practice the Dharma. In the rest of his book he unfolds how to go about practicing by assembling the necessary factors—the basic material, the support, the circumstance, and so forth—in a way that includes all the topics of contemplation and practice. You will also find these explained in this book.

The Light of Wisdom summarizes everything in this one sentence: "It has that to be understood, that which causes realization, and the final result"—that which you need to know, the path that makes it known, and the result of having fully realized it. These three we usually call ground, path, and fruition.

From *The Light of Wisdom*, Volume I:

> The ground to be understood is the all-pervasive sugata essence.
> Uncompounded, luminous, and empty, it is the natural state of awareness.
> Beyond confusion and liberation, it is completely quiescent like space.
> Although it abides without separation in samsara or joining in nirvana,
> Due to the great demon of coemergent and conceptual ignorance,
> From the solidified habitual patterns of grasping and fixation,
> And the different perceptions of worlds and inhabitants,
> The six classes of beings appeared as a dream.
> Although this is so, you have never moved and will never move
> From the original condition of the essence.
> Endeavor therefore in purifying the temporary stains.[9]

Here we have the basic framework, the very reason to practice the path. The rest of *The Light of Wisdom* contains explanations of the various levels of practice, as well as buddhahood itself—the preliminaries; main part; view, meditation, and conduct; empowerment and samaya; and so forth.

Very often, people are unsure why they should practice: "What is the reason? Where does it lead? Where are we now?" Therefore, I feel it is essential to understand our basic potential, the buddha nature, what obscures us, how to remove obscurations, and the outcome. Using this simple framework we can understand the path as well as what enlightenment is.

Tulku Urgyen Rinpoche's special quality was to begin with the view rather than end with it; to train in devotion, compassion, and renunciation, perfecting the accumulations, and removing obscurations, all within the framework of the view. The practitioner was encouraged to see all these aspects of practice as the very expressions of the view itself. That was Tulku Urgyen's unique style. The two major scriptures I have mentioned here do not categorically begin with the view. What these two scriptures present is the tried and proven path suitable to all types of practitioners. Begin with a sound understanding of buddha nature and appreciate your real support, the precious human body. Connect with the real circumstance for insight, a qualified spiritual teacher, and receive the methods, the oral instructions. This is how to progress step-by-step, all the way to the ultimate level of fruition.

Over the years I have come across many people who want to practice the Buddha's path, and they also want to understand the teachings. Often they are troubled by how these two should be combined, how to combine study and practice.

When we hear of the ten *bhumis*, for instance, there is a long list of outstanding qualities that great beings possess. These qualities sound wonderful, but then the Dharma teacher says, "Right now, you are not able to be like that. You can't practice as the mahabodhisattvas, and you don't have their qualities." Instead, here is how you can practice: You can train in being calm and mindful during the meditation state, and then during the postmeditation you can study all the scriptures. After you have reached a certain level of steadiness in *shamatha*, you can progress to *vipashyana* during the meditation state while you carry on your studies in the postmeditation. During that time you bring the topics that you have studied into the vipashyana practice. Once your level of insight, the training in vipashyana, has progressed, you can then continue into Mahamudra or Dzogchen. This means that after having received the pointing-out instruction, you then try to sustain the state of *rigpa* primarily during the meditation session. This should be obvious because that is the time you have set aside to do just that. However, you do not discontinue your studies during the postmeditation; you simply carry on learning more and more. I personally feel that this is a very pragmatic way of combining study and practice: practice during the sessions, study during the breaks. As you proceed step-by-step in this manner, you will notice that it is quite effective.

We start out as beginners, of course, and that is when we clarify the basics. Once we understand the broad picture, we can step onto the path. The very first meditation training is shamatha, while in the postmeditation you should try your best to grow familiar with the facts of life in samsara in order to gain the will to be free. That is what we call renunciation. Next, study how to seek and find a real spiritual teacher. You need to know and be the judge of who is and who isn't worth following. You also need to understand the value of training in bodhichitta. You study and understand all these topics during the post-meditation.

When you begin to progress into vipashyana, rather than just being calm, I suggest you combine it with the study of emptiness during the postmeditation. What does it mean that phenomena never arose, do not remain, and never cease? What does it mean that there is no tangible identity, neither in things nor in individuals? How do we cut through ego-clinging? How do we avoid spiritual materialism? Please study all these topics.

Once you connect with a true vajra master and not only receive the pointing-out instruction but also recognize what is being pointed out, that is the time for training in letting be in the state of self-existing awareness. What kinds of books should you then read during the post-meditation? Read Dzogchen teachings, pointing-out instructions, *The Flight of the Garuda*, and similar kinds of literature. You should read them very slowly, maybe out loud to yourself, alternating this with training in the meaning.

At this point, you still use intelligent judgment during the postmedi-tation; you scrutinize the meaning to become increasingly clear about the natural state. The intellect needs to be convinced, and you carry on and on until you are totally convinced, to the point of oversaturating yourself. This is very helpful because when we again sit during the medi-tation session there is a tendency to become dull or absentminded. Those tendencies must be tamed, and once they are, you will have wonderful results.

The great master Jigmey Lingpa mentions that in former times, during the so-called Golden Age, people were generally more content, with less craving and less of a tendency to be caught up in external distractions. Accordingly, their emotions were less tumultuous. That was a time when Dharma practitioners did not need to force themselves too much in study and practice, but could rely on a few words of pithy instruction from a master. For the most part, they were able to attain enlightenment through just that. It was a time of stability, much more so than today. Maybe this has to do with the absence of scientific development, gadgets, and sophisticated things, so there were far fewer objects to be distracted by. Therefore, there was a natural tendency to be at peace. When someone has a sense of inner calm, it is much easier to be decisive in one's practice and less skeptical.

Today it is quite different. There are a tremendous number of external things that can capture our attention. There is a vast array of preoccupations and an untold number of different philosophical systems, old religions, and new religions as well. People are faced with a huge choice and must judge and decide which is better for them. It is a very difficult choice to make. What should we rely upon? It seems that we must fall back upon our individual intelligence, rather than immediately trusting whatever we get served, even if it is Buddhism. Of course I could tell you that Buddhism is best, much better than all the others, and list its special qualities, but it is still up to you to judge, decide, and trust. However, that isn't easy. As a matter of fact, it is quite difficult to have simple trust. Therefore, it is a good idea to study.

Let me continue paraphrasing Jigmey Lingpa. If you really want to understand the Dzogchen teachings in these present times, please understand that we are not in the Golden Age any longer. These days some study is necessary. We study, then we practice, then we study some more, and then we practice again. This is a time to combine the two, rather than rigidly holding on to the idea that practice is right and study is wrong. Jigmey Lingpa says that such an attitude does not work these days, nor will it in the future. That is why he wrote that people of future generations who want to realize the Great Perfection exactly as it is must listen and reflect on the Buddha Dharma, at least to a certain degree.

When I look at this selection that Marcia Binder Schmidt has made, I am quite pleased with her choices. There is a very good reason for this: people who exclude learning and focus on nothing but sitting practice have a very hard time whenever doubts creep into their mind. They wonder, "Hey! Am I really practicing the right way?" I am not talking about someone whose stream-of-being is already liberated, but the stage before that. Doubts and uncertainty do hinder progress. It is during the post-meditation that doubts gain a foothold. A doubt is a type of question for which the unlearned person has no answer. Someone who has gained some sound understanding of the Dharma will think a little and then come up with an intelligent reply to his or her own doubt; then it is settled.

Modern people tend to reach a point in life when they get tired by more sensory input, more things, more adventures and life experiences. Often people feel, "I am so tired of all this! I just want to rest and take some time off." This attitude is like a prescription to begin shamatha practice, the aim of which is to relax deeply.

Once one has settled down and found some peace of mind, which is quite pleasant, it is common to give up "the Dharma." Why? Because one already got what one wanted, and one didn't really understand what the Dharma is all about. "I wanted some relief, some happiness. I found it, and that is good enough for me. There is nothing more I need right now." That kind of contentment can easily dismiss the possibility of further progress.

There is, however, another type of person who reflects, "What is the big deal about a little bit of happiness? That's not very profound. I don't believe that is the whole Dharma. What is the true essence of the Bud-dha's teachings?" With this kind of attitude study and practice can be combined in a fruitful alliance. During the postmeditation you study to fill in the map of what is true and what isn't. You will use this map for your further journey. However, there is no use drawing a map if you don't use it. The value of a map is proven when you are actually on the road going somewhere. When you discover that what is on the map and what you see as you move through the landscape coincide exactly, you gain a stronger sense of confidence that can become unshakable. With-out the map it is hard to feel sure. If you know how to practice correctly, you may have no doubts during the meditation state, but doubt may still arise during postmeditation.

Many people tell me about their various doubts, and it would be wonderful if they could just answer their doubts immediately each time. When they wonder, "What should I do? What is the right way?" it would be great if they could have an answer ready. The absence of doubt is true confidence. This confidence strengthens your composure during meditation. As you train more and more, your realization deepens until your stream-of-being is unbound and free. In this way, there is a rela-tionship between study and liberation, between drawing the map and arriving at the destination.

This is how I feel these days: combine study and practice. Otherwise, we may end up unable to choose anything or to trust in anything. It could happen that a valuable karmic link to Buddhist practice is lost through some small incident. Therefore, use your intelligence to strengthen such a link, so that you can overcome negative emotional habits, be free, and become enlightened. I feel that is the better choice.

It is also possible to study and study and study, leaving no time for practice. If you do this, the real purpose of the Buddha's teachings will be lost. This is like studying and redrawing maps until you get old but never visiting any beautiful places. What's the point in that? It is also possible to begin walking without any map, just hoping to end up in the right place. If you do happen to get to Tibet, you might not even realize it; you might not recognize Lhasa. If you knew a little bit about places in Lhasa, you would be able to recognize them when you got there.

I would like to conclude with the wish that your studies will be like a lamp dispelling the darkness of ignorance, while your practice eliminates the tendencies of negative emotions and obscurations, so that you will not only attain peace of mind but will also proceed to the enlightenment of all buddhas. Those who use this book as a basis for a study program might be my students or they might be students of my father, Tulku Urgyen Rinpoche, or Chökyi Nyima Rinpoche. Moreover, you might be students of Chögyam Trungpa Rinpoche, Sogyal Rinpoche, or any of the other masters of our time, and I would like to encourage all of you to be free from a sectarian attitude when you study the Dharma. Thinking things like, "I am a student of Chökyi Nyima Rinpoche and no one else!" "I belong to Tsoknyi Rinpoche and there isn't much by him here, so I won't use this book!" "I am a follower of Trungpa Rinpoche; there's not much by him here, so this book is not for me!" is not the right attitude. Please be more open-minded in your approach, appreciating value where there is value, wherever it might be. This will also ensure that, in the future, your benefit to others will be similarly unbiased.

A nonsectarian attitude is not only practical; it is also close to the truth. We should continue following our particular lineage, but rather than becoming more narrow-minded and prejudiced, we should appreciate all other lineages of teachings as well. When you enter the Vajrayana teachings, pure perception is essential, so please study with pure perception and an open mind. The extraordinary perspective of Vajrayana is, in itself, pure perception through which the "impurity" of mistaken experience, piece by piece, becomes the pure mandala of original wakefulness. Please allow that to happen.

PART TWO

STARTING POINT

Analyze my teachings as carefully as you would test gold before buying it. Do not accept my words without questioning. You must discriminate and examine them for yourself.

—BUDDHA SHAKYAMUNI

I

BUDDHA NATURE

Khenchen Thrangu Rinpoche

In general, a person is considered sensible and even honorable when he strives to benefit himself, but sometimes people intend to harm others in order to gain happiness for themselves. In the context of Dharma, this is called a "wrong intention." A "good intention" is simply the wish to benefit others. Nevertheless, if we interpret the word *others* to indicate only a select few, like our friends, relatives, and countrymen, then our intention is biased. We should never be partial to some beings while harming others; instead, we should try to cultivate an attitude that embraces all sentient beings with good wishes, including animals. In this way, our good intentions will develop into all-encompassing bodhichitta.

Some say that the Buddhists are not really serving society. For example, Christian organizations build schools and hospitals. From this point of view, it may indeed appear as though the Buddhists are not working in a concrete way to benefit the community. Yet, the main objective of Buddhism is to accomplish the welfare of others through practices

Adapted from Thrangu Rinpoche, *Buddha Nature* (Boudhanath: Rangjung Yeshe Publications, 1988), Introduction.

engaged in mentally. The Buddhist practitioner serves others through his good intentions. Perpetuating wholesome motives, he or she can truly benefit beings. Therefore, whether we are listening to Dharma teachings, reading about them, or putting them into practice, it is extremely important to develop the attitude of bodhichitta.

Although we plan to search out and follow the true and perfect path, without a qualified guide we will never discover this path. If we try to find the path by ourselves or follow an imperfect teacher, we are in danger of making a grave mistake. Therefore, we must first carefully seek out a genuine spiritual master and then adhere to his advice.

Each of us possesses *buddha nature*. We each have the seed of enlightenment within ourselves, and because this potential can be actualized, we possess an enlightened essence. At the time of the ground, we possess buddha nature. At the time of the path, the enlightened essence continues. At the time of fruition—complete buddhahood—the sugata-essence continues. The enlightened essence is a continuity that extends throughout our journey along the stages of ground, path, and fruition.

The Buddha gave graduated teachings to help sentient beings recognize the real condition—the nature of things. To understand this basic state of affairs, the Buddha first taught that samsara, conditioned existence, is replete with various kinds of suffering. Suffering originates with mistakenness, delusion. His initial teachings, which characterized this world as having the nature of impermanence and suffering, are called the First Turning of the Wheel of Dharma.

After his students had familiarized themselves with these fundamental teachings, the Buddha taught that although the truth of impermanence is undeniable, it also has no concrete existence. Thus, he explained the Second Turning of the Wheel of Dharma, which emphasizes emptiness—that all things lack both concrete substance and self-nature.

Later, the Buddha taught that emptiness does not signify a mere state of blankness. If that were the case, how could any phenomena appear at all? How could an entire universe arise? At that point, he taught the last set of teachings—the Third Turning of the Wheel of Dharma, which accentuates the luminous aspect of mind, the ability to know all manifested things. This profound, ultimate teaching emphasizes wisdom, innate wakefulness.

The Buddha started by giving advice that emphasized the benefits for oneself. These are the focal point of Hinayana, the lesser vehicle. Later, the Buddha presented teachings that stress the attempt to attain enlightenment for the benefit of all sentient beings equal in number to the vastness of the sky. These are featured in the Mahayana vehicle. Finally, he taught the Vajrayana. In order to practice Vajrayana teachings, one must first establish the basis for practice, which is twofold: arousing bodhichitta and resolving the correct view. Without a firm foundation in these two aspects, one cannot truly practice the path of Vajrayana.

2

THE BASIS: BUDDHA NATURE

Tulku Urgyen Rinpoche

We need to clearly understand what is meant by the terms *samsara* and *nirvana*. Nirvana means the fully realized buddha nature that consists of Body, Speech, and Mind aspects. The Body is the essence that simply is. Speech is its nature, the cognizant quality that is vividly present, and Mind is the capacity, which is radiant. These three aspects comprise the basic presence of all buddhas. They are none other than their essence, nature, and capacity. All sugatas are of this same identity. In the same way, samsara is the body, speech, and mind of all sentient beings, which are the deluded expressions of their essence, nature, and capacity.

Buddha nature is all-encompassing: this means it is present or basic to all states, regardless of whether they belong to samsara or nirvana. Remember, "nirvana" refers to the Body, Speech, and Mind of all the awakened ones. Body is the abiding essence, Speech is the vividly present nature, and Mind is the radiant capacity. These three, the Body, Speech, and Mind of all buddhas, are also known as the *three vajras*.

This buddha nature is present just as the shining sun is present in

Adapted from Tulku Urgyen Rinpoche, *As It Is*, Volume I, (Boudhanath: Rangjung Yeshe Publications, 1999), "The Basis, the Buddha Nature."

the sky. It is indivisible from the three vajras of the awakened state, which do not perish or change. Vajra Body is the unchanging quality, vajra Speech is the unceasing quality, and vajra Mind is the undeluded, unmistaken quality. So, the buddha nature or dharmadhatu is the three vajras; at the same time, its *expression* manifests as the deluded body, speech, and mind of all beings.

In the normal sense of the word, "body" refers to something perishable composed of flesh and blood. "Speech" refers to intermittent utterances that come and go and eventually perish. And "mind" refers to thought states and emotions that come and go, come and go, under the power of dualistic attitude, like beads on a rosary. These mental states are also transient. Everyone agrees that the body, speech, and mind of living beings are constantly changing, continually coming and going. Still, the basis of our ordinary body, speech, and mind is the buddha nature, the *dharmadhatu* that encompasses all of samsara and nirvana. There isn't a single being for whom this isn't so.

Looking from the pure angle, then, this buddha nature is present in every being, the expression of the victorious ones, just like the rays of light are present from the sun. The light is emanated by the sun, isn't it? If it weren't for the sun, there wouldn't be any light. Similarly, the origin of the body, speech, and mind of beings is the expression of the buddha nature that pervades both samsara and nirvana.

It is said that all sentient beings are buddhas, but they are covered by their temporary obscurations. These temporary obscurations are our own thinking. Buddha nature, rigpa, encompasses all of samsara and nirvana—not just the awakened state of nirvana, but everything, every single thing. The ordinary body, speech, and mind of sentient beings temporarily arose from the expression of the qualities of enlightened body, speech, and mind. As space pervades, so awareness pervades. If this were not so, then space would pervade but rigpa wouldn't. Just like space, rigpa is all-encompassing: nothing is outside it. Just as the contents and beings are all pervaded by space, rigpa pervades the minds of beings.

It is essential to start out with a basic understanding of the profundity of what is meant here in order to be able to authentically practice the teaching of the Great Perfection. Unless we know what is what, at least intellectually, it might seem to us as if sentient beings are disconnected, alien entities, and we have no idea of where they come from, where they belong, or what they actually are. They are not disconnected at all. The difference between buddhas and sentient beings lies in the latter's narrowness of scope and attitude. Sentient beings confine themselves to their own limited little area of samsara through their own attitude and thinking.

It is said that the difference between buddhas and sentient beings is like the difference between the narrowness and the openness of space. Sentient beings are like the space held within a tightly closed fist, while buddhas are fully open, all-encompassing. Basic space and awareness are innately all-encompassing. Basic space is the absence of mental constructs, while awareness is the *knowing* of this absence of constructs, recognizing the complete emptiness of mind essence. Space and awareness are inherently indivisible. It is said, "When the mother, the basic space, does not stray from her awareness child, have no doubt that they are forever indivisible."

The ultimate Dharma is the realization of the indivisibility of basic space and awareness. That is the starting point, and that is what is pointed out to begin with. It is essential to understand this; otherwise, we might have the feeling that the primordial buddha Samantabhadra and his consort are an old blue man and woman who lived aeons ago. It's not like that at all! Samantabhadra and his consort are the indivisible unity of space and awareness.

As you know, the nine gradual vehicles and the four schools of philosophy—*Vaibhashika, Sautrantika, Mind Only,* and *Middle Way*—are designed to suit the various mental capacities of different people. The term *Great Perfection,* on the other hand, implies that everything is included in Dzogchen, that everything is complete. Dzogchen is said to be unexcelled, meaning that there is nothing higher than it. Why is this? It is because of knowing *what truly is to be as it is*—the ultimate naked state of *dharmakaya.* Isn't that truly the ultimate? Please carefully understand this.

The Great Perfection is totally beyond any kind of pigeonholing anything in any way whatsoever. It is to be utterly open, beyond categories, limitations, and the confines of assumptions and beliefs. All other ways of describing things are confined by categories and limitations. The ultimate destination to arrive at in Dzogchen is the view of the kayas and wisdoms. Listen to this quote: "Although everything is empty, the special quality of the Buddha Dharma is to not be empty of the kayas and wisdom." All other systems expound that all things are empty, but truly, the intention of the Buddha is to use the word *emptiness* rather than *empty.* This is a very important point.

For instance, in the *Prajñaparamita* scriptures you find the statements, "Outer things are emptiness, inner things are emptiness, emptiness is emptiness, the vast is emptiness, the ultimate is emptiness, the conditioned is emptiness, the unconditioned is emptiness. . . ." "Emptiness" here should be understood as "empty cognizance." Please understand this. The suffix -*ness* implies the cognizant quality. We need to understand this word in its correct connotation.

Otherwise, it sounds too nihilistic to simply say that outer things are empty. If we understand "emptiness" as empty or void, rather than "empty cognizance," we are leaning too much toward nihilism, the idea that everything is a big, blank void. This is a serious sidetrack.

The Buddha initially taught that all things are empty. This was unavoidable; indeed, it was justifiable, because we need to dismantle our fixation on the permanence of what we experience. A normal person clings to the contents of his experiences as solid, as being "that"—not just as mere "experience," but as something that has solidity, that is real, that is concrete and permanent. But if we look honestly and closely at what happens, experience is simply experience, and it is not made out of anything whatsoever. It has no form, no sound, no color, no taste, and no texture; it is simply experience—an empty cognizance.

The vivid display in manifold colors you see with open eyes is not mind, but "illuminated matter." Similarly, when you close your eyes and see something dark, it is not mind but "dark matter." In both cases, matter is merely a presence, an experience of something. It is *mind* that experiences the external elements and everything else.

An appearance can only exist if there is a mind that beholds it. The "beholding" of that appearance is nothing other than experience; that is what actually takes place. Without a perceiver, how could an appearance be an appearance? It wouldn't exist anywhere. Perceptions are experienced by mind; they are not experienced by water or earth. All the elements are vividly distinguished as long as the mind fixates on them. Yet they are nothing but a mere presence, an appearance. It is mind that apprehends this mere presence. When this mind doesn't apprehend, hold, or fixate on what is experienced—in other words, when the real, authentic *samadhi of suchness* dawns within your stream-of-being— "reality" loses its solid, obstructing quality. That is why accomplished yogis cannot be burned, drowned, or harmed by wind. In their experience all appearances are a mere presence, since fixation has disintegrated from within. Mind is that which experiences, that within which experience unfolds. What else is there to experience? Mind means individual experience. All experience is individual, personal.

For instance, the fact that one yogi's delusion dissolves doesn't mean everyone else's delusion vanishes as well. When someone gets enlightened, that person is enlightened, not everyone else. When a yogi transcends fixation, only the deluded individual experience of that one person dissolves. Please think about this. There is, however, another aspect called "others'experience," or the "general experience" of sentient beings.

In all of this seemingly solid reality [Rinpoche knocks on the wood of his bed], there is not a single thing that is indestructible. Whatever is material in this world will be destroyed in fire at the end of the kalpa; there is no exception. This fire then vanishes by itself. [Rinpoche chuckles.]

Try to spend some time on *Nangjang* training,[10] and you will discover that all of reality is insubstantial and unreal. By means of Nangjang training, we discover that all experience is personal experience, and that all personal experience is seen as unreal and insubstantial when not fixated upon. In this entire world there is no created appearance that ultimately remains. Seemingly external visual forms do not really remain anywhere. These mere perceptions are dependent karmic experiences. All of relative reality is by definition dependent upon something other, upon causes and conditions, isn't it? When explaining relative phenomena, you have to mention their causes and conditions; there is no way around that. In the end, we realize that their nature is ultimately beyond causes and conditions. What is "ultimate" cannot possibly be made out of causes and conditions.

Only the authentic state of samadhi can purify or clear up this self-created confusion. More appearances and further fixating will not destroy this. This profound state is present in each individual, if only they would know it! The ultimate nature is already fully present. It is given names like *dharmakaya, sambhogakaya,* and *nirmanakaya.* Our deluded state hides this from us, but really it is this that destroys the delusion. Isn't this really amazing! [Rinpoche chuckles.]

Once we attain stability in samadhi, delusion is destroyed, since samadhi dismantles the entire drama of delusion. In other words, this mind has basically created the delusion, but by recognizing the nature of this mind we clear up our delusion, since at that moment no delusion can be re-created. If everyone could just understand this! This is amazing! [Rinpoche laughs.] It is the mind itself that creates this whole delusion, but it is also the mind itself that can let the whole delusion collapse. [Rinpoche laughs again.] Besides buddha nature, what else is there to be free from delusion? Buddha nature is the very basis for delusion. It is also that which dissolves the delusion. Please try carefully to understand this! This is something you *can* understand!

Delusion seems to separate all sentient beings from their buddha nature. But it is this very buddha nature that clears up the delusion. It is basically a matter of recognizing it or not. We speak of those who were never deluded: the buddhas and the hundred sublime families of peaceful and wrathful sugatas, including Buddha Samantabhadra. When failing to recognize, one is deluded. Delusion dissolves the very moment you recognize the identity of that which is deluded.

Delusion is like becoming possessed by a spirit during a seance, when someone starts to suddenly hop around and do all kinds of crazy things. This is exactly what has happened to all of us. Sentient beings are possessed by the "spirit" of ignorance and the 84,000 disturbing emotions, and they are all dancing around doing incredible things. They have undergone all different kinds of pain and misery for so long, aeons upon aeons. But it is a self-created possession. It is not really something from outside. Buddha nature has lost track of itself and created samsara, but it is also buddha nature, recognizing itself, that clears up the delusion of samsaric existence. The moment of recognition is like the spirit leaving. All of a sudden the possession vanishes. We can't even say where it went. This is called the collapse of confusion.

We have undergone so much misery—oh my! Spinning around on the wheel of samsara, we have suffered so much trouble! Roaming and rambling about among the six classes of beings, of course we have suffered! [Rinpoche laughs.] A yogi is like a formerly possessed person whom the spirit has left. While "possessed," this mind thinks and acts in delusion, but the very moment you recognize the nature of this mind—rigpa—the possession immediately vanishes. [Rinpoche laughs.]

3

THE GROUND

Drubwang Tsoknyi Rinpoche

The most important aspect in Buddhism is mind, and mind means attitude. We need to form a genuine attitude about engaging in the Buddhist path. Once we've decided to enter it, we should think, "What a fortunate situation I've encountered! I'm very happy about this, and I'll make full use of it. I'll use this situation not merely to make me temporarily happy or to achieve something for myself, but in order to diminish my disturbing emotions and progress toward enlightenment for the sake of all sentient beings." This kind of attitude is something we need to train in.

Having formed this attitude, we need to work on realizing that everything is pure just the way it is. Everything is intrinsically free and perfect, and this is not merely our imagination. The very nature of all things is an original purity. Whether we are talking about the nature of mind or the nature of all things, it is basically pure. This purity is not somehow separated from the impure aspect of things. Nor is it some

Adapted from Tsoknyi Rinpoche, *Carefree Dignity* (Boudhanath: Rangjung Yeshe Publications, 1998), "The Ground."

product that we need to create or achieve. It is a natural purity, already present. Do you understand this principle? This is very important.

This original purity is not to be regarded as a product, a creation of something new, something that is not already present. It's not like that at all. Original purity is not something created or accomplished. We may imagine that because we so obviously experience impurity there must be purity somewhere else that we can get to, as if we are in a foul-smelling room and we imagine a beautiful fragrance in another place. That's not it. This purity does not fall into any category; it belongs to neither samsara nor nirvana. In this context, it is not as if samsara is some impure state and nirvana is some pure place somewhere else. The purity of our intrinsic, innate nature is present throughout all states—not falling into the category of samsara, not falling into the category of nirvana, but pervasive throughout. I will talk more about this later.

This term, innate nature or basic substance or basic element, buddha nature, essence of all buddhas—this is what buddhas actually are. This is what the purity is, and this is what the training is in, what the Dzogchen training is all about.

Ground, path, and fruition—all of these terms are basically about this innate nature, which is not confined to only samsara or only nirvana. Our basic state is something that is present in every situation, whether samsaric or nirvanic, without belonging to either. In a way one could say it's the shared or common ground of these two states. So that is the purity, the purity of the basic state. The most important thing to understand at first is the ground, the basic state.

This nature, what is it? It is pure. Purity. Is this something that we can accomplish? No, it isn't. Does it belong to samsara? No. Does it belong to nirvana? No. Yet it's present throughout all states. That basic nature is what we should fully realize. It's difficult to find an accurate example of how this innate nature really is. One comparison that is often used is space. Space is not limited to being only between the walls and the pillars, not just between the floor and the ceiling—space is throughout everything.

I would now like to define the word *mind*. The Tibetan word is *sem*. Basically it means *that which knows*, that which thinks that things are "nice" or "not nice." Because there is some sense of knowing, there is some identity, some property of that which knows. Exactly what is it, how is it? In essence, it is your innate nature, which is all-pervasive, ever-present.

Most important is to remember we don't have to think of mind as a concrete "thing." It's really more a quality of knowing—of knowing and thinking. This word *mind* is going to be used a lot, but please remember every time you hear or read it that it simply means some act of knowing or thinking. It's really pretty simple. Knowing, just that.

There are many ways that knowing takes place. There can be dualistic knowing, or knowing that is free of duality. In either case, our mind is simply knowing. The word *sem* means dualistic knowing. Maybe you feel like a lot of words are being thrown out at you right now, but please just catch them and keep them. We will put them together later.

Now let's look at ground, path, and fruition. The basic nature is described as something that does not belong to either samsara or nirvana, and yet is present throughout all states, whether samsaric or nirvanic. It doesn't belong to either, yet is all-pervasive. Ground is something that is present as the very nature of this knowing mind. You can say this knowing is something that is empty and yet cognizant. These two aspects, emptiness and cognizance, are indivisible—you can't separate them. Sometimes three indivisible aspects are described: empty in *essence*, cognizant by *nature*, and unconfined in *capacity*. This indivisible nature of mind is always present and it is called by different names: the natural state, the basic nature, the real condition, the enlightened essence, or buddha nature. Regardless of what name it goes by, this is what is meant by ground.

Path, in this context, is called confusion. From the Buddhist perspective we are not talking about only one lifetime of confusion, but innumerable lifetimes. The primary confusion is this: not recognizing the basic state, the ground, to be as it is, one confuses it or mistakes the basic state for being something other. An example would be if I mistook the rosary that I am holding in my hand for something else, believing it to be a snake, or a piece of rope, mistaking its concrete physical form, smell, texture, and so forth.

This process of solidifying that which obscures our basic state has gone on for many, many lifetimes, not just for a short while. Our confusion is long-term. It's through training in the view, meditation, and conduct that we rediscover what is already present. Through training, we are reintroduced to the basic state.

Ground means the nature of our mind, our basic state, which has the capacity to be enlightened, to be awakened. By "enlightened" we mean able to be free. Everyone has this kind of potential. That is our ground.

The ground is the nature of things.
This nature, *dharmata*, is self-existing.

This dharmata nature is not fabricated.
It's not something that was once constructed.
It is not something that originally didn't exist and was then created.
It is not something that we can improve or modify in any way.
It simply is what is.
What naturally is.
The natural state, itself.
Not made by the Buddha.
Not made by sentient beings.
Not made by the four elements.
It is a nature that just is, by itself.

The Buddha did not come into this world and create this basic nature. Everything is naturally pervaded by emptiness. Likewise, mind is naturally and always pervaded by a nature that is empty and cognizant. By "everything," I am referring to material or concrete things as well. They're all permeated by an empty quality, and it is this very quality that allows things to come into being. That empty quality is still present even when things exist. In the same way, all states of consciousness are permeated by a nature that is both empty and cognizant.

The empty quality of things means the openness that allows for the thing to come into being, to unfold, to be present. You can move your hand around in midair because the space is open, right? Another word for this open quality is "empty." Here's another example: this stick I'm holding in my hand can disintegrate. It has a perishable nature, right? The fact that its existence is impermanent proves that it is empty in nature. These examples provide a rough idea of what the empty quality means in this context.

Our nature—and now we're back to talking about mind, this mind right here—is something that is basically both empty and cognizant, indivisibly. What happens in a normal moment of perception, when we are looking at a flower, for example, is that our basic identity, this unconfined, empty cognizance, becomes confined in the moment of perceiving. Somehow the empty quality becomes limited to being the perceiver, while the cognizance of the perceived, of what is present, is confined to being the object. The original unconfined and empty cognizance becomes apparently split up into perceiver and perceived, subject and object.

Of course, this isn't really the case; it just *seems* like that. This mistaking of what seemingly is as being real is confusion. That is what confusion really is: mistaking something that seems to be for what it isn't. At the same moment, one fails to recognize what actually *is*. Delusion is this ongoing, moment-to-moment conceptualizing activity of fabricating a subject and object that don't really exist.

It's as if we see a colored rope lying on the ground, mistake it for a snake, and panic. The rope and the snake look alike, and because of not directly seeing what is what, we become confused. On the other hand, when we recognize that the rope is simply a rope—when we recognize it for being what it is—the notion that it is a snake vanishes. That is only possible because the *snakeness* doesn't exist in any way whatsoever in the rope. Therefore, that which so terrified us was merely a construct created by our own thoughts.

That is why it is said that disturbing emotions have no real existence in the ground itself. Disturbing emotions, which are the basic cause of samsara, only come about during the path through mistakenness, through delusion. Path is synonymous with being confused. Path is to be mistaken. Ground is our basic state, which is pure in nature. It's because we don't know this purity—because we don't acknowledge it—that we confuse it with impurity. So, confusion occurs on the path. When this confusion is cleared up, that's called fruition.

Among these three, where are we right now? We are at the path stage—being confused. Why do we practice the Dharma? Because we have the basic state, the essential nature as ground. It is like the oil present in sesame seeds, which can be released with the proper procedure of pressing. It's not something completely nonexistent or imaginary, like oil in sand. All that is necessary is to acknowledge what we have as what we have. We need a method for recognizing this, and such a method does exist.

What do we need to recognize? We need to recognize our basic state, the ground. This basic state encompasses enlightened body, speech, and mind—body present as essence, speech present as nature, and mind radiantly present as capacity. Because the enlightened body, speech, and mind are already present as the identity of the ground, as a mere dependent relationship with that, right now, when we are on the path, our identity is one of having a body, a voice, and a mind.

To go back to the example, without the rope there wouldn't be the notion of snake. In fact, it would be impossible to have the notion of something being this snake if there wasn't a rope. In the same way, enlightened Body, Speech, and Mind, in the form of essence, nature, and capacity, are already present as our basic state, the ground. Only because of this is it possible to be mistaken about what we are. In a country where there is no rope, you would never mistake a piece of rope for a snake, because there would be no basis for misunderstanding.

Let's go one step deeper into exploring our confusion. Because we've failed to acknowledge that the enlightened body is present as essence, it has turned into a physical body. The enlightened body as essence lies beyond arising and disintegration, birth and death. It has not been acknowledged, and now it appears in the form of something that takes birth and later dies. It is the same with our voice and mind.

To reiterate, the path stage is one of confusion. We are on the path right now, and this confusion needs to be clarified. The method used to clarify confusion on the path is threefold: view, meditation, and conduct. This is where recognizing *rigpa* comes in.

This rigpa that needs to be realized is actually an aspect of the ground, an aspect of our dharmakaya nature. But rigpa can also be considered something to be recognized during the path. In this regard, path and ground are identical in essence. It is only a difference of one's essential nature being covered by confusion, or not covered by it.

When recognizing the naked state of rigpa, we are like this [Rinpoche shows a piece of blue cloth]. This is the ground, but it is covered by the path [Rinpoche covers the blue cloth with pieces of white, green, red, and yellow paper]. You can see there are many different types of coverings, including emotional obscurations and cognitive obscurations. The notions we have—first "I," as in "I am," which is followed by "my," "mine," and so forth—these notions are like opaque veils that cover the basic ground.

There are various ways to remove these obscurations, including the meditation practices of shamatha and vipashyana, the development stage, training in the completion stage with attributes, utilizing the key vajra points of *channels, energies, and essences,* and so forth. A single meditation technique removes a single layer of obscuration. When at some point we arrive at what is called the first *bhumi,* also known as the "path of seeing," realization dawns in our stream-of-being. Gradually all the covers are removed, so that eventually the ground is totally revealed. That is the realization of dharmakaya.

It's generally believed that this process takes a tremendously long time. There must be a more direct method than gathering merit and purifying obscurations through three incalculable aeons! The Dzogchen approach to removing obscurations and uncovering our basic nature is indeed direct and quick. The Dzogchen view involves cutting through to primordial purity. The Dzogchen teachings have three sections: mind section, space section, and instruction section. Within the instruction section there are two aspects: *kadag trekchö,* the cutting through of primordial purity, and *lhündrub tögal,* the direct crossing of spontaneous presence.

From the Dzogchen perspective, everything that covers or obscures the pure basic ground is called thought, or conceptual mind. Regardless of whether it is karma or habitual tendencies, it is contained within conceptual attitude. *Trekchö* is the thorough cut of cutting through, cutting the obscurations completely to pieces, like slashing through them with a knife. So the past thought has ceased, the future thought hasn't yet arisen, and the knife is cutting through this stream of present thought. But one doesn't keep hold of this knife either; one lets the knife go, so there is a gap. When you cut through again and again in this way, the string of thought falls to pieces. If you cut a rosary in a few places, at some point it doesn't work any longer.

If you cut Tsoknyi Rinpoche's head off, and cut his arms and legs off, and continue cutting, cutting in this way, at some point there is no longer any Tsoknyi Rinpoche. If you only cut off Tsoknyi Rinpoche's head, you can say here is Tsoknyi Rinpoche's head and here is his body, those two pieces. But if you cut the head up again and say here are the cheeks and here are the eyes and so on, soon you won't be able to call those pieces a head any longer. And if you cut those pieces up really finely, if you mince them up completely, finally there are no separate things left at all. Eventually it becomes emptiness. There is only the name left of Tsoknyi Rinpoche; there is no thing to attach that to. If Tsoknyi Rinpoche is not that famous, after a few generations even the name vanishes as well. Everything vanishes, even the name.

Confusion needs to be chopped into pieces in the same way. The conceptual frame of mind is not one solid lump; it's not a single concrete thing. It's actually made up of small pieces that are connected in a vague sort of way. You can call that vague sort of connection karma or habit or the thinking mind. But if you know how to really recognize, a gap immediately appears. Then it's like your obscurations have been removed, allowing a little piece of your basic nature to be visible. So it gets covered again, and again you need to recognize rigpa. You'll find that as you chop more and more, the ability of the obscurations to return actually becomes less and less.

Even if only a little piece of the basic state is visible, if it is the genuine, real thing, that is the recognizing of dharmakaya. But whether we actually recognize or not is dependent solely upon ourselves. The Dzogchen teaching on how to recognize is available and is being taught. But how it is applied by a person is something entirely up to the individual. One cannot say that everyone recognizes or everybody doesn't recognize—exactly who recognizes and who doesn't is not fixed. We can know that for ourselves.

We need to recognize in a way that is not mixed up with concepts, with attachment, with clinging, with resting or dwelling on something. And in a way that is not mixed up with analysis either. Everything is perceived, yet we are not stuck in the perceiving. This is a very important sentence: "Everything is perceived, yet we are not stuck in the perceiving." The natural expression of the basic essence of mind can move or manifest in two different ways. One is as a conceptual frame of mind, a thought. The result of that is confusion. The other is the expression showing itself as intelligence or knowledge. That becomes original wakefulness, which results in liberation.

I'm using the word *conceptual* a lot here. A concept is a thought formed about a subject and object. A conceptual attitude is based on this holding-on-to of subject and object. The subject and object can be many different things. Most obviously, they can be material objects that we see or hear. For instance, when looking at this mandala plate in front of me, the mind fixes its attention on the plate as an object. Through the medium of the eyes occurs the visual cognition of the mandala plate by a perceiver, the subject, and inevitably some thought is formed about it. The process is the same for all the senses. That is an example of conceptual mind at work.

There is another, more subtle way conceptual mind operates. Basically, conceptuality implies duality—duality of this and that, of subject and object. This does not only refer to external material things: it could also be that the previous thought is the object and the present thought is the subject. Conceptual also implies the notion of time, whether it be in the gross materialistic sense of an external interaction or the more subtle internal sense of one thought looking at the previous thought or looking back into a past memory. While it's not overtly dualistic, there is still some lapse there, some sense of time. The sense of time is always conceptual. Something that is temporal is always conceptual; thus, the notion of time is conceptual. The notion of time is a conceptual state. Is that clear?

Now I will introduce what is meant by the path. Path here refers to not knowing the basic nature—thinking of our basic state as being something other than what it actually is. That is called path. Path is delusion. This delusion or confusion essentially means we fail to know our basic nature as it is, and instead mistake it for something else. That is the confusion: not recognizing what is to be what it is, but regarding it as something other. Mind, as the nature of mind, is fundamentally pure. When we fail to recognize the identity or nature of what knows as something pure, free, egoless, and insubstantial—and when we instead regard the nature of this knowing as being "me" or "I," and hold on to that concept—this is a small view, and it is confused, mistaken. Introducing the idea of me/I is mistaking our essential nature for something that it isn't.

At some point, by means of some method, we are introduced to our basic nature and recognize what is to be as it is. When confusion has thoroughly been cleared up, that is fruition. When this mistakenness is dissolved, where does it go? Nowhere, because the confusion never existed in the first place. If the confusion were a real entity, then when it went away we could follow it and see where it went. But it wasn't real at all.

Among these three, ground, path and fruition, ground is purity, pure. Path is confusion, and fruition is being free from confusion. If anybody asks us what spiritual practice is about, we should reply that it is to clear up confusion. If someone asks what is confusion, what are you going to say?

STUDENT: Conceptual thought.

RINPOCHE: What is conceptual thought?

STUDENT: Delusion.

RINPOCHE: What is delusion?

STUDENT: Thinking something to be what it isn't.

RINPOCHE: How do you know what is to be what it is? What is the use of being free from confusion? What is wrong with confusion?

STUDENT: It is suffering, and knowing that is the path.

RINPOCHE: The Buddha said that, didn't he? Okay, let's hear from somebody else: what is the use of being free from confusion? How many of you agree that we are confused? Why are we confused? Why do you accept this?

STUDENT: Although we intellectually understand what you said about things to be as they are, we don't have the personal experience.

RINPOCHE: One more answer?

STUDENT: Not getting what we want causes pain.

RINPOCHE: Just because what you want doesn't happen, does it mean there is something wrong with what you want? Who decides how things should be? Who knows whether that's right or not?

TRANSLATOR: Can I just interject that when Rinpoche uses the word *trül,* I translate it in three different ways: delusion, confusion, or being mistaken.

RINPOCHE: There is being confused and there is being free. What do you understand by being free?

STUDENT: No thought.

RINPOCHE: That's one point of being free.

STUDENT: Not falling under the power of habitual tendencies.

RINPOCHE: Good.

STUDENT: Being awake and having an open heart.

RINPOCHE: How do you explain being awake and having an open heart?

STUDENT: Doing virtuous activities for the benefit of beings and avoiding the negative.

RINPOCHE: These are all aspects of freedom. Free of confusion means being free from the bonds of karma, whether it be good karma or bad karma. To be free and independent. Freedom means independence, a state in which one is totally unassailable, not impeded or obstructed by anything. Not even the tiniest little thing can obstruct your freedom in the least. That you can call true freedom.

Feeling at peace is of course a freedom, or at least has the flavor of freedom, but real freedom, total freedom, means to be completely independent, not subject to or conditioned by anything whatsoever. In the complete realization of the three kayas—dharmakaya, sambhoga-kaya, nirmanakaya—one is free to send out one hundred billion nirma-nakayas simultaneously or not, as one pleases. One is also able to dissolve all of them at will. To be totally in charge, to have full mastery over all that appears and exists in this way—that you can say is complete freedom, total freedom.

In order to attain this freedom, we need to abandon conceptual mind. Honestly, conceptual mind belongs to the path; it is mistaken, it is confused. Conceptual mind is temporal, it belongs to time, it is bound, it is bondage. This is something to think about.

You are probably all tired by now after all this discussion. Relax, make yourselves comfortable! Be unoccupied, but not in a dry, rigid way, being very stiff and unmoving, not like that. Try to be unoccupied and kind of moist with some inner joy, so that a little smile can come out, like that.

4

RE-ENLIGHTENMENT

Tulku Urgyen Rinpoche

Unfortunately, all sentient beings are not one; they don't become enlightened when one person does. Individual karmas and habitual patterns are innumerable, and just because one person has purified his wrongdoings, obscurations, and habitual tendencies does not mean that everyone else has purified theirs. Ultimately, everybody has to travel the path themselves and purify their own obscurations. The buddhas of the past were not able to liberate all sentient beings, not even *Avalokiteshvara*. But, if one does attain enlightenment, through the power of one's compassion and vast aspirations, one will slowly be able to guide an incredible number of sentient beings toward enlightenment. In particular, when a practitioner attains the rainbow body it is said that 3,000 sentient beings attain liberation simultaneously with the manifestation of the rainbow body.

There are a few cases in the past where many people attained enlightenment simultaneously because they already had the karmic conti-

Adapted from Tulku Urgyen Rinpoche, *Repeating the Words of the Buddha* (Boudhanath: Rangjung Yeshe Publications, 1996), "Re-enlightenment."

nuity of former practice. In the country of Uddiyana 100,000 people simultaneously achieved enlightenment. But these cases are very rare.

There is no other way to reach enlightenment than by recognizing buddha nature and attaining stability in it. Buddhas of the past did that, and the present-day practitioners who will be the buddhas of the future will do so by recognizing their own nature and attaining stability in it. There is no other way. Nobody else can accomplish enlightenment for us or pull us into liberation. It is completely up to ourselves.

For example, if there were a group in which everybody received the pointing-out instruction, recognized the nature of mind, exerted themselves diligently in practice, and grew accustomed to the buddha nature, certainly the whole group could attain enlightenment within this very lifetime. But people have different capacities and different karmic dispositions, so it is never 100 percent certain how many actually recognize the buddha nature in the correct way upon having it pointed out. Nor is it ever fixed how many will truly exert themselves in practice after having recognized the buddha nature. For this reason, it is not 100 percent guaranteed that everybody will accomplish enlightenment in one lifetime.

There have been an incredible number of practitioners in the past who attained accomplishment and liberation, the great bodhisattvas and mahasiddhas of India as well as the Tibetans of different lineages. Just read the life stories of how many practitioners did so; they are like the stars we can see in the night sky. Definitely it is possible—but it is in our own hands.

For sentient beings as a whole, samsara is endless. But for each individual person who practices and awakens to enlightenment there is an end to samsaric existence. There are two possibilities: the endless path of samsara, and the path with an end to samsara. Right now we have the choice between the two. We can practice, gain accomplishment, and attain enlightenment, cutting all ties to our existence in samsara as deluded sentient beings. For the person completely under the power of discursive thinking, the path of samsara continues endlessly. When one gains mastery over the essence of mind by perfecting one's practice of *rigpa*, samsaric existence is brought to an end.

Three key words summarize all Dharma teachings: ground, path, and fruition. The ground, the buddha nature, the dharmakaya of all the buddhas, is like a wish-fulfilling jewel. It is the basis for buddhas and sentient beings; there is no difference whatsoever. It is said that the nature of mind is like a wish-fulfilling jewel. Those who fail to recognize this are called sentient beings; those who realize it are called buddhas. In other words, the jewel of the buddhas did not fall in the mud, whereas the jewel of sentient beings fell in the mud and was covered by dirt. First there was a jewel, then it fell in the mud, under the power of delusion.

Being under the power of delusion or confusion is called the path. All the attempts to clean the jewel in order to remove the dirt obscuring it are the example for spiritual practices that enable one to gain realization.

The term *buddha* refers to someone who has realized the ground to begin with. In this context, buddha refers to primordial enlightenment. Sentient beings have no chance for primordial enlightenment since they already have soiled their jewel. But, by cleaning the jewel through engaging in the practices of visualization, recitation, and meditation, one purifies the obscurations of body, speech, and mind and gathers the accumulations of merit and wisdom. Thus there is the possibility to become "re-enlightened" and that is called fruition.

Phrased in another way, buddhas do not stray into the deluded state of a path. Because their jewel is not dropped in the mud, it does not have to be cleaned. The state of sentient beings is like a jewel that fell in the mud. The dirt has to be removed in order to re-establish the purity of the jewel. The story of the wish-fulfilling jewel is that once it is cleaned it can be placed on top of a victory banner. One can make offerings to it, and it will then fulfill all wishes—that is the fruition.

The ground is the buddha nature, which is like a wish-fulfilling jewel. It is present in all beings just like oil is present in any sesame seed. All beings have buddha nature, but this alone is not enough. The second thing needed is the support of a physical body, the precious human body. It is only as a human that one is able to practice and awaken to enlightenment. Insects and animals do have an enlightened essence, but their body is not a support for realizing it because they cannot receive teachings or speak—they don't come to Dharma talks and receive teachings. Only humans do this. The third factor needed is the positive circumstance of a spiritual teacher. These three need to coincide: having buddha nature, being a human possessing a precious human body, and connecting with a spiritual teacher. Then it's possible to receive the pith instructions on how to recognize and realize the nature that we already have. Although we cannot be primordially enlightened, we can become re-enlightened.

We presently possess all three of these factors: we have the buddha nature, we are humans, and we are connected to a spiritual teacher. If we let this precious opportunity slip away, don't practice, and just watch life pass by until we die, that would be like returning empty-handed from an island full of jewels. Sentient beings are lost; we've lost our buddha nature. An example of this is a stupid person who loses himself in a crowd of people and doesn't know who he is until someone tells him, "Here you are!" If we don't recognize our true nature, we are like the stupid person lost in a crowd, asking, "Where am I?" We need to "find" ourselves. Even though we seem to be lost, by virtue of the positive circumstance of the spiritual teacher we can be introduced to our "lost" nature. The spiritual teacher doesn't hand us something we don't already possess. We have it, and yet we have lost it, so to speak. There is no greater misfortune than losing what we already have, the buddha within ourselves. The qualities of an enlightened buddha are not *his* qualities; they are the qualities of the buddha nature fully manifest. We also possess that same potential, but it is hidden, lying dormant.

If our buddha nature is beyond delusion and liberation, can't we also say that we are in essence primordially enlightened? We could possibly succeed in convincing ourselves with such a philosophical trick, but it's not really true, because we have already strayed onto the path. If we had never fallen into confusion, we could rightfully claim to be primordially enlightened. But unfortunately it is too late to make that claim. Our precious wish-fulfilling jewel has already fallen into the stinking mud.

Primordial enlightenment means that ground and fruition are identical and there is no path of delusion to be cleared away. This is definitely different from the situation of us who have already strayed onto the path and therefore need to clear away delusion in order to reach fruition. Take the example of a myriad of jewels: some are covered with mud, some are clean. All of them are jewels, but each is distinctly individual. Sentient beings' minds cognize individually, so we have to say that they are separate.

This is quite a good example, to view all beings and buddhas as countless jewels, some covered with dirt, some clean. They are not identical even though they have the same qualities. If the minds of all sentient beings were one, then when one individual attains enlightenment, everybody else would be liberated at the same moment. But if you attain enlightenment it doesn't mean that I will be enlightened. Understand it this way: although beings have similar qualities, we are not one. We have the same essence, which is empty and cognizant, but our form of manifestation is separate, distinct from that of another sentient being.

If I recognize buddha nature and attain enlightenment it doesn't mean that another person also recognizes and attains enlightenment. Sorry about that! If beings shared both the same essence and manifestation, when one reached enlightenment everyone else would too. We are like pure gold scattered in different places: equal quality, but separate pieces. Likewise with water: the properties of water are identical, but there is water in many diverse locations in this world. Or think of the space inside our different houses—the same space but with various shapes. The empty cognizance is identical, but the "form" around it is distinctly individual. Some jewels were lucky, others fell in the mud.

5

MEDITATION

Chökyi Nyima Rinpoche

I would like to begin by defining the qualifications for the Dharma teacher and the Dharma student. I will talk about the different types of teachers we can learn from and the need to integrate learning and reflection within meditation training.

The teacher, who is sometimes referred to as the "spiritual friend," should possess numerous great qualities. In brief, he or she should have gone through the proper training of learning, reflection, and meditation involving the view, meditation, conduct, and fruition of each of the vehicles. The master who possesses confidence and experience in the view of emptiness will never err concerning the meaning of the teachings. Although some minor mistakes in the phrasing might occur, someone with stability in the view will be able to immediately correct such inaccuracies.

The spiritual friend should, of course, be perfect in learning, reflection, and meditation, but we, the students, also should never separate these three. Learning alone is not sufficient: what has been learned should be firmly established within one's being through reflection. What

Adapted from Chökyi Nyima Rinpoche, *Indisputable Truth* (Boudhanath: Rangjung Yeshe Publications, 1996), "Meditation."

is meant by the word *reflection*? It means to investigate and examine the teaching. So please discern what is said and what is meant. Investigate what the words and the meaning indicate. Understand the purpose as well as the benefit of the teaching—really work it over and ponder it. This kind of reflection clarifies our understanding of what we study.

Without some degree of study and reflection, our devotion to the spiritual master and to enlightened beings is inconsistent. Likewise, our love and compassion for others tends to be fickle and transient. Especially concerning the view of the ultimate nature, without study or reflection it's very hard to be really stable. Without a proper basis in studying and reflecting, we can easily be interrupted by doubts and hesitation. Maybe we don't get completely wrong views, but subtle wrong views can easily sneak in. Therefore, it's very important to gain some intellectual comprehension of the teachings through studying and reflecting upon them. However, if we simply leave the matter with learning and reflection, we are still mere intellectuals. There is no doubt that we need meditation training. Meditation here means the process of bringing what we have learned and reflected upon into the realm of personal experience.

When speaking of spiritual masters, there are four types of teachers that we should follow, all of whom are indispensable and can bring us great benefit. I go into greater detail about these types of teachers in my book *Indisputable Truth*, but here I will just briefly mention them. The first of these four categories is the "living lineage teacher," an actual physically embodied master who belongs to a lineage. The second type is the "teacher who is the scriptures of awakened beings," which includes the words of the Buddha and statements made by accomplished and learned masters of the past. The third type of teacher is called the "symbolic teacher of experience," our personal experiences gained from living in this world. To fully grasp the Buddhist teaching that states that samsaric existence should be discarded, we need to comprehend what the nature of samsaric existence is. By understanding the characteristics of our own daily life experiences, we come to realize that samsaric existence is futile and unreliable, not something in which to put our trust. In this way, ordinary life becomes our teacher. It instructs us in futility and impermanence. That is what is meant by the symbolic teacher of experience.

We need to meet, follow, and take guidance from these three types of teachers. Ultimately, however, there's only one true teacher. This is our enlightened essence, the self-existing wakefulness within ourselves, also called the "ultimate teacher of the innate nature." All sentient beings within the six classes of living creatures possess this enlightened essence. Among these six classes, the three inferior types—hell beings, hungry ghosts, and animals—also possess an enlightened essence, a buddha nature. But because of their unfortunate circumstances or, in the case of animals, their stupidity, they are unable to put it into practice and realize it. However, anyone who experiences and realizes this enlightened essence does attain complete enlightenment. No matter how miserable or how deluded we may be, if we can bring our buddha nature into our experience and train in it, we can be enlightened. On the other hand, if we don't experience and realize this enlightened essence, we will not attain complete enlightenment. To meet and realize this enlightened essence, we must utilize learning and reflection; most important, we need to practice meditation.

This ultimate teacher of the innate nature is present in everyone, all beings, without any exception. Although this is so, we don't acknowledge it; we don't recognize it. That is why it is said to be shrouded in a veil of ignorance. We have to use that analogy, speaking as if there were something hidden that we need to see. Since our innate nature is locked up inside an encasement of dualistic fixation, we need to destroy this dualistic experience. Now, let's examine whether this statement is true or not.

In terms of destroying this encasement of dualistic experience: unless we use some method, some technique, it just doesn't happen. The best method is of course effortlessness, but effortlessness cannot be taught. Even if we try, we do not become effortless automatically. Effortlessness just doesn't seem to spontaneously take place. But this encasement in dualistic experience falls apart the moment we simply let be in a nondualistic state. Another way to look at it is to realize that every moment of ordinary experience is governed by habit, by conditioning. Our present habit is dominated by deliberate effort. We have therefore no choice but to use our present habit of being deliberate and using effort in order to arrive at effortlessness.

When loving friends want to console or to relieve another's pain, they say, "Relax, don't worry." This is really one of the finest statements that a person can make. Relaxation—especially mental relaxation—is something basic and extremely beneficial. It is human nature to strive for material gain, sense pleasures, a good reputation, and appreciation from others, often in an intense or even desperate way. Unless we can relax and not be so caught up, our relationship to enjoyments and wealth becomes hollow and substanceless, almost as if we were robots.

When someone whose heart is troubled and worried is, out of true affection and kindness, told, "Relax, don't worry," this statement helps and can make a big difference. Telling someone to let go and relax can instill a sense of peace. This holds true not only for human beings but also for animals. When you show a genuinely loving expression on your face and kindly stroke an animal with your hand, these actions help it to feel at ease. Most important is to behave with love and compassion, expressing these feelings by being gentle and affectionate. The opposite of this is to act out of anger and to be aggressive toward others.

This is why the perfectly enlightened one, the Buddha, said, "Rest calmly." In fact, teachings on the practice of shamatha sound very much like "Relax, don't worry." When we tell each other, "Relax!" the power of just that one word has some kind of deep impact. Most people using the word don't really know the true depth of the meaning of "relax." We say, "Relax!" but that which prevents us from being relaxed is, on a coarse level, our own disturbing emotions. On a more subtle level, that which prevents an utterly relaxed state of mind is subconscious thought activity, an almost unnoticed undercurrent of conceptual thinking.

When the Buddha said, "Practice shamatha, rest calmly," he was giving affectionate advice. He was telling us to try to be at peace with ourselves, to remain like an ocean unmoved by the waves of disturbing emotions. We must realize that the degree to which our mind is occupied by disturbing emotions generates a corresponding degree of pain, of feeling unsettled and upset. If there's a medium degree of disturbing emotions, we feel that degree of pain. Even when there is simply an undercurrent of concepts, a subconscious flow of thoughts, this still prevents us from feeling totally at ease and remaining in the peaceful state of shamatha. So, the Buddha said, "Rest totally free, completely without any disturbing emotions, without any thought activity." This practice is called shamatha, and in the Sutra teachings it is taught in incredibly great detail. All the practices of shamatha can be condensed into two types: shamatha with the support of an object and shamatha without any object.

For a beginner it is difficult to simply be at peace, to rest calmly and free from a mental focus. This is because all our activities and ways of perceiving are dualistic, due to the habit of holding an object in mind. Therefore, the beginning practice of shamatha is to keep some concept or object in mind—not a complicated point of focus or multiple ones, just a single simple one.

The most widespread and generally accepted form of shamatha with support involves placing the attention on the movement of our breath or on an object like a pebble, a stick, an image of the Buddha, or the like. Focusing our mind on one simple object prevents it from being occupied by anything else. We are not planning the future, reacting to some past event, indulging in being upset about this and that, or pondering some choice object of love or hate. By concentrating on just one thing, it is possible for a feeling of peace, relaxation, and comfort to take place.

Imagine a monkey locked inside a small box with four openings; it is really restless. It sticks its head out one side after the other, so rapidly and repeatedly that someone observing from the outside might think that there are four monkeys. Our present state of mind is very much like that restless monkey. It doesn't linger in one place from one moment to the next. All the time our minds are busy, constantly thinking. When we practice this form of shamatha, focusing our attention on just one object, we become accustomed to this new habit after some time. That is how it is possible to attain stability in a calm state of mind, in shamatha.

Compared to a state of mind that is occupied by nervous, restless thoughts, it is much better to be in a focused, relaxed state of peaceful attention. The benefits of this can be seen immediately: the very moment mind is simply focused on one object, the waves of disturbing thoughts and emotions are absent. Spending a session meditating in this way is like taking a break. It becomes a time of peace and calm, of feeling comfortable with ourselves. When our attention begins to stray away, when we are unable to keep an object in mind, we get distracted, and the feeling of being at ease also disappears. Then we remember the object of attention and continue as before, and the feeling of being at peace reoccurs.

At this point of meditation training, please don't believe that dualistic fixation is absent; it hasn't collapsed yet. Yet, the moment of resting calmly with focused attention is free of gross disturbing emotions; it's free of anger, attachment, and dullness. Say we're focusing on a vase of flowers. We're not involved in reacting against the flowers, in aggressively disliking them, which is anger. We are not attracted to them either, thinking how nice they are, which is attachment. Neither are we indifferent to them, which is dullness. Although the mind is free from the gross expression of these three types of emotions, there is still some sense of focus, of "me," "that," and "I'm focused!" As long as one retains such concepts of subject and object, dualistic fixation is not absent. In this way, it's not yet the perfect type of shamatha, and it is definitely not the awakened state of mind. Nevertheless, compared to an ordinary disturbed state of mind, shamatha with an object is much preferable, because it's free from gross disturbing emotions.

As beginners, we should stay focused on the object of attention. And yet we need to understand that as long as the mind stays focused on an object, something is still incomplete. Deciding "I will rest my attention on one thing" is quite beneficial. But it would be even better if we could simply rest our attention free from focus, in a total openness free from reference point. This is the second type of shamatha. As long as we remain focused upon a particular object, we retain the idea of "that" and "I," meaning the one who focuses and the object of focus. There's still some degree of fixation or grasping occurring. In Buddhism, grasping or fixating on duality is considered the root cause of samsaric existence. Thus, to practice a meditation that is an exercise in retaining dualistic fixation can't be called perfect. Still, it is a stepping-stone. If we don't learn our ABCs in first grade, we'll never start reading. In the same way, once we grow accustomed to the practice of shamatha with focus, it becomes very simple to learn how to rest calmly free from focus. When our attention remains totally undisturbed by emotions, thoughts, and concepts, free from all reference points, and free from focus, that is called objectless shamatha.

Having cultivated this state of shamatha, the next step is to embrace it by clear seeing, by vipashyana. The practice of shamatha, of being at peace, is by itself insufficient to obtain liberation from the three realms of samsaric existence. For this reason it is extremely important to carefully study the teachings, to reflect upon them, and to become clear about how to practice. If we don't do this, if we simply identify the ultimate meditation state with shamatha, even though we may become very stable, we may never go beyond a samsaric state called the "formless meditation gods." We may remain here for a very long time, but when the experience eventually wears out we end up back in other samsaric states. So it's very important to be careful, to see clearly.

We should understand that shamatha practice has both pros and cons, a good side and a bad side. The good side of shamatha is that it is free from any disturbing emotions, free from the agonizing thought activity of the three times. The bad side of shamatha is that in itself it does not lead to liberation from samsara. It only becomes a cause for liberation when embraced by vipashyana. The realization of all the buddhas is described as the unity of shamatha and vipashyana, never as shamatha by itself.

To reiterate, first of all, when we're not involved in disturbing emotions and thoughts, there is an immediate sense of peace, of relief from suffering. The state of shamatha is unspoiled by thoughts of the past, present, or future. By not thinking of anything in these three times, we are free from disturbing emotions. In addition to shamatha, there is also the practice of vipashyana, which means "seeing clearly." The basic nature of our mind, our innate nature, is a wakefulness in which emptiness and cognizance are indivisible. Unless there is some clear seeing of this innate wakefulness, to merely rest calmly in a state of stillness is essentially to be ignorant. We need to do more than simply be free from disturbing emotions and thought activity. Excellent as it is, a tranquil feeling is not enough to clearly see our innate nature. Self-existing wakefulness, the unity of being empty and cognizant, is totally free from any fixation on subject and object. To rest evenly in that is called the unity of shamatha and vipashyana. So, straighten your back. Stop talking, and don't force or control your breathing—just let it flow naturally. The realization of all buddhas is the unity of shamatha and vipashyana.

The Buddha gave different levels of teachings aimed at different types of persons, so we should apply whatever teaching fits us. If you know how to practice the state that is the unity of shamatha and vipashyana, then you should do that. If you feel that you are better able or more ready to practice the state of shamatha without object, you should do that. And if you feel that's difficult, that you must focus on an object in order for the attention not to waver from one thing to another, then practice shamatha focused on an object. We should practice according to our individual capacity, which is something we ourselves know. It doesn't help to fool ourselves, thinking we can practice something that we don't really understand. Be honest and practice in accordance with your own level. Then the session is not wasted.

Meditation training is the opposite of the ordinary conceptual state of mind that thinks, "I am here, the world is there." Because it's so different from our ordinary state of mind, it's vital to study and reflect in order to eradicate any lack of understanding, misunderstanding, or doubt that we may have about the correct view, meaning the correct understanding of how things are. If we, after arriving at certainty in the correct view, implement that in meditation practice, even a short period of meditation will have a great impact. On the other hand, if we don't gain an authentic understanding of the view of the innate nature of things, the effect will not be that great no matter how diligent we are. In short, don't separate learning, reflection, and meditation, because these can clear away all the faults of not understanding, misunderstanding, and doubt.

PART THREE

INTEGRATION

6

INTEGRATING VIEW AND CONDUCT

Tulku Urgyen Rinpoche

Of the two aspects of view and conduct, it is said that we should "ascend with the conduct"—start with the conduct at the bottom and work up. This means first study and practice the teachings of the *shravakas*; next the teachings of the bodhisattvas, and finally those of the Vajrayana. Start with the bottom and work up—ascend with the conduct. We do this first by contemplating the four mind-changings, then practicing the specific preliminaries, then doing *yidam practice*, and finally ending with the three great views. The three great views are known as Mahamudra, the Great Seal; Dzogchen, the Great Perfection; and Madhyamika, the Great Middle Way.

The Buddha described his teachings in this way:

Just like the steps of a staircase,
You should train step-by-step
And endeavor in my profound teachings.
Without jumping the steps, proceed gradually to the end.

Adapted from Tulku Urgyen Rinpoche, *Rainbow Painting* (Boudhanath: Rangjung Yeshe Publications, 1995), "Conduct."

Just as a small child
Gradually develops its body and strength,
Dharma is in that same way,
From the steps of entering in the beginning
Up until the complete perfection.

Accordingly, we should behave in conformity with the basic teachings, starting from the bottom, just as we would on a staircase. We cannot climb a staircase by starting at the top; we must begin with the first step.

The view, on the other hand, should be unfolded from above: that is why the saying continues "while descending with the view." Imagine a canopy or parasol that is unfolded above oneself: the view should descend from above in this way.

We must be careful because there is a way of perverting this basic principle and turning it completely upside down, so that one ascends with the view and descends with the conduct. This means to behave according to the highest vehicle while holding a view that starts from the bottom. This is called perverting the teachings. We should get the highest view, but behave first like a shravaka, then like a *pratyekabuddha*, and slowly like a bodhisattva. Regarding conduct, start from the bottom, not the other way around. You will not find any teaching anywhere that says, "Keep the view of a shravaka, or an even lower view, while acting like a Dzogchen yogi." This is a very important principle: keep the view as high as possible, but behave with a very low profile. Act like a shravaka, then a pratyekabuddha, then a bodhisattva. This is called unfolding the view from above, while ascending with the conduct from below.

The view of Mahamudra, Dzogchen, and Madhyamika is identical in essence. Although it is said, "The ground is Mahamudra, the path is the Middle Way, and the fruition is the Great Perfection," in the view itself there is no difference whatsoever. In my tradition we do not select only one particular view among these three. The naked, natural state of mind does not exclusively belong to any specific category of Middle Way, Mahamudra, or Dzogchen. These three are taught here as one identical nature. The awakened state of Mahamudra does not differ from the awakened state of Dzogchen or Madhyamika. Buddhahood is the final fruition of all these regardless of which of these paths you follow, just as when you approach the Vajra Seat in Bodh Gaya from north, south, or west, you arrive at exactly that spot. It does not matter from which direction we approach it; the ultimate destination is the same.

To be a real yogi, someone who truly realizes these three great views, first recognize the natural state of awareness. Then, train to develop the strength of that recognition by sustaining its continuity. Finally, gain some degree of stability. That is the only authentic way. Some people, though, want this to happen on the spot. They do not want to undergo any of the preliminary practices, or subject themselves to the yidam training that is known as the main part of the practice. Some people want nothing but the view. That would be fine if it really were enough, but it is not.

The main reason you cannot only teach the view is that quite a few people will then miss the main point by believing, "I only need the view! There is nothing to do! I can give up all activities!" Of course, this may be true in some sense; however, what happens when someone gives up conventional Dharma practice too early is that such a person fails to do any spiritual practice in terms of purifying obscurations and gathering the accumulations. At the same time, he or she does not truly realize, progress in, and attain stability in the view. The end result is that the view remains an idea while your behavior shows no regard for good and evil. That is what Padmasambhava meant by "losing the conduct in the view."

We need to integrate view and conduct. Padmasambhava said as well, "Though your view is higher than the sky, keep your deeds finer than barley flour." Understand the expression "finer than barley flour" to mean to adopt what is virtuous and avoid what is evil, with respect for the law of cause and effect, with attention to the smallest detail. This is to keep harmony between view and conduct. The opposite, separating one's actions from the view, is to somehow convince oneself that there is no need to do the preliminary practices, no need for any good deeds, no need for making offerings, and no need to apologize for evil actions. One can fool oneself into believing one need only remain in simplicity. What this honestly means, though, is that such a person will have no spiritual progress. Ultimately, it is definitely true that there *is* nothing to do, but this is true only after one has passed through to the other side of understanding, experience, and realization. To maintain an intellectual conviction of the view without having undergone the training is a severe misunderstanding. This is how the self-professed "Dzogchen practitioner" goes astray.

In Tibet many people committed this grave error. Westerners cannot really be blamed for this fault yet, since the Dharma is only now taking hold in their countries; the understanding of practice is just being established. Tibet, on the other hand, was a country where the Dharma had been taught and understood for many centuries. Yet many people went astray in this fashion, not simply a few. Frankly speaking, there may have been more people in Tibet with a "make-believe view" than with genuine insight.

I do not feel I can really blame Westerners who heard stories about the Buddha and the Indian siddhas receiving the teachings on mind essence and nondoing, and who then think, "Well, we are the same; there is nothing to do. Everything is fine as it is."

It is honestly not such a simple matter to arrive at the correct view. You must connect with a true master; you must have the necessary intelligence. Then you must go all the way through the training. It is much easier to glare at benefactors with wide-open eyes and look about with an air of Dzogchen. Most people behaving like that are actually charlatans. Often they could not help it; without some dishonesty it could be hard to get by and gather donations. Playing the simple meditator and keeping a low profile would not be successful—who would know about your realization then? If you happened to be an upstart lama with a penchant for fame and fortune, you would have to brag a little. You would need to tell about how many Dharma lineages and teachings you held, how long you stayed in retreats, how special your realization is, how you tamed both gods and demons, and the like. Then things would happen; you would be swarmed by sponsors and followers like a piece of rotting meat covered with flies. Yes, honestly, there were more fake lamas in Tibet than authentic ones.

Some people have the habit of thinking that something is bound to happen after practicing meditation a while—like going through school—that after ten or fifteen years you end up with a degree. That's the idea in the back of people's minds: "I can make it happen! I can *do* enlightenment!" Not in this case, though. You cannot make enlightenment, because enlightenment is unconstructed. Realizing the awakened state is a matter of being diligent in allowing nondual awareness to regain its natural stability. It is difficult to reach enlightenment without such diligence, without undertaking any hardship.

Faced with the reality of not progressing in the so-called meditation practice of a conceptually constructed view, you might get discouraged: "I can't get enlightened! I spent three years in retreat and nothing has happened!" On the other hand, if you practice in an authentic fashion you will definitely become enlightened; there is no question about this. Training assiduously with devotion, compassion, and loving-kindness while repeatedly letting be in unconstructed equanimity, you will surely discover the true signs of spiritual practice. These signs are the acute feeling that life is impermanent and that there is no time to waste; that the Dharma is unfailing; that there is genuine benefit from training in samadhi; and that it is truly possible to overcome conceptual thinking.

While these are taught to be the most wonderful signs of progress, a materialistic type of person will not see them as being so wonderful. He wants a flabbergasting meditation experience. If something astounding happens that he can see or hear or maybe even touch, he thinks, "Wow! I am really getting somewhere now! This is completely different from what I am used to—such a beautiful experience! Such bliss! Such clarity! Such emptiness! I feel totally transformed! This must really be *it*!" [Rinpoche chuckles.]

On the other hand, when you reach the "even plains" of non-thought, the simple quiet after conceptual thinking dissolves, there is nothing very exceptional to see, hear, or grasp. You may feel, "Does this really lead anywhere? There is nothing special in this!" Honestly, the view is not something spectacular; on the contrary, it is free from pinpointing anything particular at all. The person who does not comprehend this fact will think, "What's the use of this? I worked so hard for years and nothing is really happening! Maybe it would be better to visualize some deity. Maybe I should chant some special mantra that would give me powers, and then I could show some results of practice, some real accomplishment!" People do fall prey to this type of thinking.

During this process, your subtle disturbing emotions remain intact; eventually they manifest again and take over your being. Why wouldn't they? Everyone is overcome by disturbing emotions unless they are stable in nondual awareness. Only the moment of the awakened state does not become caught up in deluded emotion. Nondual awareness is the most effective way, but the materialistic practitioner does not appreciate this. He wants an altered state, a special experience, an extraordinary dream. When it happens he congratulates himself, "Excellent! This is the real thing!" Such is the weakness of human nature.

My root guru Samten Gyatso once said, "I have not had a single special experience. As the years pass by, my trust in the authenticity of the Dharma grows. I am confident in the truth of the three kayas. From the age of eight I looked into the essence of mind, and since then I have never forsaken it. My diligence varied and of course I became distracted at times, but mostly I have kept to the practice of mind essence." I only heard him say this once; otherwise, he would never discuss such personal matters.

At the same time Samten Gyatso was so intelligent and learned, so attentive to every little detail, so skilled in every little task, so steady and trustworthy, that people would regard him as being like Marpa the Translator. Samten Gyatso was so precise in all matters that if you got his word on something you would never later hear him say that he forgot. That's the kind of man he was, extremely dependable, totally reliable.

His eyes burned with an astonishing brilliance, like the flame of a butter lamp at its end, somewhat like the bright eyes of a kitten. Coming into his presence, it felt as if he was penetrating your innermost core, laying bare your innermost secrets. Anyway, he was scrupulously attentive to all his daily affairs, both spiritual and secular. He never postured or put on the air of high realization. In Tibet there was no shortage of people of *that* kind—people who never lowered their vacant, glaring gaze to the ground, and who spouted random statements like "All the phenomena of samsara and nirvana are great equality!" [Rinpoche laughs.] Actually, what do you gain from such pretense!

So you see, it is possible to lose the conduct in the view. It is also possible to lose the view in the conduct. Caring for others, helping them with medicine and education, is definitely virtuous. However, it must be done out of an attitude of the *four immeasurables*, without any selfish aims for fame and respect, and without dwelling on the idea "I am doing good! I am kind to others!" To act out of the four immeasurables creates virtuous *karma* of the general conditioned kind. Helping others out of a pure selfless motivation is the best form of conditioned virtue; it is truly wonderful!

Unconditioned virtue, on the other hand, is the training in thought-free wakefulness. Many people ask, "How does sitting in meditation practice help others? It would be much better to go out and give them food and medical care and build them schools." People may have the attitude of wanting to act for the welfare of others before having accomplished anything themselves. Helping others is definitely virtuous, and it does help them somewhat. You of course create good karma by helping others, but such altruistic action does not necessarily mean you will be liberated. Only after liberation can you immeasurably benefit all beings.

The most important technique for avoiding pitfalls on the path is knowledge and trust in the Dharma. Knowledge means comprehension of what is and what is not true, through studying and understanding the teachings. The real knowledge, however, that which we should really be diligent in, is understanding the view. View, meditation, conduct, and fruition all depend on the view. Diligence in meditation involves the *development stage*, while diligence in conduct refers to the bodhisattva trainings.

A very important factor is an unchanging trust in the Three Jewels. You can gain it by considering this: without the Precious Buddha, wouldn't this world be totally blind? How could anyone reach liberation from samsara or the omniscient state of enlightenment? It is solely through studying and following his flawless words, the Precious Dharma, that our congenitally blind eyes will open. Without someone to uphold and transmit these teachings through the spoken and written word, the teachings would surely have died out. The Buddha would have appeared and taught and then nothing; the whole process would not have taken even a hundred years. That we still have the Buddha's teachings available today is thanks to the Precious Sangha, consisting mainly of the great bodhisattvas on the ten bhumis, the sons of the victorious ones, and the arhats. My role is to be teaching the Dharma, and regardless of whether it is pretense or not, I definitely have received the blessings of the Precious Sangha. When I think about it, the kindness of the Three Jewels is absolutely incredible! So how can I help having trust in them?

Knowledge, the other factor, is what helps us to distinguish between what is and what is not true. In ancient times, the Buddha taught that there were 360 religions and belief systems prevalent in the world. These were also called the "360 wrong views" because they were incorrect, consisting mainly of different varieties of *eternalism and nihilism*. The Buddha taught the true view. There is a simple reason for this: a sentient being cannot realize the correct view that is unmixed with concepts, because the mind of any sentient being is conceptual. The only way to transcend conceptual mind is to follow the words of a fully awakened one, a buddha.

Knowledge is what distinguishes between truth and untruth, between what is correct meditation training and what is not. As we gradually progress through deeper levels of learning, as our knowledge broadens, our fixation automatically diminishes. Isn't fixation and clinging the root of samsara? When there is no more clinging to painful or pleasant situations, we are free from samsara. As *Tilopa* said, "You are not bound by what you experience, but by your clinging to it. So cut through your clinging, *Naropa!*"

It is also said, "The sign of learning is to be gentle and disciplined." Imagine a piece of paper burned in the fire—it becomes totally soft. A sense of peace is the true sign of learnedness. "The sign of meditation training is a decrease in disturbing emotions," meaning that the training of looking into mind essence dissolves your three or five poisons, which is the unrecognized expression of your essence. This occurs the moment you recognize it. The disturbing emotions vanish without a trace, like flames extinguished.

Sentient beings chase around after all sorts of myriad things. Now is the time to take a rest. Otherwise, we will continue to roam around in samsaric existence. Nothing other than mindfulness can really block off or halt your karma. It is our karmic actions and disturbing emotions that force us to wander through samsara, and it is these karmic actions and disturbing emotions that we need to relinquish. Don't we need to stop being under their control? The moment of the view does not lie subject to karma and disturbing emotions. The view is the real reason the buddhas are not under the power of karma and disturbing emotions; they have captured the stronghold of the view.

Realizing the view, authentically and totally, melts away the obscurations of karma and disturbing emotions, and this allows the qualities of original wakefulness to unfold. This is the real meaning of "buddha," the awakened state of mind. If you could truly allow this to happen, wouldn't that then be the absence of all defects and the perfection of all virtues? The correct view is what clears away all faults. Stability in the view reveals the essential nature of mind free of obscurations, like the sky that cannot be dyed any color or to which nothing can adhere. Yet the sky itself is not something that can vanish. Please understand this vital point!

It is often said that to plan to practice sometime in the future is to let obstacles slip in before the practice even begins. Most people let the time slide by, thinking, "I really want to practice the Dharma more and I will surely do so later on in my life!" Other people may believe that the time has come to act for the welfare of others, while in fact they do not possess the qualifications to effectively do so. They think, "Now I will teach! I can really help others! I can make a difference!" Then they run about in the world pretending to work for sentient beings.

Generally speaking, Westerners are quite sharp when it comes to comprehending the natural state. If they would also practice it afterward! And not only the natural state: we need to train ourselves to exert effort in virtuous actions. Engaging in evil requires no effort at all; it is spontaneous. Killing others, stealing their possessions, lying, and so forth require almost no effort at all. One need not teach insects how to kill each other. No sentient being needs training in the three negative karmic actions of the body carried out on the physical plane; we engage in them quite spontaneously. Even animals needn't be taught how to kill.

Without having to study, we know quite naturally how to carry out the four negative actions of speech: lying, using harsh words, slandering, and engaging in idle gossip. No one needs to train in the three negative actions of mind: ill will, craving, and holding wrong ideas. We all seem to know quite well how to carry out these activities. Sentient beings are already experts; it happens quite spontaneously due to the ripening of past karma. Dharma, on the other hand, is something we need to study.

To roll a big boulder up to the top of a mountain, we need to push it all the way up. But to let it roll down into the valley, we need not do much; we let go and it rolls down all by itself. Nudge a stone and it will roll downhill all by itself, but there is no such thing as a stone that rolls uphill. In the same way, we do not need to study how to engage in negative actions. Sometimes, when giving in to the impetus to carry out a negative action we are under the power of karma. At other times we feel faith in the teachings; we feel good-hearted, compassionate, and devout, and so forth, yet this is very rare. That is why it is said, "Those who don't practice are as abundant as the stars at night; those who do practice are as scarce as morning stars." This is due to karma.

For those with good karma, the situation is different. A great Kagyü master sang, "Even in my mother's womb, my spiritual aspirations were awakened and I had the desire to practice. At the age of eight, I remained in equanimity." That's an example of good karma ripening.

Again, although you may have a very high view, you should still keep a refined level of training. Here, refined means that you pay close attention to and remember impermanence and your mortality. When you reach the point of not being distracted from the recognition of mind essence, impermanence is not such an important issue. If something is impermanent, let it be impermanent; if it is not, then it is not. Only when you have no distraction whatsoever do you not need to think about impermanence.

"High view" in this case means to pay close attention to how things are, such as impermanence. "Good meditation" does not only mean being skilled in the development stage or *yogic exercises*; it means facing the fact that everything is impermanent. It also means reaching the point of nondistraction. In other words, one does not sleep at night; one does not fall into the delusory dream state, but is able to recognize dreams as dreams. During deep sleep, there is a continuous long stretch of luminous wakefulness. When one reaches this point, there is no need to dwell on impermanence anymore.

The Tibetan word for enlightenment is *jangchub*, which means "purified perfection," or in Sanskrit, *bodhi*. Literally, this means the complete purification of the two obscurations, along with habitual tendencies, and the perfection of all qualities of wisdom. It is like a lotus bud that, having grown out of the mud, fully blooms. Until this occurs, we should practice as the masters of the past advise: "Go to a retreat place, either in a forest or in the mountains. In a remote, quiet spot, take a comfortable seat, supplicate your guru one-pointedly, and inspire yourself by thinking of impermanence with compassion."

In Kham, there is a saying, "When you want to boil water, you can blow on the flames or pump the bellows, as long as the water boils." In the same way, if all the different practices we do benefit our stream-of-being, then that's fine. If you can remain in nondual awareness without meditating and without being distracted, everything is fine. But if your nondual awareness is merely imagined, or if you try to construct it in meditation, it will remain merely a concept. If awareness becomes carried away, then you are in delusion. The key term here is "undistracted nonmeditation." When nondual awareness is totally free of confusion and distraction, then your water has really boiled.

7

PADMASAMBHAVA'S
OVERVIEW OF THE PATH

Jamgön Kongtrül

EXPLANATION OF THE PATH
THAT CAUSES REALIZATION

There are two parts: A short statement by means of a summary and the detailed explanation of that.

Short Statement by Means of a Summary

The *Lamrim Yeshe Nyingpo* root text says:

> The stages of the path that bring about realization are innumerable.
> Purify your being, sow the seeds, and cultivate them.
> Remove the hindrances, and likewise bring forth enhancement.
> Thus, enter the correct path through these five aspects.

An inconceivable number of stages of the paths of Sutra and Mantra have been taught as the methods that bring about realization of the

From Padmasambhava and Jamgön Kongtrül, *The Light of Wisdom,* Volume I (Boudhanath: Rangjung Yeshe Publications, 1998).

inseparability of ground and fruition. Yet, when condensing these into one vital essence, the way to purify your being is like tilling a hard virgin field; the way to sow the seeds of ripening and freeing is like planting grain free from defects; the way to nurture them is like the endeavor in the acts of farming such as giving water and fertilizer; the way to remove the hindrances of the path is like the exertion in protecting against hailstorms and the like; and the way to bring forth enhancement of qualities is like applying the means for improvement such as bringing rain, and so forth.[11]

Enter therefore thoroughly the correct path by training correctly in the path through these five aspects, and thus, you will realize the fruition of liberation, like the fully ripened crops.

Detailed Explanation

This includes five steps: purifying your being; sowing the seeds; cultivating them; removing hindrances; and bringing forth enhancement.

PURIFYING YOUR BEING
This has two points: the way to follow a spiritual guide, the root of the path, and, having followed him, the way of mind training.

8

ADVICE ON HOW TO PRACTICE
THE DHARMA CORRECTLY

Padmasambhava

Padmakara, the master of Uddiyana, resided at Samye after being invited to Tibet by the king. He gave numerous teachings to the king, his chieftains, and other devoted people in the eastern part of the central temple. Since they didn't understand correctly, he gave this advice repeatedly.

Master Padma said: No matter how much I teach, the people of Tibet don't understand; instead they engage in nothing other than perverted actions. If you want to practice the Dharma from the core of your heart, do like this:

To be a Buddhist lay person (*upasaka*) doesn't just mean to observe the *four root precepts*; it means to cast unvirtuous misdeeds far away. To be a novice (*shramana*) doesn't merely mean to assume a pure exterior; it means to practice virtue correctly. To be a monk (*bhikshu*) doesn't only mean to control body, speech, and mind in daily activities and to be forbidden to do all kinds of things; it means to bring all roots of virtue to the path of great enlightenment.

From Padmasambhava, *Advice from the Lotus-Born* (Boudhanath: Rangjung Yeshe Publications, 1996), "Advice on How to Practice the Dharma Correctly."

To be virtuous doesn't simply mean to wear yellow robes; it means to fear the ripening of karma. To be a spiritual friend doesn't just mean to assume a dignified demeanor; it means to be the glorious protector of everyone. To be a yogi doesn't merely mean to behave crudely; it means to mingle one's mind with the nature of dharmata.

To be a *mantrika* doesn't just mean to mutter incantations [with a malevolent attitude]; it means to swiftly attain enlightenment through the path of uniting means and knowledge. To be a meditator doesn't simply mean to live in a cave; it means to train oneself in the true meaning [of the natural state]. To be a hermit doesn't just mean to live in the deep forest; it means that one's mind is free from dualistic constructs.

To be learned doesn't only mean to uphold the *eight worldly concerns*; it means to distinguish between right and wrong.[12] To be a bodhisattva doesn't mean to retain self-interest within; it means to exert oneself in the means of liberating all sentient beings from samsara.

To have faith doesn't mean to whimper; it means to enter the right path out of fear of death and rebirth. To be diligent doesn't mean to engage in various restless activities; it means to exert oneself in the means of leaving samsaric existence behind. To be generous doesn't merely mean to give with bias and partiality; it means to be profoundly free from attachment to anything whatsoever.

Oral instruction doesn't mean many written books; it means a few words that strike the vital point of meaning in your mind. View doesn't simply mean philosophical opinion; it means to be free from the limitations of mental constructs. Meditation doesn't mean to fixate on something with thought; it means your mind is stable in natural cognizance, free from fixation.

Spontaneous action doesn't just mean to act with crazy abandon; it means to be free from fixation on deluded perceptions as being real. Discriminating knowledge (*prajña*) doesn't mean the sharp intellect of mistaken thought; it means to understand that all phenomena are nonarising and devoid of mental constructs.

Learning doesn't just mean to receive teachings through one's ears; it means to cut through misconceptions and have realization beyond conceptual mind. Reflecting doesn't only mean to pursue conceptual thinking and form assumptions; it means to cut through your deluded clinging. Fruition doesn't only mean the *rupakayas* invited down from *Akanishtha*; it means to recognize the nature of mind and attain stability in that.

Don't mistake mere words to be the meaning of the teachings. Mingle the practice with your own being and attain liberation from samsara right now.

9

THE QUALIFIED MASTER

Tulku Urgyen Rinpoche

Before setting out on the path of liberation and enlightenment, we need to meet a true qualified master. To find such a person we must first understand the characteristics that such an individual exemplifies. When we go to school we need a good teacher. If your teacher is a complete moron without any skill, how can you learn anything from him? In the same way, the kind of spiritual teacher we are looking for is a person who can guide us all the way to liberation and the omniscient state of enlightenment. Isn't that true?

"Liberation" means taking rebirth in a pure buddhafield after this life. The "omniscient state of enlightenment" is complete buddhahood endowed with all perfect qualities and totally free from any defects whatsoever. We should be seeking the kind of teacher who can surely lead us to that state. The most qualified teacher is called a "vajra-holder possessing the three precepts." He or she should possess the perfect qualities of being outwardly endowed with the vows of individual liberation, called *pratimoksha*, while inwardly possessing the trainings of a

Adapted from Tulku Urgyen Rinpoche, *Rainbow Painting* (Boudhanath: Rangjung Yeshe Publications, 1995), "The Qualified Master."

bodhisattva. On the innermost level, the qualified master must be competent in the true state of samadhi.

A person who possesses only the vows of individual liberation that correspond to Hinayana practice is called a "virtuous guide." If a person in addition possesses the bodhisattva trainings, he or she is called a "spiritual teacher." If a person is adept in the Vajrayana practices along with these vows and trainings, he or she is called a *dorje lobpön*, or "vajra master."

A true vajra master should have already liberated his own stream-of-being through realization. This means actualizing the authentic state of samadhi. Furthermore, he or she should be able to liberate others through compassion and loving-kindness; that is a second essential quality.

To illustrate some characteristics of a qualified vajra master I will tell you about my teacher. My guru was my uncle, Samten Gyatso. Samten Gyatso was my father's older brother and was the fourth incarnation of Ngawang Trinley. I feel a little shy telling this story because there is no way I can avoid praising this person. I really don't want it to sound as if I'm indirectly praising myself by lauding a family member. However, there is a crude example I can use to illustrate this. My guru was excellent, and I am related to him, in the same way that excrement is akin to the very good food it initially was. Understand the analogy. I am just being honest. Even though I'm telling the truth, it's embarrassing because I must praise someone of my own lineage.

My uncle, my root guru, was from the Tsangsar family line on my grandfather's side. Samten Gyatso's mother, Könchok Paldrön, was the daughter of the *tertön* Chokgyur Lingpa. Samten Gyatso held as well as other lineages the lineage known as Chokling Tersar, the New Treasures of Chokgyur Lingpa. Samten Gyatso was regarded as an emanation of four-armed Mahakala. The second incarnation of Chokgyur Lingpa once had a pure vision of Samten Gyatso in which he saw him as an emanation of *Vimalamitra*. Externally, Samten Gyatso kept the *Vinaya* very purely and strictly. In his entire life, he never tasted alcohol nor ate any meat. Inwardly, in tune with the bodhisattva trainings, he always kept a low profile. He never dressed up; instead he wore the robes of an ordinary monk. He was never adorned with anything special, such as brocade.

People said he had a very high view or realization, but he did not talk about it. Once, though, he told me, "At a young age I was introduced to mind essence. Since then until now, I have not had any great problems at all in sustaining the view; as a matter of fact, there does not seem to be any difference between day and night." To repeat, a vajra-holder possessing the three levels of precepts holds the external precepts, which are the moral disciplines of individual liberation. He also holds the internal precepts, which are the bodhisattva trainings, and the inner-most Vajrayana precepts called *samaya*. Samten Gyatso had perfected all three.

It is said that the confidence of the Dharma influences other people's experience. Because of possessing this courage Samten Gyatso was never afraid of anyone. He always wore ordinary, simple clothing. He never dressed in a special fashion, no matter who came to see him or whom he went to meet, even though he encountered some of the highest mas-ters of Tibet. Although he never put on any conspicuous finery, when he entered a room people always made way for him. Even if they were important dignitaries, people were completely terrified of him. They would immediately move to the side to make a path for him to walk.

Even the Karmapa was a little afraid of Samten Gyatso. He once told a companion, "I'm really terrified of that lama. I don't know why, but he really scares me." Even I would have to tell myself, "I don't have to be afraid; after all, he's my uncle!" Yet every morning when I stood before the door to my uncle's quarters, I would always hesitate and think twice before daring to open the door. There was nothing to really be afraid of, but everyone, including me, was somehow intimidated by Samten Gyatso. He possessed some remarkable quality, an intensely commanding presence.

One of Samten Gyatso's gurus, Karmey Khenpo Rinchen Dargye, was reborn as the son of Samten Gyatso's sister. He was called Khentrül, meaning the incarnation of Karmey Khenpo. This young incarnation once said to me, "Why should we be scared of him: Samten Gyatso is our uncle." The young Khentrül was quite courageous, and eloquent in a remarkable way. However, whenever he came into Samten Gyatso's presence and saw his bald head, Khentrül would forget what he was about to say. He would lower his gaze and start to tremble very slightly.

Since he was guru to the king, Samten Gyatso was often summoned to the palace, where he would preside over the various religious cere-monies. He would stay in the old palace, while the king and his family resided in the new palace. In the new palace was an assembly hall called the Square Hall, where the big chieftains, ministers and dignitaries sat with their haughty airs. The king, who was quite eccentric, would not allow any upholstered seating in this room—only hard wooden benches. No matter how special the ministers might be, they had to sit on bare wooden planks. Nevertheless, they sat there in their fine brocade *chuba*s with long sleeves. When they strutted about, they kept their noses in the air and did not pay any attention to ordinary people.

When Samten Gyatso came to see the royal family each morning, he had to pass through this hall. He would often cough slightly before entering. When the dignitaries heard the "cough" approaching, they would all try to stand up at once. Sometimes they tried to stand up by leaning on the shoulder of the person next to them. Then, because they were all using the same support system, they would all tumble here and there and make a mess of themselves. They were all completely terrified of Samten Gyatso.

I was often one of the two attendants who accompanied Samten Gyatso on his visits to the living quarters of the royal family. When Samten Gyatso entered their room, the queen, prince, and princesses would all immediately abandon whatever they were doing and leap to their feet. The king himself had long before turned over his rule to the prince and was seldom seen because he remained in meditation retreat.

Samten Gyatso never flattered others by playing up to them or telling them how wonderful they were. He spoke in a very straightforward manner. If something was true, he would say it was; if it was not, he would say it was not—without adding or subtracting anything. He never talked around the subject. If anyone started to speak to him directly concerning his amazing qualities, he would not allow them an opening. For instance, if they began to say, "Rinpoche, you are very learned . . ." or "You must be very realized . . ." he would scold them immediately. He never tolerated that.

Samten Gyatso kept to the "hidden yogi style" whereby he did not show his accomplishments to anyone, and definitely did not behave as if he was someone special. He never blessed people by placing his hand on their heads, he did not permit others to prostrate to him, and he never sat on a high seat. He spent most of his early life living in caves. If he had any understanding or special powers, he did not ever show them to anyone. He did not build temples or erect statues. During the first part of his life, he always had four or five private scribes with him. He had the entire *Chokling Tersar*, almost forty volumes, copied out. In fact, this is the only thing he actually put any effort into, having the whole *Chokling Tersar* written down exactly.

How then was Samten Gyatso installed as a vajra master? It happened in the following way. The fifteenth Karmapa had wanted to receive the transmission of the Chokling Tersar from Chokgyur Lingpa's son, Tsewang Norbu. At that time, Tsewang Norbu had arrived in Central Tibet and was staying in Lhasa at a benefactor's home. Khakyab Dorje sent for him and Tsewang Norbu agreed to go. Unfortunately, his self-important benefactor, not wanting to let go of his resident priest, made it difficult for Tsewang Norbu to leave. Tsewang Norbu died soon after without ever having the chance to travel to Tsurphu and transmit the Chokling Tersar.

Karmapa then sent for Tsewang Norbu's nephew, Tersey Tulku. He was a reincarnation of Tsewang Norbu's brother, another son of Chokgyur Lingpa, who died while still very young and was eventually reborn as the son of Chokgyur Lingpa's daughter, Könchok Paldrön. He was the youngest of her four sons, being my uncle and the brother of Samten Gyatso. Tersey Tulku was extremely learned and paid great attention to details. He was totally qualified to give the Chokling Tersar in a very precise way. After he arrived in Central Tibet, the Karmapa sent him a message to come to Tsurphu.

Karmapa sent Tersey Tulku his most trusted servant, a monk from the Golok province named Jampal Tsültrim, to make this request. Jampal Tsültrim was of very good stock and character. Though he served as Karmapa's servant, he was a master in his own right. He was the Karmapa's scribe and a very pure monk. He was a very impressive and reliable personage, so the Karmapa sent him on this mission. However, since he was from Golok, he was quite tough-minded and extremely self-assured. When he visited Tersey Tulku, he told him, "The Karmapa requests that you come and give him the Chokling Tersar." Tersey Tulku was, like his brother Samten Gyatso, a hidden yogi type, so he refused outright, saying, "This is utterly ridiculous! How can a dog put his paw on a man's head? Why are you making this demand?" Gelong Jampal Tsültrim said, "I'm not asking you to do this; it's the Karmapa giving you the command. Do you want to break samaya with him?" Tersey Tulku said, "No, he's a bodhisattva on the tenth bhumi. I'm the same as a dog. I'm nothing. How can I act as his guru, giving him empowerments? There is absolutely no question about this—how can I do it?" Then they got into a heated argument and Gelong Jampal Tsültrim finally slapped him across the face and said, "You lowlife!" He then walked away. He returned to Khakyab Dorje and said, "This man is impossible—the lowest of the low! I argued with him, but he totally refuses to come." The fifteenth Karmapa was not upset about this. He merely said, "That's all right. We'll see. Maybe it will work out in the end."

Khakyab Dorje then invited Samten Gyatso to come to Tsurphu, but he didn't tell him exactly what the purpose of the visit was supposed to be. Sometime after Samten Gyatso had arrived at Tsurphu, he was invited to come to Khakyab Dorje's private chambers. When he got there, he saw a throne set out with brocade robes, a crown, and all the paraphernalia of a vajra master. He was told to sit on the throne. At first there was much protesting back and forth, but finally Khakyab Dorje said, "I command you to sit there. From now on, I install you in the position of vajra master."

It was not only the Karmapa who forced the role of vajra master on Samten Gyatso; Tsewang Norbu did so as well. Tsewang Norbu was once invited to *Riwoche* to give the *Rinchen Terdzö* empowerments. Since Chokgyur Lingpa had already passed away, they wanted to receive this cycle from, at best, Jamgön Kongtrül, but he was quite elderly and weak. Next best, they wanted Khyentse, but he was too old. Then both Khyentse and Kongtrül decided to send the son of Chokgyur Lingpa, Tsewang Norbu, as their representative to give the *Rinchen Terdzö*. Many great tulkus were present there, including the two reincarnations of Chokgyur Lingpa.

Each evening after the ceremonies, the tulkus and great lamas would gather in Tsewang Norbu's private room for discussions and question-and-answer sessions. One night, they were discussing the future of the Chokling Tersar. Tsewang Norbu was a very large man, with a commanding presence and piercing eyes. He just glared at them. Then he pointed his finger at Samten Gyatso, who had been sitting silently near the door, keeping a low profile. Tsewang Norbu said, looking at Tersey Tulku [*Tersey* means the son of the tertön], "You think that you are the incarnation of Chokgyur Lingpa's son!" Looking at the two Chokling tulkus he said; "You two think you are incarnations of Chokgyur Lingpa himself. All three of you think you are someone very special! But you aren't compared to that one over there!" Pointing to Samten Gyatso, he continued, "He will be much more influential in maintaining the lineage." Samten Gyatso was very frightened by this statement. Although Tsewang Norbu was his maternal uncle, everyone was a little afraid of him. When he made a statement like this, it was like a prophecy that really sank in.

When Tsewang Norbu left for Central Tibet many years later, he seemed to know he would never meet Samten Gyatso again. He enthroned Samten Gyatso privately in his chambers and, giving him his vajra and bell, Tsewang Norbu said, "I entrust you with the lineage of the Chokling Tersar. You will have to pass it on in the future." Although

Samten Gyatso protested, he was still invested with this responsibility. That's why he didn't refuse later on when Khakyab Dorje invited him to come to Tsurphu. He said, "All right," and he gave the empowerments.

When Samten Gyatso was giving Khakyab Dorje the entire transmission of the Chokling Tersar, Khakyab Dorje was not staying at Tsurphu proper, but remained in his retreat place above Tsurphu. He was elderly at this time. He had recently remarried, and his consort was called Khandro Chenmo, meaning the Great Dakini of the Karmapa. She was only about sixteen years old then; the Karmapa died three years later when she was nineteen. Tersey Tulku was also there at that time. He was no longer shy about coming to Tsurphu once his brother had agreed to give the empowerments. In the evenings they would often talk with Khakyab Dorje, sometimes until midnight or later. Khakyab Dorje would then leave Samten Gyatso's retreat hut and return to his quarters. One night, after they had parted, Khakyab Dorje joined his palms and told his consort, "At this time and during this age, probably no one except Samten Gyatso has authentic realization of the innermost essence of the Great Perfection." That was the kind of pure appreciation the Karmapa had for Samten Gyatso. The Great Dakini herself told this to me later.

To be established in the role of a vajra master can be a bit problematic. In the case of Samten Gyatso, he was forcefully installed in that position by Tsewang Norbu, his root guru, and by Khakyab Dorje. Samten Gyatso never said much about this to anyone. Shortly before Samten Gyatso died, I spent many evenings in his room. Samten Gyatso would lie in his bed, and I would sleep at his feet on the floor near him. One night we were talking, and Samten Gyatso began to speak for the first time about his innermost realization. He also told the details I've just related above about his relationship with Khakyab Dorje, Tsewang Norbu, and so forth. Apart from this time he never related this personal information to anyone.

"From that point on," he told me, "I really fell under the power of one of the *four Maras*, the demon of distraction called the 'heavenly son.' Before that, my only ambition was to remain in a cave and do practice. But since Karmapa forced me into this, I now have to behave like a vajra master and give empowerments, reading transmissions, etc." This is something he had never done before. He had always sidestepped it completely. But from then on, he had to undertake that position. When looking back, there is now no doubt that he became the one responsible for widely propagating the Chokling Tersar teachings.

Samten Gyatso himself said, "I was happy just to live in caves. I never had the intention or desire to act like a lama. At the age of eight I was introduced to mind nature, and I have remained in it as much as possible till this time." So when Samten Gyatso grew older, he often thought, "I should have stayed in caves; instead, I fell under the power of hindrances." It was not empty talk when he said this; he actually did feel that way. He had no ambition to become a vajra master or sit above anyone else. He once told me, "Being successful is actually called the 'pleasant obstacle.' While unpleasant obstacles are easily recognized by everyone, the pleasant obstacle is rarely acknowledged to be an obstacle." Unpleasant obstacles are, for example, being defamed or implicated in scandals, falling sick, meeting with misfortune, and so forth. Most practitioners can deal with these. They recognize these situations as obstacles and use them as part of the path. But pleasant obstacles, such as becoming renowned, collecting a following of disciples, and superficially acting for the welfare of others, are much more deceptive. One starts to think, "My goodness! I'm becoming really special. I'm benefiting many beings. Everything is perfectly fine!" One does not readily notice that one is falling prey to pleasant obstacles, and this is why they are a major hindrance for progress. Samten Gyatso warned that people rarely recognize these hindrances. They usually only think, "My capacity for benefiting others is expanding!" Well, this is what one tells oneself while failing to notice that one has fallen prey to an obstacle.

IO

THE GURU, THE VAJRA MASTER

Chögyam Trungpa Rinpoche

Coming to the study of spirituality we are faced with the problem of our relationship with a teacher, lama, guru, whatever we call the person we suppose will give us spiritual understanding. These words, especially the term *guru,* have acquired meanings and associations in the West that are misleading and that generally add to the confusion around the issue of what it means to study with a spiritual teacher. This is not to say that people in the East understand how to relate to a guru while Westerners do not; the problem is universal. People always come to the study of spirituality with some ideas already fixed in their minds of what it is they are going to get and how to deal with the person from whom they think they will get it. The very notion that we will *get* something from a guru—happiness, peace of mind, wisdom, whatever it is we seek— is one of the most difficult preconceptions of all. So I think it would be helpful to examine the way in which some famous students dealt with the problems of how to relate to spirituality and a spiritual teacher.

From Chögyam Trungpa, *Cutting Through Spiritual Materialism* (Boston: Shambhala Publications, 1973), "The Guru," and *Journey Without Goal* (Boston: Shambhala Publications, 1981), "The Vajra Master."

Perhaps these examples will have some relevance for our own individual search.

One of the most renowned Tibetan masters and also one of the main gurus of the Kagyü lineage, of which I am a member, was Marpa, student of the Indian teacher Naropa and guru to Milarepa, his most famous spiritual son. Marpa is an example of someone who was on his way to becoming a successful self-made man. He was born into a farming family, but as a youth he became ambitious and chose scholarship and the priesthood as his route to prominence. We can imagine what tremendous effort and determination it must have taken for the son of a farmer to raise himself to the position of priest in his local religious tradition. There were only a few ways for such a man to achieve any kind of position in tenth-century Tibet—as a merchant, a bandit, or especially as a priest. Joining the local clergy at that time was roughly equivalent to becoming a doctor, lawyer, and college professor, all rolled into one.

Marpa began by studying Tibetan, Sanskrit, several other languages, and the spoken language of India. After about three years of such study he was proficient enough to begin earning money as a scholar, and with this money he financed his religious study, eventually becoming a Buddhist priest of sorts. Such a position brought with it a certain degree of local prominence, but Marpa was more ambitious and so, although he was married by now and had a family, he continued to save his earnings until he had amassed a large amount of gold.

At this point Marpa announced to his relatives his intentions to travel to India to collect more teachings. India at this time was the world center for Buddhist studies, home of Nalanda University and the greatest Buddhist sages and scholars. It was Marpa's intention to study and collect texts unknown in Tibet, bring them home, and translate them, thus establishing himself as a great scholar-translator. The journey to India was at that time and until fairly recently a long and dangerous one, and Marpa's family and elders tried to dissuade him from it. But he was determined and so set out accompanied by a friend and fellow scholar.

After a difficult journey of some months, they crossed the Himalayas into India and proceeded to Bengal, where they went their separate ways. Both men were well qualified in the study of language and religion, and so they decided to search for their own teachers, to suit their own tastes. Before parting they agreed to meet again for the journey home.

While he was traveling through Nepal, Marpa had happened to hear of the teacher Naropa, a man of enormous fame. Naropa had been abbot of Nalanda University, perhaps the greatest center for Buddhist studies the world has ever known. At the height of his career, feeling that he understood the sense but not the real meaning of the teachings, he abandoned his post and set out in search of a guru. For twelve years he endured terrific hardship at the hands of his teacher Tilopa, until finally he achieved realization. By the time Marpa heard of him, he was reputed to be one of the greatest Buddhist saints ever to have lived. Naturally Marpa set out to find him.

Eventually Marpa found Naropa living in poverty in a simple house in the forests of Bengal. He had expected to find so great a teacher living in the midst of a highly evolved religious setting of some sort, and so he was somewhat disappointed. However, he was a bit confused by the strangeness of a foreign country and willing to make some allowances, thinking that perhaps this was the way Indian teachers lived. Also, his appreciation of Naropa's fame outweighed his disappointment, and so he gave Naropa most of his gold and asked for teachings. He explained that he was a married man, a priest, scholar, and farmer from Tibet, and that he was not willing to give up this life he had made for himself, but that he wanted to collect teachings to take back to Tibet to translate in order to earn more money. Naropa agreed to Marpa's requests quite easily, gave Marpa instruction, and everything went smoothly.

After some time Marpa decided that he had collected enough teachings to suit his purposes and prepared to return home. He proceeded to an inn in a large town where he rejoined his traveling companion, and the two sat down to compare the results of their efforts. When his friend saw what Marpa had collected, he laughed and said, "What you have here is worthless! We already have those teachings in Tibet. You must have found something more exciting and rare. I found fantastic teachings that I received from very great masters."

Marpa, of course, was extremely frustrated and upset, having come such a long way and with so much difficulty and expense, so he decided to return to Naropa and try once more. When he arrived at Naropa's hut and asked for more rare and exotic and advanced teachings, to his surprise Naropa told him, "I'm sorry, but you can't receive these teachings from me. You will have to go and receive these from someone else, a man named Kukuripa. The journey is difficult, especially so because Kukuripa lives on an island in the middle of a lake of poison. But he is the one you will have to see if you want these teachings."

By this time Marpa was becoming desperate, so he decided to try the journey. Besides, if Kukuripa had teachings that even the great Naropa could not give him and, in addition, lived in the middle of a poisonous lake, then he must be quite an extraordinary teacher, a great mystic.

So Marpa made the journey and managed to cross the lake to the island where he began to look for Kukuripa. There he found an old Indian man living in filth in the midst of hundreds of female dogs. The situation was outlandish, to say the least, but Marpa nevertheless tried to speak to Kukuripa. All he got was gibberish. Kukuripa seemed to be speaking complete nonsense.

Now the situation was almost unbearable. Not only was Kukuripa's speech completely unintelligible, but Marpa had to constantly be on guard against the hundreds of bitches. As soon as he was able to make a relationship with one dog, another would bark and threaten to bite him. Finally, almost beside himself, Marpa gave up altogether, gave up trying to take notes, gave up trying to receive any kind of secret doctrine. And at that point Kukuripa began to speak to him in a totally intelligible, coherent voice and the dogs stopped harrassing him and Marpa received the teachings.

After Marpa had finished studying with Kukuripa, he returned once more to his original guru, Naropa. Naropa told him, "Now you must return to Tibet and teach. It isn't enough to receive the teachings in a theoretical way. You must go through certain life experiences. Then you can come back again and study further."

Once more Marpa met his fellow searcher and together they began the long journey back to Tibet. Marpa's companion had also studied a great deal and both men had stacks of manuscripts, and, as they proceeded, they discussed what they had learned. Soon Marpa began to feel uneasy about his friend, who seemed more and more inquisitive to discover what teachings Marpa had collected. Their conversations together seemed to turn increasingly around this subject, until finally his traveling companion decided that Marpa had obtained more valuable teachings than himself, and so he became quite jealous. As they were crossing a river in a ferry, Marpa's colleague began to complain of being uncomfortable and crowded by all the baggage they were carrying. He shifted his position in the boat, as if to make himself more comfortable, and in so doing managed to throw all of Marpa's manuscripts into the river. Marpa tried desperately to rescue them, but they were gone. All the texts he had gone to such lengths to collect had disappeared in an instant.

So it was with a feeling of great loss that Marpa returned to Tibet.

He had many stories to tell of his travels and studies, but he had nothing solid to prove his knowledge and experience. Nevertheless, he spent several years working and teaching until, to his surprise, he began to realize that his writings would have been useless to him, even had he been able to save them. While he was in India he had only taken written notes on those parts of the teachings that were part of his own experience. It was only years later that he discovered that they had actually become a part of him.

With this discovery Marpa lost all desire to profit from the teachings. He was no longer concerned with making money or achieving prestige but instead was inspired to realize enlightenment. So he collected gold dust as an offering to Naropa and once again made the journey to India. This time he went full of longing to see his guru and desire for the teachings.

However, Marpa's next encounter with Naropa was quite different than before. Naropa seemed very cold and impersonal, almost hostile, and his first words to Marpa were, "Good to see you again. How much gold have you for my teachings?" Marpa had brought a large amount of gold but wanted to save some for his expenses and the trip home, so he opened his pack and gave Naropa only a portion of what he had. Naropa looked at the offering and said, "No, this is not enough. I need more gold than this for my teaching. Give me all your gold." Marpa gave him a bit more and still Naropa demanded all, and this went on until finally Naropa laughed and said, "Do you think you can buy my teaching with your deception?" At this point Marpa yielded and gave Naropa all the gold he had. To his shock, Naropa picked up the bags and began flinging the gold dust in the air.

Suddenly Marpa felt extremely confused and paranoid. He could not understand what was happening. He had worked hard for the gold to buy the teaching he so wanted. Naropa had seemed to indicate that he needed the gold and would teach Marpa in return for it. Yet he was throwing it away! Then Naropa said to him, "What need have I of gold? The whole world is gold for me!"

This was a great moment of opening for Marpa. He opened and was able to receive teaching. He stayed with Naropa for a long time after that and his training was quite austere, but he did not simply listen to the teachings as before; he had to work his way through them. He had to give up everything he had, not just his material possessions, but whatever he was holding back in his mind had to go. It was a continual process of opening and surrender.

In Milarepa's case, the situation developed quite differently. He was a peasant, much less learned and sophisticated than Marpa had been when he met Naropa, and he had committed many crimes, incuding murder. He was miserably unhappy, yearned for enlightenment, and was willing to pay any fee that Marpa might ask. So Marpa had Milarepa pay on a very literal physical level. He had him build a series of houses for him, one after the other, and after each was completed Marpa would tell Milarepa to tear the house down and put all the stones back where he had found them, so as not to mar the landscape. Each time Marpa ordered Milarepa to dismantle a house, he would give some absurd excuse, such as having been drunk when he ordered the house built or never having ordered such a house at all. And each time Milarepa, full of longing for the teachings, would tear the house down and start again.

Finally Marpa designed a tower with nine stories. Milarepa suffered terrific physical hardship in carrying the stones and building the house and, when he had finished, he went to Marpa and once more asked for the teachings. But Marpa said to him, "You want to receive teachings from me, just like that, merely because you built this tower for me? Well, I'm afraid you will still have to give me a gift as an initiation fee."

By this time Milarepa had no possessions left whatsoever, having spent all his time and labor building towers. But Damema, Marpa's wife, felt sorry for him and said, "These towers you have built are such a wonderful gesture of devotion and faith. Surely my husband won't mind if I give you some sacks of barley and a roll of cloth for your initiation fee." So Milarepa took the barley and cloth to the initiation circle where Marpa was teaching and offered them as his fee, along with the gifts of the other students. But Marpa, when he recognized the gift, was furious and shouted at Milarepa, "These things belong to me, you hypocrite! You try to deceive me!" And he literally kicked Milarepa out of the initiation circle.

At this point Milarepa gave up all hope of ever getting Marpa to give him the teachings. In despair, he decided to commit suicide and was just about to kill himself with Marpa came to him and told him that he was ready to receive the teaching.

The process of receiving teaching depends upon the student giving something in return; some kind of psychological surrender is necessary, a gift of some sort. This is why we must discuss surrendering, opening, giving up expectations, before we can speak of the relationship between teacher and student. It is essential to surrender, to open yourself, to present whatever you are to the guru, rather than trying to present yourself as a worthwhile student. It does not matter how much you are willing to pay, how correctly you behave, how clever you are at saying the right thing to your teacher. It is not like having an interview for a job or buying a new car. Whether or not you will get the job depends upon your credentials, how well you are dressed, how beautifully your shoes are polished, how well you speak, how good your manners are. If you are buying a car, it is a matter of how much money you have and how good your credit is.

But when it comes to spirituality, something more is required. It is not a matter of applying for a job, of dressing up to impress our potential employer. Such deception does not apply to an interview with a guru, because he sees right through us. He is amused if we dress up especially for the interview. Making ingratiating gestures is not applicable in this situation; in fact it is futile. We must make a real commitment to being open with our teacher; we must be willing to give up all our preconceptions. Milarepa expected Marpa to be a great scholar and a saintly person, dressed in yogic costume with beads, reciting mantras, meditating. Instead he found Marpa working on his farm, directing the laborers and plowing his land.

I am afraid the word *guru* is overused in the West. It would be better to speak of one's "spiritual friend," because the teachings emphasize a mutual meeting of two minds. It is a matter of mutual communication, rather than a master-servant relationship between a highly evolved being and a miserable, confused one. In the master-servant relationship the highly evolved being may appear not even to be sitting on his seat but may seem to be floating, levitating, looking down at us. His voice is penetrating, pervading space. Every word, every cough, every movement that he makes is a gesture of wisdom. But this is a dream. A guru should be a spiritual friend who communicates and presents his qualities to us, as Marpa did with Milarepa and Naropa with Marpa. Marpa presented his quality of being a farmer-yogi. He happened to have seven children and a wife, and he looked after his farm, cultivating the land and supporting himself and his family. But these activities were just an ordinary part of his life. He cared for his students as he cared for his crops and family. He was so thorough, paying attention to every detail of his life, that he was able to be a competent teacher as well as a competent father and farmer. There was no physical or spiritual materialism in Marpa's lifestyle at all. He did not emphasize spirituality and ignore his family or his physical relationship to the earth. If you are not involved with materialism, either spiritually or physically, then there is no emphasis made on any extreme.

Nor is it helpful to choose someone for your guru simply because he is famous, someone who is renowned for having published stacks of books and converted thousands or millions of people. Instead the guideline is whether or not you are able actually to communicate with the person, directly and thoroughly. How much self-deception are you involved in? If you really open yourself to your spiritual friend, then you are bound to work together. Are you able to talk to him thoroughly and properly? Does he know anything about you? Does he know anything about himself, for that matter? Is the guru really able to see through your masks, communicate with you properly, directly? In searching for a teacher, this seems to be the guideline rather than fame or wisdom.

There is an interesting story of a group of people who decided to go and study under a great Tibetan teacher. They had already studied somewhat with other teachers, but had decided to concentrate on trying to learn from this particular person. They were all very anxious to become his students and so sought an audience with him, but this great teacher would not accept any of them. "Under one condition only will I accept you," he said. "If you are willing to renounce your previous teachers." They all pleaded with him, telling him how much they were devoted to him, how great his reputation was, and how much they would like to study with him. But he would not accept any of them unless they would meet his condition. Finally all except one person in the party decided to renounce their previous teachers, from whom they had in fact learned a great deal. The guru seemed to be quite happy when they did so and told them all to come back the next day. But when they returned he said to them, "I understand your hypocrisy. The next time you go to another teacher you will renounce me. So get out." And he chased them all out except for the one person who valued what he had learned previously. The person he accepted was not willing to play any more lying games, was not willing to try to please a guru by pretending to be different from what he was. If you are going to make friends with a spiritual master, you must make friends simply, openly, so that the communication takes place between equals, rather than trying to win the master over to you.

In order to be accepted by your guru as a friend, you have to open yourself completely. And in order that you might open, you will probably have to undergo tests by your spiritual friend and by life situations in general, all of these tests taking the form of disappointment. At some stage you will doubt that your spiritual friend has any feeling, any emotion toward you at all. This is dealing with your own hypocrisy. The hypocrisy, the pretense and basic twist of ego, is extremely hard; it has a very thick skin. We tend to wear suits of armor, one over the other. This hypocrisy is so dense and multileveled that as soon as we remove one layer of our suit of armor, we find another beneath it. We hope we will not have to completely undress. We hope that stripping off only a few layers will make us presentable. Then we appear in our new suit of armor with such an ingratiating face, but our spiritual friend does not wear any armor at all; he is a naked person. Compared with his nakedness, we are wearing cement. Our armor is so thick that our friend cannot feel the texture of our skin, our bodies. He cannot even see our faces properly. There are many stories of teacher-student relationships in the past in which the student had to make long journeys and endure many hardships until his fascination and impulses began to wear out. This seems to be the point: the impulse of searching for something is, in itself, a hang-up. When this impulse begins to wear out, then our fundamental, basic nakedness begins to appear and the meeting of the two minds begins to take place.

It has been said that the first stage of meeting one's spiritual friend is like going to a supermarket. You are excited and you dream of all the different things that you are going to buy: the richness of your spiritual friend and the colorful qualities of his personality. The second stage of your relationship is like going to court, as though you were a criminal. You are not able to meet your friend's demands and you begin to feel self-conscious, because you know that he knows as much as you know about yourself, which is extremely embarrassing. In the third stage when you go to see your spiritual friend, it is like seeing a cow happily grazing in a meadow. You just admire its peacefulness and the landscape and then you pass on. Finally the fourth stage with one's spiritual friend is like passing a rock in the road. You do not even pay attention to it; you just pass by and walk away.

At the beginning a kind of courtship with the guru is taking place, a love affair. How much are you able to win this person over to you? There is a tendency to want to be closer to your spiritual friend, because you really want to learn. You feel such admiration for him. But at the same time he is very frightening; he puts you off. Either the situation does not coincide with your expectations or there is a self-conscious feeling that "I may not be able to open completely and thoroughly." A love-hate relationship, a kind of surrendering and running-away process develops. In other words, we begin to play a game, a game of wanting to open, wanting to be involved in a love affair with our guru, and then wanting to run away from him. If we get too close to our spiritual friend, then we begin to feel overpowered by him. As it says in the old Tibetan proverb: "A guru is like a fire. If you get too close you get burned; if you stay too far away you don't get enough heat." This kind of courtship takes place on the part of the student. You tend to get too close to the teacher, but once you do, you get burned. Then you want to run away altogether.

Eventually the relationship begins to become very substantial and solid. You begin to realize that wanting to be near and wanting to be far away from the guru is simply your own game. It has nothing to do with the real situation, but is just your own hallucination. The guru or spiritual friend is always there burning, always a life-fire. You can play games with him or not, as you choose.

Then the relationship with one's spiritual friend begins to become very creative. You accept the situations of being overwhelmed by him and distant from him. If he decides to play the role of cold icy water, you accept it. If he decides to play the role of hot fire, you accept it. Nothing can shake you at all, and you come to a reconciliation with him.

The next stage is that, having accepted everything your spiritual friend might do, you begin to lose your own inspiration because you have completely surrendered, completely given up. You feel yourself reduced to a speck of dust. You are insignificant. You begin to feel that the only world that exists is that of this spiritual friend, the guru. It is as though you were watching a fascinating movie; the movie is so exciting that you become part of it. There is no you and no cinema hall, no chairs, no people watching, no friends sitting next to you. The movie is all that exists. This is called the "honeymoon period" in which everything is seen as a part of this central being, the guru. You are just a useless, insignificant person who is continuously being fed by this great, fascinating central being. Whenever you feel weak or tired or bored, you go and just sit in the cinema hall and are entertained, uplifted, rejuvenated. At this point the phenomenon of the personality cult becomes prominent. The guru is the only person in the world who exists, alive and vibrant. The very meaning of your life depends upon him. If you die, you die for him. If you live, you survive for him and are insignificant.

However, this love affair with your spiritual friend cannot last forever. Sooner or later its intensity must wane and you must face your own life situation and your own psychology. It is like having married and finished the honeymoon. You not only feel conscious of your lover as the central focus of your attention, but you begin to notice his or her lifestyle as well. You begin to notice what it is that makes this person a teacher, beyond the limits of his individuality and personality. Thus the principle of the "universality of the guru" comes into the picture as well. Every problem you face in life is a part of your marriage. Whenever you experience difficulties, you hear the words of the guru. This is the point at which one begins to gain one's independence from the guru as lover, because every situation becomes an expression of the teachings. First you surrendered to your spiritual friend. Then you communicated and played games with him. And now you have come to the state of complete openness. As a result of this openness you begin to see the guru-quality in every life situation, that all situations in life offer you the opportunity to be as open as you are with the guru, and so all things can become the guru.

Milarepa had a vivid vision of his guru Marpa while he was meditating in very strict retreat in Red Rock Jewel Valley. Weak with hunger and battered by the elements, he had fainted while trying to collect firewood outside his cave. When he regained consciousness, he looked to the east and saw white clouds in the direction where Marpa lived. With great longing he sang a song of supplication, telling Marpa how much he longed to be with him. Then Marpa appeared in a vision, riding a white snow lion, and said to him something like, "What is the matter with you? Have you had a neurotic upheaval of some sort? You understand the Dharma, so continue to practice meditation." Milarepa took comfort and returned to his cave to meditate. His reliance and dependence upon Marpa at this point indicates that he had not yet freed himself from the notion of guru as personal, individual friend.

However, when Milarepa returned to his cave, he found it full of demons with eyes as big as saucepans and bodies the size of thumbs. He tried all kinds of ploys to get them to stop mocking and tormenting him, but they would not leave until Milarepa finally stopped trying to play games, until he recognized his own hypocrisy and gave in to openness. From this point on you see a tremendous change of style in Milarepa's songs, because he had learned to identify with the universal quality of guru, rather than solely relating to Marpa as an individual person.

The spiritual friend becomes part of you, as well as being an individual, external person. As such the guru, both internal and external, plays a very important part in penetrating and exposing our hypocrisies. The guru can be a person who acts as a mirror, reflecting you, or else your own basic intelligence takes the form of the spiritual friend. When the internal guru begins to function, then you can never escape the demand to open. The basic intelligence follows you everywhere; you cannot escape your own shadow. "Big Brother is watching you." Though it is not external entities who are watching us and haunting us; we haunt ourselves. Our own shadow is watching us.

We could look at it in two different ways. We could see the guru as a ghost, haunting and mocking us for our hypocrisy. There could be a demonic quality in realizing what we are. And yet there is always the creative quality of the spiritual friend which also becomes a part of us. The basic intelligence is continuously present in the situations of life. It is so sharp and penetrating that at some stage, even if you want to get rid of it, you cannot. Sometimes it has a stern expression, sometimes an inspiring smile. It has been said in the tantric tradition that you do not see the face of the guru, but you see the expression of his face all the time. Either smiling, grinning, or frowning angrily, it is part of every life situation. The basic intelligence, *tathagatagarbha,* buddha nature, is always in every experience life brings us. There is no escaping it. Again it is said in the teachings: "Better not to begin. Once you begin, better to finish it." So you had better not step onto the spiritual path unless you must. Once you have stepped foot on the path, you have really done it, you cannot step back. There is no way of escaping.

The Vajrayana teacher is referred to as the vajra master. The vajra master is electric and naked. He holds a scepter in his hand, called a *vajra,* which symbolizes a thunderbolt. The teacher holds the power to conduct lightning with his hand. By means of the vajra he can transmit that electricity to us. If the cosmos and the student are not connecting properly, the vajra master can respark the connection. In this sense the teacher has a great deal of power over us, but not such that he can become an egomaniac. Rather, the teacher is a spokesman who reintroduces the world to us: he reintroduces us to our world.

The vajra master is like a magician in the sense that he has access to the cosmic world and can work with it, but not in the sense that he can turn earth into fire, or fire into water, just like that. The vajra master has to work with the actual functions of the universe. We could say that the cosmos contains a lot of magic, and because the vajra master has some connection with the world and the happenings of the world, there is magic already. Therefore, the vajra master could be considered a supervisor of magic rather than a magician.

Relating with the vajra master is extremely powerful and somewhat dangerous at this point. The vajra master is capable of transmitting the vajra spiritual energy to us, but at the same time, he is also capable of destroying us if our direction is completely wrong. *Tantra* means "continuity," but one of the principles of tantric discipline is that continuity can only exist if there is something genuine to continue. If we are not genuine, then our continuity can be canceled by the vajra master. So we do not regard our teacher in the Vajrayana as a savior or as a deity who automatically will give us whatever we want.

The vajra master could be quite heavy-handed; however, he does not just play tricks on us whenever he finds a weak point. He conducts himself according to the tradition and the discipline: he touches us, he smells us, he looks at us, and he listens to our heartbeat. It is a very definite, deliberate process done according to the tradition of the lineage. That process—when the vajra master looks at us, when he listens to us, when he feels us, and when he touches us—is known as *abhisheka* or empowerment.

Abhisheka is sometimes translated as "initiation," but that does not actually convey the proper meaning. As we discussed earlier, abhisheka is a Sanskrit word that literally means "anointment." It is the idea of being bathed in holy water that is blessed by the teacher and the mandala around the teacher. However, abhisheka is not an initiation or rite of passage in which we are accepted as a member of the tribe if we pass certain tests. In fact, it is entirely different. The vajra master empowers us and we receive that power, depending both on our own capability and the capability of the teacher. Therefore the term "empowerment" is more appropriate than "initiation," because there is no tribe into which we are initiated. There is no closed circle; rather, we are introduced to the universe. We cannot say that the universe is a big tribe or a big ego; the universe is open space. So the teacher empowers us to encounter our enlarged universe. At this point the teacher acts as a lightning rod. We could be shocked or devastated by the electricity he transmits to us, but it is also possible that we could be saved by having such an electric conductor.

In the Vajrayana, it is absolutely necessary to have a teacher and to trust in the teacher. The teacher or vajra master is the only embodiment of the transmission of energy. Without such a teacher we cannot experience the world properly and thoroughly. We cannot just read a few books on tantra and try to figure it out for ourselves. Somehow that does not work. Tantra has to be transmitted to the student as a living experience. The tantric system of working with the world and the energy of tantra have to be transmitted or handed down directly from teacher to student. In that way the teachings become real and obvious and precise.

A direct relationship between teacher and student is essential in Vajrayana Buddhism. People cannot even begin to practice tantra without making some connection with their teacher, their vajra, indestructible, master. Such a teacher cannot be some abstract cosmic figure. He has to be somebody who has gone through the whole process himself—somebody who has been both a panicking student and a panicking teacher.

We could say that the vajra master exists because he is free from karma, but that through his compassion such a teacher establishes a relative link to his world. However, in a sense no one is actually free from karma, not even the enlightened buddhas. The buddhas are not going to retire from their buddhahood to some heavenly realm. They have to help us; they have to work with us. That is their karma and our karma as well.

That is one of the interesting differences between the theistic and the nontheistic approach. In the theistic approach, when we retire from this world, we go to heaven. Once we are in heaven we do not have anything to do with the world. We have no obligations, and we can be happy ever after. But in the nontheistic tradition, even if we attain the state of liberation or openness, we still have debts, because the rest of our brothers and sisters in the world are still in trouble. We have to come back. We can't just hang out in nirvana.

So the vajra master is a human being, someone who has a karmic debt to pay as a result of the intensity of his compassion. The Dharma cannot be transmitted from the sun or the moon or the stars. The Dharma can only be transmitted properly from human to human. So there is a need for a vajra master who has tremendous power—power over us, power over the cosmos, and power over himself—and who has also been warned that if he misdirects his energy he will be cut down and reduced into a little piece of charcoal.

It is extremely important to have a living vajra master, someone who personally experiences our pain and our pleasure. We have to have a sense of fear and respect that we are connecting and communicating directly with tantra. Making that connection is a very special thing. It is extremely difficult to find a true tantric situation and to meet a true tantric master. Becoming a true tantric student is also very difficult. It is very difficult to find the real thing.

II

WAKE-UP PRACTICE

Tulku Urgyen Rinpoche

In the morning we should begin with the practice of stirring from the sleep of ignorance.

Chant the liturgy called *Awakening from the Sleep of Ignorance* from the Barchey Künsel teachings, and then, after exhaling the stale breath, visualize the guru on top of your head.

Next recite the *Buddha of the Three Times*, after which the guru dissolves into yourself.

From beginningless time until now, the wisdom *prana* has been obscured by the *klesha* prana, the wind of disturbing emotions. This klesha prana continually leads to thoughts of attachment, aggression, and delusion, thereby creating habitual patterns. To avoid this, expel the stale breath.

At the outset of practice straighten the body. As the right nostril is the major path for the movement of the strong kleshas, first exhale through the right nostril, then the left and finally through both. Exhale the stale breath three or nine times, whichever is suitable. The exhalation

Adapted from Tulku Urgyen Rinpoche, *Vajra Heart* (Boudhanath: Rangjung Yeshe Publications, 1988), "Wake-up Practice."

should be accompanied by a hissing sound, and the inhalation should be done slowly. When exhaling, imagine that all the karmas, kleshas, evil deeds, obscurations, sicknesses, and negative forces flow out like smoke from a chimney. When inhaling, imagine that five colored rainbow lights of the blessings, wisdom, loving compassion, activities, and qualities of all the victorious ones and their sons dissolve into yourself. Negativity leaves your body through all the pores, but mainly through the nostrils.

Then, while imagining your root guru above the crown of your head, chant *Buddha of the Three Times*, an incredibly blessed supplication especially suited for these times. Most people in Tibet did not have to learn this supplication to the guru, because the Dharma was so widespread that even small children could chant it without deliberate study. When we chant,

> *Düsum sangye guru rinpoche*
> Buddha of the three times, Guru Rinpoche,

we are supplicating Guru Rinpoche, who carries out all the activities of all the buddhas in order to tame beings. When we chant,

> *Ngödrub kündag dewa chenpö shab*
> Lord of all accomplishments, great blissful one,

we recognize his attainment as the Guru of Great Bliss—Guru Dewa Chenpo. We know that he can conquer all when we chant,

> *Barchey künsel düdül drakpo tsal*
> Dispeller of all obstacles, wrathful tamer of Maras.

This is the external practice. The treasures of Chokgyur Lingpa include the external practice, called *Barchey Künsel*, "Clearing Away the Obstacles," the inner practice, *Sampa Lhundrub*, and the secret practice, *Dorje Draktsal*. These lines contain all three. The first line, "Buddha of the three times, Guru Rinpoche" is the outer practice, Barchey Künsel. The next line is the Sampa Lhundrub, the inner practice, and the third line is the secret practice, Dorje Drakpo Tsal. One supplicates all three.

> *Solwa debso jingyi lobtu sol*
> I supplicate you, please grant your blessings.

Chinang sangwey barchey shiwa dang
Please pacify the outer, inner, and secret obstacles.

The outer obstacles are the obstacles of the outer elements. The inner obstacles are those of the channels and winds. The secret obstacles are those of grasping and fixation. So the essence of the Barchey Künsel, the external practice, is to pacify or dispel these three kinds of obstacles.

Sampa lhüngyi drubpar jingyi lob
Bless me with the spontaneous fulfillment of my wishes.

Through this blessing, whatever you wish for, such as the supreme and common siddhis, may be spontaneously accomplished. In fact, when obstacles are cleared away, the siddhis will be spontaneously accomplished.

The Barchey Künsel sadhana is contained in the *Essence Manual of Oral Instructions*. However, the essence of this instruction is condensed into the supplication, "Buddha of the three times, Guru Rinpoche." One wishes to accomplish the *common and supreme siddhis*. One supplicates wholeheartedly, with a single-pointed frame of mind, without any doubt. One resolves there is no hope or refuge elsewhere than in the guru.

In Tibetan, the word *glorious* refers to the splendor or the glory of having realized the dharmakaya for the benefit of oneself, and the glory of manifesting the rupakaya for the benefit of others. This is the twofold benefit. In Tibetan, the expression "glorious and precious root guru" is always used since it is the root guru who confers the empowerments, expounds the tantras, and imparts the oral instructions. Among root gurus, the one who introduces the unborn dharmakaya of one's own mind is called the precious root guru.

After repeating the supplication to Guru Rinpoche three times, recite one rosary of *Lama Khyenno*. That means "Lama, think of me" or "take care of me" and is "I supplicate you" or "I take refuge in you." Finally, the guru melts into light, and one considers oneself inseparable from him. One's body, speech, and mind and the guru's Body, Speech, and Mind become inseparable.

After this come the two clarifications of attitude: the bodhisattva attitude of vast thought, the Sutra path, and the Secret Mantra attitude of profound method, the Mantra path.

The two precious kinds of bodhichitta are the foundation of all the vehicles. According to the Sutra path, one accomplishes enlightenment through emptiness and compassion. Emptiness is the path of *prajña*; compassion is the path of *upaya*. According to Mantra, upaya is the *development stage* and prajña is the *completion stage*. Through development and completion one attains the unified level of Vajradhara. These are the special principles of Sutra and Mantra. The relative and absolute bodhichitta are the root of both Sutra and Mantra, which again are complete within the attitude of compassion. The link between buddhas and beings is compassion. It is never the case that buddhas, after attaining enlightenment, leave sentient beings behind. This is because of the power of compassion. Once enlightened, buddhas have not even a hair-tip of self-interest; they accomplish only the benefit of others.

Whether a Dharma practice carries one toward a perfect path or not depends upon one's attitude. Taking on the bodhisattva attitude of vast thought, resolve: "May all the sentient beings as vast as the sky possess happiness and be free from suffering. So they may obtain complete and perfect enlightenment, I will practice this profound path of meditation." The vast thought of the bodhisattva attitude refers to the Sutra teachings of the bodhisattvas, the Mahayana vehicle.

Through the Secret Mantra attitude of profound method, envision the external world as the celestial palace and the inhabitants, all sentient beings, as having the nature of dakas and dakinis. The thoughts of all sentient beings have the nature of primordial purity, the original wakefulness of enlightened mind. This is called the threefold mandala: appearances as the mandala of the deity, sounds as the mandala of mantra, and thoughts as the mandala of wisdom. It is also called the three things to carry. This pure perception is what is meant by the Secret Mantra attitude of profound methods.

The principle of Secret Mantra is nothing other than pure perception of that which has existed since the very beginning. One should never be separated from pure perception. The outer world is pure; all sentient beings are dakas and dakinis. Even dogs and pigs, although appearing to be impure beings, possess the enlightened essence. They also possess the constituents of flesh, blood, heat or warmth, breath, and vacuities, the five properties of the five elements. In fact, the *five aggregates* are of the nature of the *five male buddhas* and the *five elements* are of the nature of the *five female buddhas*. Even the Hindu religion perceives the five elements as fire gods, water gods, and so forth. Worldly Hindus will take refuge in the gods of the elements, fire gods, wind gods, or water gods. We do not blame them for that; they don't know any better. Their gods include the sun and moon, and so on. We can actually understand something from that. Their deities are worldly deities; ours are wisdom deities, which means that the aggregates and the elements do not possess even a dust mote of impurity.

If one looks into the Vajrayana teachings and understands the intent of the *Guhyagarbha Tantra*, then all of the outer and the inner, the world and the beings, are the continuity of pure deities, which have existed as the nature of the three vajras since the very beginning. It is not that we must change the phenomenal world and its inhabitants from something that "is" into something that "is not," nor must we transmute impurity into purity. We need not superimpose our own view on phenomena; pure perception is simply a recognition of the primordial state itself. Due to the difference between the confusion and liberation of thoughts, however, we have been unable to make this distinction and have become confused. This has not been to our benefit. In fact everything, all that appears and exists, is *all-encompassing purity.* It is said that in the all-encompassing purity of the phenomenal world, the very name of obstructing forces does not exist. So the attitude here is that everything is all-encompassing purity.

First we dissolve the guru into ourselves, then we form the attitudes of bodhichitta. The training in awakening from the sleep of ignorance is a practice widespread in all the Buddhist traditions of Tibet, both the old and the new schools. Different liturgies are used, but the practice is the same. The Barchey Künsel terma of Chokling was spoken by Guru Rinpoche. We incorporate it here, since waking up in just an ordinary manner has little benefit.

Actually we have been sleeping since beginningless time. Sleep is an aspect of ignorance, a subsidiary aspect of closed-mindedness. The sleeping state is not stupidity itself because stupidity means being unaware or ignorant of the true meaning. Sleep is one of the seven thought states, whereas the real stupidity is ignorance of the true meaning. This king of stupidity has sleep as his minister.

At the very moment of waking up one should think of Guru Rinpoche with all the dakas and dakinis, voices singing and ornaments dangling. With ornaments of jewel and bone, they play hand drums and bells. "This is what wakes me up." Thus should one wake, not just in an ordinary manner. This is the meaning of stirring from sleep. Due to their compassion and powers, one is awakened, not merely from ordinary sleep but from the sleep of ignorance. So: "Now I have awakened into the space of awareness wisdom."

Rinpoche sings the liturgy:

Guru Padma together with his host of dakas and dakinis, accompanied by the music of hand drums and bells, have arrived with great splendor in the sky before me. Their bodies in dancing postures, their voices as melodies of symbolic language and mantra songs, and their minds as the essence of self-occurring awareness are all directed toward me.

Lord guru and host of dakinis
Gaze upon me with your compassionate eyes.
Now all sentient beings of the three realms are asleep,
Their minds in a state of indifference.
When waking up, they wander through experiences of confusion.
So that I, your child, a yogi who realizes natural awareness,
May guide my mothers, the sentient beings of the six realms,
To the pure land of celestial realms,
I will follow you, the father guru.
Not remaining indifferent in thought, word, or deed,
I will gain certainty through learning, reflection, and meditation,
And arrange my life around the four sessions.
In this delightful realm of a mountain retreat
I will accomplish the two benefits of self and others.
Guru, may you and your host of dakinis,
Bless my body, speech, and mind.

Then, expel the stale breath three times.

THE FIRST OF THE FOUR DHARMAS OF GAMPOPA

Tulku Urgyen Rinpoche

Grant your blessings that my mind may follow the Dharma.

—GAMPOPA

Before receiving teachings, let's motivate ourselves with the precious enlightened attitude of bodhichitta. Form this wish: "I will study the Dharma and correctly put it into practice in order to establish all my mothers, sentient beings as many as the sky is vast, in the state of liberation and the precious, irreversible supreme enlightenment."

I would like to present a teaching called "The Four Dharmas of Gampopa," which is identical with four instructions given by *Longchen Rabjam*. If a practitioner receives these instructions and is diligent, he or she will be able to attain complete enlightenment within a single

Adapted from Tulku Urgyen Rinpoche, *Repeating the Words of the Buddha* (Boudhanath: Rangjung Yeshe Publications, 1996), "Four Dharmas of Gampopa," and *As It Is,* Volume I (Boudhanath: Rangjung Yeshe Publications, 1999).

lifetime. It is amazing how extraordinary the vital teachings of the buddhas and accomplished practitioners are.

The buddhas have totally perfected all the qualities of abandonment and realization; they have abandoned the obscurations and realized the wisdom qualities. Out of their great love and kindness for other beings, similar to the love a mother has for her only child, the awakened ones taught the Dharma. The source of Buddhism on this earth is Buddha Shakyamuni, the completely enlightened one. His teachings have been transmitted through a lineage of bodhisattvas abiding on the bhumis, the bodhisattva levels. Thus these teachings have been passed down through an unbroken lineage of accomplished practitioners up to my own root teacher.

The first of these is how to turn one's mind toward Dharma practice. Included within this are the four mind-changings. The second Dharma is how to ensure that one's Dharma practice becomes the path. This includes teachings on the preliminary practices of the four times 100,000. Within the third Dharma, how to make the path clarify confusion, are the teachings on development stage, recitation, and completion stage. And within the fourth, how to let confusion dawn as wisdom, are teachings on how to gain certainty, realization of the natural state by means of the three great views. It is said that the ground is Mahamudra, the path is the Middle Way and the fruition is the Great Perfection. These Four Dharmas of Gampopa contain a complete path for an individual to attain full enlightenment within one body in one lifetime.

Now for the first, "Turn your mind toward following the Dharma!" This is done by reflecting on the four mind-changings. The first of these describes the difficulty of obtaining a precious human body endowed with the eight freedoms and ten riches. Since we are already human beings it might seem that we effortlessly obtained a human body; however, that was not the case. It takes a tremendous amount of positive karma accumulated in former lifetimes for an individual to be born in a precious human body. It is only due to our former meritorious karma combined with pure aspirations that we now have a precious human body. There are as many human beings as there are stars in the sky at night. But among these humans, those who have interest in practicing the sacred Dharma, beings with a precious human body, are extremely few, like the stars in the morning sky. Among people with interest in Dharma, those who have sincere diligence are even fewer. Genuine Dharma practice means to give up all worldly ambitions and to pursue instead the attainment of complete enlightenment in this very lifetime.

Although we have obtained a precious human body, it is governed by impermanence. Impermanence means that nothing, neither the world nor the beings in it, lasts. In particular, the life span of a human is extremely short, as unpredictable and insubstantial as a flash of lightning or a bubble in water. On this earth no one lives forever; one after the other, people pass away. After death, if we end up in the three lower realms we will undergo unbearable, indescribable misery and pain. Currently we strive for perfect conditions, pleasure and wealth. But no matter what incredible state of worldly luxury and happiness we might now attain, we lack the power to bring any of it—our friends, family members, or wealth—into the afterlife.

Although we feel love and affection for our family and our friends, at the moment of death we journey alone to an unknown place. We have repeated the same experience in all our past lives, leaving behind all our acquaintances and abandoning our possessions. No matter what happiness and abundance we achieve in this lifetime, it is as insubstantial as the dream we dreamt last night. To understand that nothing lasts, that everything passes by like a dream, is to understand impermanence and death.

If it simply were the case that our life ended in nothingness, like water drying up or a flame being extinguished, that would be perfect. There wouldn't be anything to worry about. But I'm sorry to say it does not happen like that, because our consciousness is not something that can die. After death we are forced to experience the effect of our former karmic actions. Due to ignorance we have wandered endlessly in samsara, unable to be liberated, continually circling between the three lower and three higher realms, one after the other. In order to free ourselves from the six realms of samsaric existence, we need to practice the sacred Dharma now while we have the chance.

Reflect on the meaning of these four topics I have just mentioned: the difficulty of obtaining a precious human rebirth, the fact that nothing lasts, that we are all mortals, that everyone is governed by the consequences of karmic actions, and that there is no place within samsaric existence with permanent happiness. Those are called the four mind-changings. They are extremely important to take to heart before starting to practice the precious Dharma. They are not fiction or fantasy. They are facts; they explain the circumstances and conditions that we live under within samsaric existence.

It's not impossible to understand that we do die, nor the details of what follows. We are all really just standing in line for that, waiting for it to happen. We need to face these facts in a very realistic way. It is very important to take these to heart.

13

RENUNCIATION MIND

Dzongsar Khyentse Rinpoche

I think the word *ngöndro* or *preliminary* is encouraging because it is something that is taught for beginners. However, this word *preliminary* seems to have misled a lot of people who think it is not the main course, and hence many students tend to consider the preliminary practices to be unimportant. That is quite unfortunate because ngöndro consists of all the practices of the three yanas. For instance, there is refuge, which broadly speaking is the essence of Hinayana practice. Refuge saves us from choosing a wrong path and leads us to the right path, view, and meditation. Bodhichitta is the essential practice of Mahayana, which, as stated in the *Mañjushri Sutra*, is the only way to realize nonduality. Vajrasattva practice and mandala offering purify our perception and our being and also accumulate merit so that we become a perfect vessel to practice the profound yogas. Finally, there is the quintessential practice of Vajrayana, the sacred outlook laid out very skillfully in the last stage of the ngöndro, the guru yoga. We should not forget that ngöndro is not merely a preliminary; it is a main practice.

If ngöndro practice were only a preliminary practice, then why would someone like His Holiness Dilgo Khyentse Rinpoche need to practice it even at a very late stage of his life? Yet he never gave up doing several ngöndros, *Longchen Nyingtig, Chetsün Nyingtig,* and at one point I also saw him doing *Kunzang Tuktig.* Those of you who seriously want to pursue the path of this dangerous, enigmatic Vajrayana, be ready to practice the ngöndro for a long time, not merely until you finish a certain required amount.

The preliminaries have a very special structure that I will explain according to some of the writings by Jamgön Kongtrül. Ideally, someone who wishes to practice the ngöndro should, at least intellectually, come to the right view. Recognition of the correct view is difficult. I am not asking you to have recognized the view without any doubts—such confidence is very difficult, especially for beginners like us. All I am asking you is to at least get an intellectual understanding of the right view.

For instance, the term *Longchen* indicates a view and has infinite meanings. Here, for the time being, the word *Longchen* is openness, a very big space. Basically, space is where things can fit. Right now, in our mindstreams, our space is very limited because we are either engrossed in the past, anticipating the future, or distorting the present. Lifetimes upon lifetimes, years upon years burdened by all our various influences, we have limited and narrowed our space; now nothing fits in our mindstream, and the result is a constant anxiety and lack of courage. We undergo all the standard sufferings. We clutch very strongly. We grasp at things even though these tightly held, seemingly very attractive, solid, and tangible objects and experiences always fail us. No matter how many of them have failed us, somehow there is always this hope that the next object that we are clutching on to is not going to fail us. This tendency has continued for many, many lifetimes. Therefore, our mindstream is very limited and without space. Of course there is no space for others, nor is there is any space for one's own fickle expectations, hopes and fears, and so on. Our practice is to clear this space. To know in reality that space is possible, that space does exist, even though seemingly there is no space, that much understanding is what I call an intellectual understanding of view.

That much acceptance is very important and has to come through hearing teachings, contemplating, and reading books. Once we are vaguely convinced of this kind of view, then, as Jamgön Kongtrül says, it is really important to get used to this view. Practice means getting used to this view. Otherwise, as I was saying earlier, it is easy to get distracted, easy to think that the next object that we are going to clutch or grasp on to is going to work, maybe not this time but surely next time.

Jamgön Kongtrül said that, in order to begin our practice of getting used to the view, laying the foundation is most important. The foundation is renunciation mind. Renunciation means revulsion for this endless, meaningless, worldly life that is constantly creating suffering, whether directly or indirectly. Some amount of renunciation mind is very necessary as a foundation. This is a very important remark by Jamgön Kongtrül because we really cannot take refuge until we have renunciation mind. As long as we do not have renunciation mind, we always think that there is an alternative, a different way to solve the problem. It is like we are falling from a cliff and as we drop we grab anything in front of us: grass, branches, dried wood, whatever. All of these fail, but we don't give up because we think that the next tuft of grass is going to work. As long as we don't stop, as long as we don't see that none of these are going to work, we can't really surrender totally to the Triple Gem. This is why renunciation mind is a foundation. It is so easy to talk about and so difficult to practice.

How can you people develop renunciation mind? You live in this world where things work, the traffic lights work, the toilets flush properly. How can renunciation happen here? It doesn't even begin to happen with people like us. Given the places where we grew up and the conditions we endured, you might think that renunciation mind is easy, but actually it is not. Rather it is just as bad, if not worse, because people like us are hoping to become people like you, so renunciation mind in fact is totally absent.

Jamgön Kongtrül said, as a foundation of the practice we need renunciation mind, and as a door to the practice we need devotion or trust. Not only trust in the guru, we also need to trust the path and the method. Now, that is very crucial. Jamgön Kongtrül continues, as the main path itself we need compassion, and as a soul or life-stream of the path we need diligence. When diligence is lost, the path dies. The path is very short-lived, very fragile, so diligence is necessary. That which ensures that we are on the path is mindfulness. To dispel the obstacles to the path we need complete surrender to the Triple Gem. To enhance the power and the strength of the path we need devotion toward the guru, and to not get sidetracked we need to understand that our guru's pith instructions are the path. This is very important advice because most of the time we forget that the pith instructions are the path. We always think that the path is in the sutras, shastras, and tantras, but the path can be the simple instructions coming from the guru. In short, lay the foundation with renunciation mind, open the door with devotion, remain on the path with compassion, persist with diligence, and avoid sidetracks with mindfulness. All these are structured in the preliminaries. This is why the preliminaries are so important, because other than these there is no path or any other actual Vajrayana practice.

When you begin whatever ngöndro practice you choose to do, instead of immediately beginning to read the liturgy it helps a lot to contemplate renunciation mind, to contemplate all the preliminary thoughts such as impermanence, karma, and the faults of samsara. Somehow doing so will properly create the atmosphere of that day's practice. I have noticed that many students, since their time is very limited, especially for those who have so many sadhanas to practice, do not do this contemplation at the beginning of the practice. For instance, in the *Longchen Nyingtig* there is a technique of blessing the tongue, and even before that there is the technique of purifying the stale air; these are all skillful means to invoke this contemplation. If you don't have the time to do all those practices, at least sit and contemplate for a few minutes.

When you contemplate, do so sincerely. We read so much about impermanence and the faults of samsara, the hell realms and the hungry ghost realms, that somehow we become jaded by this information. Contemplating these things or merely thinking or even reading a few pages about them does help a little bit. However, it does not really invoke the yearning or strong wish to actually give up everything worldly and to concentrate on practice. These contemplations do not seem to really penetrate our mind. Whatever makes you feel revulsion for samsaric life, whatever makes you have some kind of enthusiasm toward the path is something you should invoke, no matter what it happens to be on that particular day. It could be that you have had a ridiculous misunderstanding with a friend or sibling, and so that might invoke renunciation mind. Consider that now you are over forty or fifty years old and you have tried so many methods, changed so many clothes, and had so many partners, but none of it works. Usually we think, "Ah, this next partner is going to be different!" This is my own personal experience as well as the experience of those people who happen to be close to me. [Rinpoche smiles.] Really, genuinely contemplate. Let's say you are practicing this in the evening, then consider what you have done that day, what you have gone through. It should bring some kind of notion that what you have been doing is ridiculous, that there is actually something better to do. I think this is quite important.

I am only reminding the older Dharma students who have gathered so much information. Honestly, how many times have you heard these preliminary teachings? How many years now have you sat through explanations of *The Words of My Perfect Teacher*? Isn't it at least three years that I have been teaching this? Somehow, we are jaded by this information. I have known a few of you for twenty years, and ever since we met we have talked about how samsara is futile; but look, we are still stuck. We still get hurt if we are even slightly ignored. We still get bothered if someone steps on our toes. That just goes to show that we do not have renunciation mind. We have sat through the teachings; we have heard and read so much about it, but we are not really taking it to heart. Really, this is quite important.

On the other hand, I like to encourage myself that I have been quite fortunate to have this opportunity and some kind of merit to have met great masters, and so much of the information they passed on to me is stored in my being. Now personally, I have given up on myself, but at least if I speak up about this information then maybe along the way it might help some of you.

But as I speak this I feel so embarrassed. I feel embarrassed because when I was talking about getting hurt, getting agitated, getting paranoid, getting blissed-out, getting satisfied, or getting annoyed, I myself go through all of these, and each and every one of them is actually a big deal for me. When I get annoyed it is a big deal, it is a *very* big deal; in fact, when I get annoyed several people get annoyed. At least you are in a better situation; you at least sort of hide yourself in your own closet and get annoyed, so who cares? Nobody gives a damn about it. But I might even get annoyed if I am the only one who is annoyed. All this shows that there is no renunciation mind. This is how I contemplate, though of course not all the time. It is once in a blue moon when all the movies are watched, when there is nothing interesting on television, and when no interesting people are calling me except a few devoted but somewhat neurotic students. Anyway, then I try to practice.

That I easily become annoyed and agitated shows that I do not have renunciation mind. Renunciation mind is very simple in a way. We have renunciation mind when we realize that all this is not a big deal. Somebody steps on your toe, what's the big deal? The more we get used to this notion, the more we have renunciation mind. At least I try to see why I make all this into such a big deal. I am merely giving you a model of how to invoke renunciation mind.

It is a bit like this example. We have been walking in this desert for so long, and anything that flows, anything that is watery, is *so* important for us. Even if we see a mirage our only wish is to get near the water without ever realizing that it is a mirage. If you don't know that it is a mirage and you go there, all you end up with is a big disappointment. So, knowing that it is only a mirage is renunciation mind.

Renunciation somehow has this connotation of giving something up. But it is like the example of the mirage. You can't give up the water because there is none; it is only a mirage. Moreover, you don't have to give up a mirage because what is the point of giving up a mirage; one need simply know that it is a mirage. Such understanding is a big renunciation. The moment you know that it is a mirage, most likely you will not even go there because you know it is fake; or even if you do go, there is no disappointment because you already know what is there. At the very least you will only have a little disappointment. That is why Jamgön Kongtrül said renunciation mind is like a foundation.

Renunciation mind has nothing to do with sacrificing. As I just mentioned, when we talk about renunciation, somehow we get all scared because we think that we have to give up some goodies, something valuable, some important things. But there is nothing that is important; there is nothing that is solidly existing. All that you are giving up is actually a vague identity. You realize that this is not true, not the ultimate, and this is how and why to develop renunciation.

14

IMPERMANENCE

Tulku Urgyen Rinpoche

> The world outside is impermanent, as are the beings contained
>   in it.
> Definitely death lies at the end of birth.
> The time of death lies uncertain,
> But when death arrives only the Dharma can help me.
> I will therefore endeavor in one-pointed practice without
>   wasting time.
>
> —KARMEY KHENPO RINCHEN DARGYE

Whether we are beginners or not, we should know that nothing in this world lasts. To understand this fully and to really take it to heart is the foundation of all Buddhist practice. Not taking impermanence to heart prevents our Dharma practice from being successful. The starting point, the first step through the door to Dharma practice, is the understanding that life is impermanent, that our time is running out.

We believe that what we have will last for some time, but no matter where we look in this world, we find nothing that is stable or permanent. As soon as the sun and moon rise, moment by moment they draw closer

---

Adapted from Tulku Urgyen Rinpoche, *Repeating the Words of the Buddha* (Boudhanath: Rangjung Yeshe Publications, 1996), "Impermanence."

to setting. They don't linger in between for even an instant. Seasons change; the days, months, and years pass by. The whole universe is in flux as it goes through the stages of formation, subsistence, disintegration, and disappearance. All living things perpetually change. Life is like a candle that slowly burns down, getting shorter, not longer. Life doesn't wait; it is like a waterfall that is continuously running, never stopping. Every moment we are drawing closer to death. We probably understand this intellectually, but it's very important to think carefully about it so that it remains vividly present in our mind.

Not really taking impermanence to heart, we make long-term plans and take them seriously. Consider yesterday, today, and tomorrow. Yesterday will never come back; it is part of our life that is gone. Past moments, hours, and days never return. Tomorrow becomes today and today fades into yesterday. When today has become yesterday, nobody in the whole world can bring it back to the present. Our life passes, and the fact that it can end at any moment means we are in a most precarious and dangerous situation.

We can be certain that not a single person alive now will be alive 150 years from now. Nevertheless, nobody believes he will eventually die. We are always preoccupied with plans to create and establish something that can be continued, maybe not just for ourselves, but for our children and grandchildren.

If we could just live forever in this present body, we wouldn't have to worry about any aftermath. But death is unavoidable. No one is immortal. Each and every one of us must someday die. We are like a tree that appears to be growing but is decaying inside. Sooner or later the rot takes over and the tree falls.

Undeniably, our present life will end in death. The time before death is more comfortable than what follows. No matter how bad our situation may be while we are alive, we can always try to improve it through our ingenuity. At this time we have free will and the opportunity to change our circumstances. But the events that occur after death depend totally on our personal karma. We are absolutely powerless and choiceless regarding the experiences that will arise.

After death, depending on the karma accumulated by our past actions, we are thrust into a new existence. If we desire rebirth in a good situation, we should realize that the causes for this are currently in our own hands. What can be of help after death? Only the Dharma practice that we invest our time in right now can ensure positive future circumstances. Nothing else will be of any benefit; we can't rely on anything else.

In Buddhist training, revulsion and renunciation are called the "two feet of meditation practice." Revulsion is losing our appetite for samsaric existence and realizing that samsaric pursuits are futile and pointless and do not yield any permanent pleasure and happiness whatsoever. Renunciation means to understand that time is running out and everything passes.

Revulsion is the feeling people suffering from jaundice or liver disease experience when served fried food; they are either very nauseous or they vomit. In the same way, when we realize that all the achievements of the six realms of samsara are futile, insubstantial, and meaningless, we lose our appetite for them.

Renunciation, wanting to be free from samsara, is to realize that all conditioned samsaric states are painful and everything is impermanent. We need to acknowledge sincerely and honestly that our life is a fleeting, fragile existence. Our present body is as perishable as a rainbow in the sky, our breath is like mist on the mountains, and all our thoughts and feelings are like bubbles that appear one moment and vanish the next. From the core of our heart, we need to have this conviction.

Worldly people are only interested in having nice clothes to wear, getting good food to eat, and securing a good reputation. But food, clothing, and a good name are very unstable achievements. In fact, although we really only need enough clothes to keep warm and not freeze, somehow we feel the minimum is not enough. We don't just want ordinary clothes: we want special, fashionable, designer clothes. Regarding food, we only need to eat so that the body survives and doesn't starve. However, mere sustenance doesn't really satisfy us. We want something extraordinary to eat, gourmet food. We also want to be sure to have all the necessities of life when we grow old. We constantly worry about the future, stashing our money away for our old age. When we die, if we have always dressed nicely we will leave behind a well-dressed corpse. If we only wore ordinary clothes, we leave a corpse in ordinary clothing. But a corpse is a corpse, and the attire doesn't make any real difference. We can't take our clothes, supply of food, or bank account with us.

Of these three, food, clothing, and reputation, the worst is craving a good name and respect. When one moves in lower social circles, one longs for the prestige of being talented, influential, clever, or beautiful. One wants to be regarded as somebody. When one circulates among kings and ministers in the highest ranks of society, one desires world fame. The need for a good name is even more pointless than the other two because at least one can eat the food and wear the clothes. One can't really do anything with reputation; it's like thunder in the sky or an echo that vanishes the moment after resounding.

Our reputation is totally useless. When we die, even if we have been the king of a great nation, although those still alive will say, "Oh, our king died," in the *bardo* state we won't be greeted by any official welcoming party. The terrifying figures appearing in the bardo, the Lord of Death and his henchmen, do not respect anyone, regardless of his or her social standing. On the contrary, the more we indulge in superficial self-esteem in this life, that much more loss will we reap in the bardo state. At that time there will be nothing whatsoever left to support such a conviction. Practitioners regard the craving for food, clothing, and reputation as detrimental. They curtail their preoccupation with these things and are satisfied with the bare necessities of life.

Until now, we have had so many past lives, one after the other. There are no immortals in this world; everyone dies. After death we will be reborn among one of the six classes of beings, remain there for some time, then die once again to be reborn elsewhere. On and on it goes, through countless future lives. This chain of birth, death, rebirth, and death again is powered by our karmic deeds and their fruition. This whole cycle is called samsara, which means "spinning" or "circling" like a cog in a machine.

That which decides where we will be reborn is called our karmic debt. If we have committed many positive or "white" karmic deeds, the effect is that we are reborn in one of the three higher realms of samsara. If, on the contrary, we have committed many negative actions, the karmic effect will be rebirth in one of the three lower realms of samsara. The three higher realms are the realms of human beings, demigods, and gods. An even higher achievement is liberation from samsara, which refers to rebirth in one of the buddhafields. Higher than even liberation is buddhahood, complete enlightenment itself.

In accordance with the severity of one's negative karma, one could take rebirth in one of the three lower realms, as an animal or, if the karmic misdeeds are even worse, as a hungry ghost or a hell being in one of the hot or cold hells. All of these realms are created by our own karmic actions. The one who knew that our good and evil actions have an effect and that there are higher and lower realms was the perfectly Awakened One, the Buddha.

The Buddha named the world we are born into *Saha*, which means "indiscernible," that which cannot be seen clearly. If we do an evil action, its effect does not appear immediately. When we do something good, that result is not evident to anybody. If the result of a negative action would ripen the moment after enacting it, nobody would commit evil. Likewise, people would not hold back from positive deeds because the effect would be instantaneous. However, the results of actions do not ripen immediately; they are not instantly discernible, but only ripen slowly. Due to not realizing the positive and negative results of actions and not understanding impermanence, we are completely oblivious to the consequences of our actions. We don't see what is happening, we don't see the result of our actions, we don't see how much or how little merit we have, so we walk around like stupid cows. If the effect of an action were to manifest immediately, then even if someone said "Please do a negative action," there is no way we would do so because we would instantly see the result. If we have eyes and stand on the brink of an abyss, we will not jump, because we see that by jumping we would die. If we could see the effect of our good and evil actions, we would never commit negative actions. But this world is not like that: here, the results of actions appear unclear and vague.

If the effect of an action could be immediately discerned, we would not need a teacher to act as a substitute for the Buddha and tell us to be careful, do good, and avoid evil actions. What is right and wrong would be self-evident. But because we are in a world where the effects of actions are not self-evident, it is important to listen to a teacher repeating what the Buddha said. He repeats words that are not lies, such as "good actions give good results, negative actions give negative results." But it's not enough just to hear that. We need to believe it as well, because unless we trust what has been said, we won't act in accordance with it. Some people think that when a Buddhist teacher says something like "good actions lead to good results," he is lying or doesn't know what he's talking about. It's important to trust because we ourselves cannot see clearly. Due to ignorance we don't see the effect of our positive or negative actions. We don't know what we did in the past or if we will die tomorrow.

The Buddhist teachings were given by the Buddha Shakyamuni, who could see the past, present, and future as clearly as something placed in his own hand. He gave teachings on how to act as a legacy to future generations. He said there are buddhafields, there are lower realms, there is karma, the cause and effect of actions. Normal people can't see clearly, so to help them he told them things like "Avoid negative actions, they will bring negative results; do what is correct and positive, it will bring positive results." He also told us that this life is not the only one;

that there are future lives, there were past lives. The Buddha was extremely kind. In between the time the Buddha lived and now there have been people who followed his teachings, not only the teachings on how to behave, but also the more subtle teachings. They attained special results: some could fly through the sky and pass through solid rock; some died without leaving a physical body and became rainbow light. It is not only because I am Buddhist that I believe the Buddha. It is because there have been so many since him who showed very special signs of accomplishment. That is why I feel I can safely believe all his words.

Because the teacher was so great, Buddhism became widespread in many countries, including Tibet. Apart from Buddhism, Tibetans don't know much. They don't know how to make airplanes, cars, or other technical wonders. But mundane things bring only superficial benefit and lack ultimate value. Instead of making outer machinery, Tibetans focused on spiritual machinery. Many attained the *rainbow body*. There was the great master Karmapa who defeated the four demons, the first Karmapa called *Düsum Khyenpa*. There is one praise to him that says, "Victor over the four demons, knower of the three times," Düsum Khyenpa. In short, it's very important to have trust in the Buddha's teachings if one wishes to apply them. If one tries to apply them without trust, they won't help much.

So what is truly meaningful in this life? Only the pursuance of buddhahood, the state of complete enlightenment. The Three Jewels are truly meaningful: the Precious Buddha; his teachings, called the Precious Dharma; and those who explain the teachings and keep the tradition alive through practice, the Precious Sangha. From the core of our heart, we should place our trust and confidence in these three. When we genuinely feel from deep within there is nothing more precious and valuable than the Three Jewels, this is called "taking refuge." These three Precious Ones will never deceive us or abuse our trust in this life, at the moment of death, in the bardo state, or in our following lives.

How is everything perceived in the state of complete enlightenment? Imagine a crystal ball in your hand: the ball does not obstruct anything but is completely transparent. Everything all around can be seen simultaneously in the crystal ball and is vividly clear. In the same way, the enlightened state perceives everything in all directions at the same moment and in a completely unobstructed fashion. The Dharma teachings are an expression arising from this state and are totally free from any falsehood or pretense.

There was not just one buddha. In the past there have been countless awakened ones. In the present world aeon, one thousand buddhas will appear. In future aeons, a countless number of buddhas will appear. When a fully enlightened one appears and teaches, the words he utters, which are totally free of any deception, are called the Precious Dharma. Those who uphold those teachings and pass them on to others are called the Precious Sangha. In this world, we can find nothing more valuable than the Buddha, Dharma, and Sangha.

The Dharma teachings given by the Enlightened One would be nothing more than writing on paper without someone to uphold and propagate them. Those who uphold the teachings one after another, like the holders of a family line, are called the Precious Sangha. Without great bodhisattvas and masters to teach others, there would be no living tradition. Throughout the centuries these beings have given many commentaries clarifying the Buddha's words, so that today many hundreds of volumes of these books can be found. The Precious Sangha is made up of the teachers and masters who can explain what the Dharma teachings mean and how we can implement them. We need living beings who can communicate the profundity of the Dharma.

The spiritual blessings of the Buddha, Dharma, and Sangha are not far away. The sun in the sky is quite distant, but the moment we hold a mirror up to it, a reflection of the sun immediately appears. In the same way, the very moment we feel faith and devotion, the blessings of the Buddha, Dharma, and Sangha are with us. These blessings are said to be like a hook, while the openness that occurs in the moment of faith is compared to a ring. The hook catches the ring, just as faith and devotion open us fully to the blessings.

To strengthen their connection to the Buddha, Dharma, and Sangha, a great number of people have relied on three unmistaken qualities: the unmistaken quality of the Buddha's words, the unmistaken quality of the statements of noble beings and the enlightened masters, and the unmistaken quality of their own root guru's oral instructions that they put into practice. By combining these unmistaken qualities with their own experience, innumerable people have been able to reach a state totally free from doubt. Moreover, they attained great accomplishments so they could fly through the sky, pass freely through solid rock, and, without leaving a physical body behind, go to the celestial realms at the time of death. Some could travel to distant places without leaving their bodies. For example, at the time of the first Karmapa, several Indian panditas came to Tibet. After meeting the Karmapa, they told others, "We know this old guy with the monkey face very well. He came to India many times and participated in the feast offerings with our guru. We have met him many times before in India." In fact, the Karmapa had never been known to leave Tibet, but a great master like him had the ability to fly off to visit a faraway feast offering and return at his leisure.

By combining the unmistaken qualities with our own experience, we can reach a state totally free from doubt. It's not like we are told, "Don't doubt! Just believe!" It's not like that. It is possible to be completely free from doubt through these three unmistaken qualities. Countless practitioners have achieved that. I myself have no doubt whatsoever in the words of the Buddha.

There are past lives and future lives; there are definite effects from good and evil actions; there are higher realms above and lower realms below. The reason I feel certain of these things is the unmistaken qualities mentioned above. If I were only to rely on myself, I would be unable to reach this certainty because I have never visited the higher realms or been to the hells, nor can I perceive past or future lives. Therefore I do not rely solely on my own judgment. The reason I am able to appear so confident is because I use these unmistaken qualities as confirmation.

What is really valuable? Our precious human rebirth, this body, given to us by our father and mother. We have all our senses intact, we are intelligent and capable of understanding—it is an incredible advantage, like a wish-fulfilling jewel. Another analogy compares being endowed with a precious human rebirth to arriving on an island where jewels abound. As this is the case, it's extremely important not to stand around with our hands in our pockets or folded across our chest. This life should be put to use and be taken full advantage of, so that we don't return empty-handed.

Right now, because we possess a human rebirth, we are clever, practical-minded, and able to carry out most of our intentions. But what if we were animals living in a forest or on a mountaintop? What would be our ability to determine our own future? We would be unable to receive teachings and put them into practice. Right now, we do possess the precious human body and have the power and opportunity to practice the Dharma. Definitely we should do so.

Right now we are at a crossroads where we can go either up or down. Going down requires no effort on our part; it is easily accomplished because it is our natural tendency to continue old patterns of negative emotions. Dharma practice, on the other hand, requires effort; it needs to be cultivated. It is like trying to roll a great boulder uphill. It won't arrive there on its own; it must be pushed up. If we let it go, it will roll all the way downhill under its own power. We don't need to help it. In the same way, we don't have to put much effort into accomplishing negative actions; they come about automatically because it is our natural tendency. Practicing virtue and avoiding negativity is what requires effort.

The Buddha spoke of the ultimate view that cuts through the root of the three poisons. If we want to bring an end to samsaric existence and cross the ocean of samsaric pain and suffering, we need to practice the Precious Dharma that the Buddha taught. If, on the other hand, we are happy and content to continue in the three realms of samsara and we are not tired of undergoing endless suffering, of course we don't need to practice the Dharma. If we think, "I've been circling around taking birth, growing old, getting sick, and dying, taking birth, growing old, getting sick, and dying again and again endlessly, and I'll just go on like that," we can certainly continue doing so, and we don't need to practice the Dharma. When we end up as an ox or cow, we just have to eat grass, fall asleep, wake up, and abide in stupidity until we are slaughtered and eaten. Samsaric existence does not require our efforts in order to perpetuate itself. It will continue automatically. In the chant called the *Rudra's Lamenting Apology*, a line says, "In the past, I have cried enough tears to fill an ocean. The bones of my past skeletons, if heaped together, would be higher than the world's tallest mountain."

To put it bluntly, if we want happiness we need to engage in Dharma practice, but if we are satisfied with pain and suffering we needn't bother practicing. While driving, when we reach a fork in the road where we can go either right or left, it is our own hands that will steer right or left; the choice is ours. In the same way, whether we want to steer a course that will bring happiness in the future or continue on a course that brings us endless pain is entirely up to ourselves. No one else can steer for us. But if we can turn toward enlightenment and attain buddhahood, at that point we will be able to benefit not just ourselves but countless other sentient beings.

Another word for buddha is *sugata*, meaning "having gone to bliss," to a place where not even the word *suffering* is heard. Happy in this life, happy at the time of death, happy in the bardo state, and happy in the future lives is one way to travel. On the other hand, samsaric existence is painful now with the suffering of illness, and later with the experience of death and the confusion of the bardo state that leads us into the lower realms where we experience even more suffering. Samsara only goes from bad to worse.

An advanced practitioner will be happy even when facing illness or at the moment of death. He will be joyful at the prospect of dying because he knows that what comes after will only be better and better. A good practitioner is confident enough to be joyful during sickness and joyful at the moment of death, whereas an ordinary person is depressed by illness and desperate at the moment of death. When he must leave behind his relatives, children, and possessions, he suffers tremendously. All the nice things he worked so hard to acquire will now be carried off and enjoyed by others—truly, how sad.

In Tibet there's a saying, "When seen from afar, yaks look healthy and handsome; close up, they look like sickly sheep; but under the fleece, they are infested with lice and scabies." In other words, when we look at others from afar they may appear to have happiness, prestige, friends, and wealth. But when we get closer we see that they are not really very happy and their situation is not so ideal. There is always something to complain about, and when we get very close and examine their inner feelings, each person has his own set of worries and carries his own burden around with him. No one is in perfect happiness. That's why the Buddha called samsara an ocean of suffering, not an ocean of bliss. But I don't need to convince you of this; you can understand it from your own experience.

Don't just take my word for it, but decide for yourselves what is really meaningful to pursue in this life. I am only trying to refresh your memory and clarify what you already know very well. Nonetheless, appearances, what we smell, hear, see, taste, and touch, are seductive. If we allow ourselves to be carried away by our fickle mind, even though we may really want to practice the Dharma, it is somehow postponed. We think, "Well, if not today, I can practice tomorrow or maybe next month, or next year." Or never. Things don't occur exactly in accordance with our plans. It is said, "When I was young, I was controlled by others and couldn't practice the Dharma. When I grew up, I played around and couldn't practice the Dharma. Now, I'm old and too weak to practice the Dharma. Alas, alas! What shall I do?" Decide for yourselves: are you able to practice the Dharma?

If we apply the teachings, the first beneficiary will be ourselves. Later, after we have taken care of ourselves, we will be capable of helping countless other beings. On the other hand, if we don't succeed in benefiting ourselves and others through Dharma practice, we are not really adding more beings to the ocean of samsara, but only adding ourselves to the multitudes already roaming through the lower realms. That is not of such great benefit. Wouldn't it be better to attain enlightenment and leave samsara behind, rather than just adding ourselves to the countless beings suffering in the lower realms?

15

THE SECOND OF THE FOUR DHARMAS OF GAMPOPA

Tulku Urgyen Rinpoche

> *Grant your blessings that my Dharma practice*
> *may become the path.*
>
> —GAMPOPA

We continue in samsaric existence as long as we are covered by the obscuration of disturbing emotions and the cognitive obscuration. These two obscurations are precisely what hinder us from attaining the state of omniscient buddhahood. In order to remove them we engage in the practices known as the preliminaries. These practices are included under the second Dharma of Gampopa, "Make your Dharma practice become the path!"

Through the four mind-changings we develop the wish to be liberated from samsaric existence and attain the precious state of enlightenment, not merely for ourselves, but for all beings. We have become ready

Adapted from Tulku Urgyen Rinpoche, *Repeating the Words of the Buddha* (Boudhanath: Rangjung Yeshe Publications, 1996), "Four Dharmas of Gampopa," and *As It Is,* Volume I (Boudhanath: Rangjung Yeshe Publications, 1999).

to take refuge in the Three Precious Ones. The Buddha is the completely and perfectly awakened state of omniscience. The Dharma is the path that leads to that, the teachings. The Sangha are all the masters who have upheld, propagated, and made the teachings flourish from the time of the Buddha up until our kind personal master with whom we have managed to connect. To take refuge in these with full trust and confidence ensures that we have the possibility to also become awakened ones ourselves. Taking refuge and seeking guidance under the Three Jewels is what opens the way to becoming enlightened.

Connected with this, as a branch, is the development of bodhichitta. Without bodhichitta, we cannot proceed on the Mahayana path. The understanding that all other sentient beings are in fact our own mothers and fathers from past lives provides a very important basis for our progress. Every little insect that we meet, without a single exception, has been our own mother and father—not just once, but many times. And all of them are on the wrong track. They want to be happy, but do not know how to accomplish this. To develop bodhichitta means to form this most courageous resolve: "I will personally take responsibility to lead all sentient beings to the state of enlightenment!" This bodhisattva vow is what makes the difference between a Hinayana and a Mahayana follower. To take this vow is called generating bodhichitta. Taking refuge and developing bodhichitta are therefore the very essence of the path.

When we truly apply ourselves to the preliminary practices, we can remove obstacles on the spiritual path and create all the conducive conditions for quickly realizing the ultimate fruition. That is exactly what is meant by the second of the Four Dharmas of Gampopa: how to ensure that one's Dharma practice becomes the path.

Some people regard themselves as exclusively Mahayana or Vajrayana practitioners. Others say they only follow Theravada, that they don't know anything beyond that. But talking in this way only exposes one's lack of understanding. The three vehicles are not meant to be separated at all. We can practice all of them simultaneously—in fact, we need to in order to have a solid foundation. Without really applying ourselves to the four mind-changings and taking refuge, we have no real foundation from which to connect to the Buddhist teachings. Similarly, if you want to drink tea, you need a place to put the cup. You need a table, which is the same as the foundation of the shravaka or Hinayana teachings. You also need the cup to contain the tea, which is the Mahayana attitude. And you need the tea as well—otherwise there is nothing to drink, and you *do* need a drink. Vajrayana teachings are like the liquid poured into the cup.

In the same way, in order to become enlightened we first need to connect to the Three Jewels. Taking refuge involves entrusting ourselves to the Buddha, Dharma, and Sangha; the taking of refuge contains the Hinayana teachings. After that, what is the use of being the only one who is enlightened while all our mothers roam about in samsara? That would be totally shameless. It is said that the Hinayana orientation is like the little puddle of water contained in the hoofprint of a cow, while the Mahayana attitude is as vast as the entire ocean. Everyone needs to be enlightened—not only ourselves. Thirdly, without the very profound teachings of Vajrayana, including deity, mantra, and samadhi, there is no way we can achieve full enlightenment in this same body and lifetime. Thus, we need all three vehicles together: Hinayana, Mahayana, and Vajrayana. There is no point at all in regarding oneself as some kind of superior practitioner who doesn't need "low" or "inferior" teachings. Such an attitude would be very unrealistic.

Ensuring that one's Dharma practice becomes the path means purifying the obscurations and misdeeds that create obstacles and block the path to the attainment of complete enlightenment. There is a profound reason to practice the preliminaries, even though some may think of them as unnecessary. It is through the preliminary practices that we are truly able to clear away obstacles and make our Dharma practice become the path of enlightenment.

16

INSTRUCTIONAL ADVICE ON
TRAINING IN BUDDHISM

Patrül Rinpoche

O root lama, the great vajradhara, who is the embodiment of
The triple refuges and all the buddhas in reality,
Please always remain inseparably on the crown of my head, and
Bestow blessings without separation from me in the three times.

O friend who is devoted to Dharma from the heart,
You have requested me again and again with these heartlike words:
"Please write and give us your heart-advice."
So I offer you this affectionate message from the heart.

The first entrance to the path of liberation from samsara
Depends on having a perfect lama.
So, with proper devotion without changes,
To follow whatever he teaches is important.

From *Enlightened Living*, translated by Tulku Thondup (Boudhanath: Rangjung
Yeshe Publications, 1997).

However, in these days, the age of dregs,
There are many people who are attached to having lamas
    deceptively,
Cherishing the desires for this life in their hearts.
It is crucial to reverse such a manner.

Therefore, whatever is the essence of your wish,
Without concealing it, again and again
From the bottom of your heart
Recollecting it, you should speak to the lama and implore him for
    the wish.

Although a gem is all wish-fulfilling,
If it is not anointed and displayed atop a victory banner
And prayed to, and aspirations are not made for the wishes,
A gem it may be, but no wishes will be fulfilled.

The lama is the source of the teachings,
But if there is no one who requests the teachings,
There won't be any occasion for giving the profound teachings.
So it is important to request the sublime teaching, whichever
    one wishes.

Without practicing the teachings you were given earlier,
To keep yearning to receive further teachings
Is to do nothing but bother the lama and provoke scoldings,
So it is crucial to exhort yourself in practice all the time.

You should do practice by knowing the crucial aspects of the
    teaching.
The essence of the teaching is going for refuge and development of
    the mind of enlightenment
Through these two one accomplishes buddhahood.
There is no need to yearn for many other so-called profundities.

If the fourfold turning of the mind to Dharma, the entrance
    to Dharma,
Is not born in the stream of your mind perfectly,
Even to hear other teachings is only to waste them.
So it is crucial to exhort yourself to tame your mindstream.

Those people who don't eat what is given and who steal what
    is preserved,
Who abandon the Dharma teachings that they have studied

But pretend to be practicing something else,
Are doing nothing but causing others to be indifferent to Dharma
    and breaking the sacred pledge.
Without taming one's mind through mental disciplines,
The practices of body and speech do not benefit the mind.
Therefore it is crucial to contemplate with your mind again
    and again
The fourfold turning of the mind and the development of the mind
    of enlightenment.

If these contemplations are perfectly born in your mind,
And if your mind has entered into the Dharma without wavering,
Then the excellent lama gradually will give you
The entire profound instructions of higher and higher teachings.

From the difficulty of obtaining fortunate human birth
Up to the development stage, the perfection stage, the practices on
Channels, energy, and heat of the esoteric path,
And the training on cutting through of Great Perfection, which is
    the direct approach—
There is no Dharma that is not included in this.

Therefore, besides the teachings you have already received,
There is no need to request more.
However, it is crucial to receive clarifications and refinements
To resolve any doubts on the teachings you have received.
Having trained in the fivefold hundred thousand practice, such as
    going for refuge,
To complete the guru yoga, the esoteric path of devotion,
With recitation of the mantra ten million times
Is the tradition of this lineage.

So if you have completed just the preliminary practice
Properly as it is and thoroughly,
Hereafter the certainty of your birth in Zangdog Palri
Is promised. See the instruction texts.

The unmodified, self-aware, and ordinary mind,
Which is thorough, free, and innate, is the Dharmakaya.
Realize that suchness of the mind nakedly
And maintain the thoughts, the appearing power of the awareness
    of liberation-at-arising.

Apart from this, some crucial points on meditation
I have given you again and again in the past, as you asked.
As there is no teaching higher than that to give you,
Please do practice on those instructions.

Thus, having been urged by a friend, who has lived in accordance
  with the Dharma.
This is written by that shallow wanderer.
Although lacking in definitiveness, profundity, or excellent meaning,
It is an honest and direct message from the heart.

By the merits of writing this, in all the successive lives,
In the presence of the consorts of the Lord of Accomplished Ones,
In the single assembly, without separation,
I pray, may we be reborn and taste the joy of Dharma.

  Thus, as prayed by Patrül, may all be auspicious and may all be
  virtuous.

THE TRUE FOUNDATION

Tulku Urgyen Rinpoche

Let me tell you another essential point: until you have truly taken to heart and assimilated their truth within your being, continue to train in the general and specific preliminaries. These are the reflections on the four mind-changings—on the precious human body, on impermanence and mortality, on the consequences of karmic actions, and on the negative characteristics of samsaric existence. The specific preliminaries are: taking refuge and making prostrations, generating bodhichitta, Vajrasattva recitation, mandala offerings, and guru yoga. It is common to all schools of Tibetan Buddhism to begin with these.

If we truly take the four mind-changings to heart, reflecting sincerely on the sufferings of the six classes of beings, we will not find it difficult to do these preliminary practices. Otherwise we might think it was okay to just lie back and have a good time eating and drinking, with an attitude like "Why bother to do exhausting things such as prostrations and mandala offerings?" In reality, these preliminary practices are the

Adapted from Tulku Urgyen Rinpoche, *Rainbow Painting* (Boudhanath: Rangjung Yeshe Publications, 1995), "The True Foundation."

foundation for attaining complete enlightenment. When you sincerely understand that, you can see the reason for doing this "work."

However much you hear about the difficulties of obtaining a precious human body and the value of renunciation, the will to be free, such information will only benefit when you make these thoughts your own. Right now you have the freedom to do so. Make no mistake; these four reflections are the very basis for the path of enlightenment. To build a house you need a stable foundation; if the foundation is good then a hundred-storied tower can be built on top of it. If you want to become enlightened in this very body and life, you need to bring about a deep shift in attitude, a shift that can take place by your reflecting on these four mind-changings. On the other hand, if you only want to enjoy life's pleasures, you'll find Dharma practice to be extremely tiring. You will lose interest in it eventually if you think these four thoughts are unimportant. In fact, you will not have any lasting interest in a spiritual path until you take them into your stream of being.

For example you hear talk about the view, about the teachings of Madhyamika, Mahamudra, and Dzogchen. Through these, you can attain enlightenment in one body and one lifetime; such precious teachings do exist. But it is a mistake not to take the four mind-changings as your foundation. To rely only on teachings about the view is like trying to arrive somewhere that can only be reached by flying, when you only have the capacity for walking. If we do not have the proper foundation, there is no way to progress.

Almost every Dharma system contains preliminary and main practices. I will once more repeat what the Buddha said, "Just as the steps of a staircase, you should also train step-by-step and endeavor in my profound teachings; without jumping over any step, proceed steadily to the end. Progress in Dharma is similar to the way a small child gradually develops its body and strength, from entering in the beginning up until the complete perfection." First are the teachings of the shravakas and pratyekabuddhas, and the levels continue like going up a staircase all the way up to the three profound views of Mahamudra, Madhyamika, and Dzogchen.

It cannot be repeated too many times that you need a firm foundation. Unless you are someone of the highest capacity like Garab Dorje, it is not enough to have merely been introduced to the view without following that up with the preliminary practices. Needless to say, not everyone is of the highest capacity: the perfect conditions do not always manifest with a perfect teacher, a perfect student, and perfect teachings.

Taking this into account, we have to examine ourselves honestly. We are ordinary people, and we are mistaken if we think otherwise. If from the start the four mind-changings have been a motivating force, then practicing the Dharma will not be difficult at all. Without embracing these we will only tire ourselves. The very basis of our practice rests on taking these four mind-changings to heart.

Within the preliminary practices, all three yanas can be practiced in one session, on one seat. Taking refuge comprises the essentials of the Hinayana teachings; generating bodhichitta embodies the heart of the Mahayana teachings; and meditation and recitation of Vajrasattva comprise the very quintessence of the Vajrayana teachings. Thus, within a single session, we can cover all three vehicles and perform a complete Buddhist practice.

If you want to practice many extensive details, you can find hundreds of thousands of teachings in the Buddhist canonical collection. But it is impossible to practice them all in a single lifetime. Padmasambhava and other masters kindly extracted the essence of the teachings in developing the preliminary practices, which include all the instructions of the scholars and accomplished beings of India and Tibet. Every Vajrayana school contains these preliminary practices. Why? Because these are an excellent method for purifying obscurations and gathering the accumulations. Without purifying obscurations and gathering the accumulations we cannot reach the state of enlightenment. Compared to the main practice, the preliminary practices are considered more profound. If you want to grow a crop you need fertile ground: a hundred years of planting seeds on a stone will not yield a harvest. If these four thoughts, the four mind-changings, are not embedded in your stream-of-being, if you do not comprehend their depth, then you will not realize the true meaning. The highest teachings of Vajrayana have their base in the preliminary practices.

The four mind-changings are not beyond our comprehension. We are capable of understanding that having a human life is extremely rare and precious. Most people know that everything is impermanent, that with each passing day our life becomes shorter. If we have some degree of intelligence, we can trust that our actions have their karmic consequences. Finally, it's apparent that all samsaric states, being impermanent and unreliable, can never offer us lasting happiness. These are all things we can understand—but intellectual comprehension is not enough. We must take to heart and deeply assimilate this understanding within our stream-of-being.

All the great masters of the past practiced in this way. They gave up all worldly concerns and attached as much importance to mundane aims as we do to a gob of phlegm spat out onto the ground. No one ever thinks of picking up such an object, do they? We should try to cultivate that same detachment toward all samsaric states. The old Kadampa master said, "Give up your homeland; wander in unknown lands; be a child of the mountains; wear the mist as your garment; keep companionship with wild animals in jungles, forests, caves, and mountain retreats." How were practitioners able to do this? Was it just by pushing themselves into enduring these hardships? No, they simply took to heart, clearly and genuinely, the four mind-changings. When we reflect on these four points and truly take them to heart, then practicing the Dharma in an authentic way is not difficult at all.

The measure of having taken to heart the preciousness of the human body, with its freedoms and riches that are so difficult to find, is that we are unable to waste time. We are filled with deep joy at having attained something so precious and rare, and we want to put this treasure to full use. This sense of true appreciation, of rejoicing so deeply that one cannot sit idle, is the measure of having taken to heart the preciousness of the human body.

Another example for taking the four mind-changings to heart is that of a beautiful but vain maiden who notices that her hair has caught fire. She will not rest at ease for a single instant, but will immediately try to extinguish the flames. In the same way, if we have truly assimilated the four mind-changings, we will not hesitate for a single second, but will immediately try to practice the sacred Dharma.

People usually have the attitude, "Things do last; we live for quite some time." Of course, they know that there is impermanence, but they think that it does not pertain to the present; that it is something that "comes later on." For example, we might think, "This particular object will finally disintegrate; right now, however, it does exist and continues to do so. Things are therefore permanent." This attitude is contrary to how things really are.

Taking impermanence to heart means to acknowledge that nothing whatsoever lasts even from one moment to the next—especially our life. Our existence here in a physical body has no real permanence. We will die. We should develop this attitude, "I will die. I do not know when and I do not know how; but it is unavoidable!" Keep this feeling so acutely in your mind that you cannot bear to sit idle. Instead you will feel: "I have to do something truly worthwhile. I cannot let the time fly by. As each day and moment passes, I'm closer to death. Not only me—it's like this for everyone, but no one pays any attention." The measure of having taken to heart the thought of impermanence is a genuine understanding of our mortality and everyone else's. When you have this painfully acute understanding of the "suffering of being conditioned" and of the fact that time is continuously running out, you refuse to waste a single second on anything that is not Dharma practice.

As a further argument for impermanence, consider the universe in which we live. Usually people believe that the world is solid and real, but this is not true. It will not last forever, and in the meantime it is constantly changing with each passing moment. When the universe finally disintegrates, there will be an end to this world as we know it. It will be destroyed by the "seven suns" and the "one water" until the only thing remaining is space. Since space is uncompounded, it can never disintegrate, but everything within space vanishes—everything! Then a period of voidness will endure for a while until a new universe is formed. It in turn remains for a while—which is the time we are experiencing now—and again disintegrates and vanishes. These four major cycles—formation, abidance, destruction, and voidness—a world goes through constitute a great aeon, and this process is repeated again and again. Nothing material is exempt from this endless process. By our pondering this, our normal tendency to cling to permanence will naturally fall away.

Also consider the great noble beings who have appeared in this world. All the bodhisattvas of the past as well as all the buddhas who possessed incredible clairvoyance, wisdom, and the capacity to transform an aeon into a second and a second into an aeon have passed away. The bodily forms of great noble beings are not permanent either. Please ponder this.

Consider the people who possessed great merit, power and dominion. Universal rulers, *chakravartin*s, who wielded the "wheel of gold" controlled all four continents. Those possessing the "wheel of silver" reigned over three continents. Those possessing the "wheel of copper" governed two continents, and those possessing the "wheel of iron" still held command over one entire continent. They had the power to rule over all peoples. They could even dine with Indra on the summit of Mount Sumeru, seated on thrones of equal height, and then fly back into the human realm. But where are they now? They are all gone. Please realize that even people of great might also vanish.

Next, consider the many causes of death and the few circumstances for staying alive. There are 404 kinds of diseases, 80,000 kinds of attacks from evil spirits, and many other obstacles for life as well. All these surround us like gusts of wind in a great storm, while our life force is like the flame of a candle or a butter lamp. There are very few reasons for this flame to remain without being extinguished. We usually believe that medicine prolongs life, but sometimes medicine administered in the wrong way can become the cause of death. Even the means of healing can cut life short. Please consider the many causes of death and the few circumstances that sustain life.

It is a small miracle that we wake up each morning. It is said that the difference between being alive or dead is a single breath. If you exhale and don't inhale, you are dead. That's all it takes. Nagarjuna said, "Since this is the case, it's amazing, a wonder, that one wakes up in the morning." It is not enough to merely hear or read about impermanence; you need to take it to heart.

In the cycle of teachings given by Padmasambhava called *Karling Shitro*—the *Peaceful and Wrathful Deities Revealed by Karma Lingpa*—there is a very vivid image of the inevitability of our death. Imagine that you are standing on a half-inch-wide ledge on a sheer cliff overlooking an almost bottomless abyss, with a roaring river raging below. You cannot bear to look down. Only your toes can rest on the ledge, while your hands grasp two handfuls of grass the size of a goat's beard. You are hanging on to these two handfuls of scrub-grass that represent your life span and life force. At the same time, impermanence, in the form of two rats representing the Lord of Death and the Lord of Life, gnaw away the grass you are clinging to, piece by piece. Once the grass is consumed, there will be nothing left to hold on to. There is only one way to go: to plunge into the nearly bottomless abyss and the raging river. Your guardian spirits are present in the form of two crows who hover above you, but how can they help your desperate situation? So, you hang on while the rats eat up the grass, blade by blade. You have no chance of survival whatsoever.

This is our current situation. We as practitioners must vividly imagine Padmasambhava's teaching, which clearly points out our mortality and inescapable death. Please contemplate this well, because it represents how it truly is. Below is the abyss of the three lower realms. We do not have to think of anything other than that. Then ask yourself, "What can I do?" A true practitioner should take this to heart and meditate on it!

Our clinging to sense pleasures, the desirable objects of the five senses, causes us to spin around in samsara. Here's another example from the *Karling Shitro* regarding attachment to sense pleasures. Imagine you are sentenced to death and have been dragged before the executioner. Your head now lies on the chopping block and he raises the ax in the air above your neck. He's just about to strike when someone steps up to you and says, "I would like to present you with a beautiful consort, a magnificent palace, and countless luxuries and enjoyable experiences!" How will you feel, knowing the ax is about to fall? Is the prospect of enjoying all these sense pleasures enticing in the least? This example from the *Karling Shitro* illustrates in a very vivid way the futility of our attachment to the five sense pleasures of samsara. Do we really think they will last? Practitioners, combine the metaphor with the meaning!

Trust in the consequences of your karmic deeds. All that takes place—the formation of the universe and its abiding, changing, and disintegration—occurs without any creator or maker to initiate it. It is all the result of the karmic actions of sentient beings. This is an unfailing law.

Next, among the six classes of beings, all the different life forms are basically painful. There is no place of permanent happiness within samsara, regardless of where you are reborn. As a hell being, you suffer from heat and cold; as a hungry ghost, you suffer from hunger and thirst; as an animal, you suffer from stupidity and being enslaved or eaten by others; while as a human being, a demigod, or a god, you still suffer from various imperfections. If you reflect deeply upon these different samsaric states, you will find that none offers any sanctuary free from suffering and pain.

Longchen Rabjam meditated for many years in a place called Gangri Tökar, White Skull Snow Mountain, where he even lacked a proper cave. He took shelter for three years under a cliff overhang. His only possession, in terms of bedding and clothing, was a hemp-cloth sack. During the day he wore this as his garment, while at night it became his bedding. This single scrap of sackcloth also served as his seat during meditation sessions. At the entrance to this rock overhang grew a huge thornbush. Whenever he had to go out and relieve himself, the thorns pierced his body in numerous places. While he was urinating outside, he would think, "It's really uncomfortable having to push past this thornbush every day. I should hack it down!" Then, on his way back in, he would think, "On the other hand, maybe this is the last day of my life. Why should I spend it cutting down a bush? That's meaningless—I'd rather do something that has real significance, like train myself in the view, meditation, and conduct. If this is my last day, I should spend it practicing. One never knows how much time one has left in life." So, he would forget about cutting down the bush and go back inside to continue his practice session. This went on day after day, and after three years he attained complete realization. And he never cut down the thornbush. This is an example of how the reflection on impermanence can manifest itself in a great realized master like Longchenpa.

The whole point of the preliminary practices is to purify the negative karma and the obscurations we have created. This does not necessarily involve the pursuit of physical well-being. Doing prostrations and the other preliminary practices is not a matter of making ourselves as comfortable as possible. Trying to avoid pain is definitely not the style of an honest practitioner. It is the behavior of a Lhasa dignitary, who prostrates on top of a soft mattress with all kinds of cushioning devices on his knees, ribs, and elbows to ensure that the practice will not hurt in any way. This is called "VIP prostrations," and I assure you that this style does not purify any karma or obscurations whatsoever.

There is another way of prostrating, which is the style of Patrül Rinpoche (author of The Words of My Perfect Teacher). You simply prostrate wherever you are, however the landscape may be. Whether you are prostrating in the main shrine hall or outside atop rocks and grass, you bow down and stretch out, full of devotion, imagining that you are right in front of the objects of refuge. Patrül Rinpoche always practiced outdoors in the vast meadows. He lived in a black yak-hair tent and he would often do prostrations outside while chanting the Sukhavati Aspiration by Karma Chagmey, a prayer to be reborn in the pure land of Buddha Amitabha. Because Patrül Rinpoche never bothered with a prostration board or any cushioning devices, he eventually wore down through the grass and down into the soil, leaving a deep indentation in the ground the exact size of his body. This is how most Tibetan practitioners of the past prostrated. They did not dress up in special prostration gear and glide in an especially soft place so there would be no pain. Many people would draw blood from their hands. I have often seen people skin their foreheads and develop a callus, and sometimes skin their hands and knees. By performing 100,000 prostrations in this way you can definitely purify your negative karma and obscurations.

When we take a bath, we wash away the dirt and sweat that has accumulated on our skin. In fact, the whole reason for taking a bath is to clear away this accumulation. It's not that we leave half of it and say, "I took a bath so now I am clean," when we are still half dirty. In the same way, the point of the ngöndro, the preliminary practices, is to remove the obscurations and become pure. Therefore, the basic guideline for how to practice and how long to practice is the extent to which we have purified our obscurations. There is no real guideline other than total purification!

The whole reason for doing prostrations is to completely purify misdeeds and obscurations, not to do easy, comfortable Dharma practice. That is not the aim in itself; neither is it self-mutilation. The point is to focus totally on the practice with proper motivation, with full devotion for the Three Jewels and compassion for beings, combined with diligence. This is the main thing. We should not be emerging from our bath or shower still dirty; remember this!

At the time of the Buddha, which was called the Age of Perfection, it was sufficient to do one complete set of 100,000 preliminaries in order to achieve complete purification. The next two ages that followed were called the "two-endowed" and the "three-endowed," meaning two and three repetitions were necessary. The fourth period, which we are in now, is called the "period of adhering only to the superficial attributes." At this time, it is not enough to do two times 100,000 or even three times 100,000 to achieve complete purification. In this age we must do four times 100,000, meaning four full sets of preliminaries.

Motivation, your attitude, is of primary importance when going through the preliminary practices. This attitude involves devotion for the Three Jewels and compassion for sentient beings, infused with diligence. If you train in the preliminaries with proper motivation they will turn out well: that is the first point. The second point is that negative karma and obscurations are embedded in the *alaya*, the all-ground. As long as this all-ground with its ignorant aspect is not purified, it will continue to form the basis for further obscurations and negative karma. So, what truly needs to be purified is the basic ignorance of the all-ground.

To achieve complete purification is the main point, not only when doing prostrations and taking refuge, but also during the other preliminary practices. After performing the visualization, try to remember the view of Mahamudra, Dzogchen, or the Middle Way. At times, try to prostrate and chant while remaining in mind essence. This will increase the effect of the practice. It is said that when a practice is done correctly, with mindfulness rather than just doing it mechanically, the effect is multiplied 100 times. If the practice is carried out while in the state of samadhi, in other words while recognizing mind essence, its effect is multiplied 100,000 times. Since many people have great interest in recognizing the nature of mind, we need not set this aside while doing purification practices. On the contrary, we should unify the two aspects of practice: the accumulation of merit and the accumulation of wisdom.

By combining these practices with the recognition of mind nature, we combine the accumulation of conceptual merit with the accumulation of nonconceptual wisdom. By the accumulation of merit with a reference point, you manifest the twofold rupakaya and purify the obscurations of disturbing emotions. By the accumulation of wisdom free from reference point, you realize the immaculate dharmakaya and purify the ignorant all-ground. The way to do this is, after bringing to mind and visualizing the objects of refuge, to look into who is performing this practice. If we can do a full prostration without losing the view of mind essence, that single prostration is equal to 100,000 prostrations. It's how we practice that makes all the difference.

For example, reciting the 100-syllable mantra only once while resting undistractedly in mind essence has the same value as distractedly reciting the 100-syllable mantra 100,000 times. So, how one carries out the practice makes an enormous difference. By looking into mind essence while prostrating, we are able to purify not just our obscurations and negative karma, but also the very ground of ignorance upon which all obscurations and negative karma are based.

Even though you may have already done a great deal of Buddhist practice over the years, if you want to attain realization, do not hold yourself back from doing as many of the preliminary practices as possible until you are totally purified. It is not the number that matters, but the degree of purification. The way to maximize this is by combining the accumulation of merit with the view. So keep the view you have been introduced to, whether it be the view of Mahamudra, the Middle Way, or Dzogchen, in mind when you are performing the preliminary practices. No matter which of the three great views you choose to practice according to the Tibetan tradition, each includes the preliminary practices.

A famous quote sums up the whole reason for these practices: "When obscurations are removed, realization occurs spontaneously." The only thing that prevents realization is our obscurations and negative karma; and the preliminary practices remove them. When the mind is totally stripped of obscurations, realization is like a wide-open, clear sky with nothing to obscure it in any way whatsoever. Habitual tendencies are like the smell of camphor—even when it is washed away, a faint odor lingers. It is the same with the obscurations that lie latently within the all-ground. Another famous quote says, "It is delusion to depend on any other method than these practices for removing obscurations, gathering the accumulations, and receiving the blessings of a realized master."

What is more valuable—a single diamond or a room full of glass beads? Similarly, our practice does not depend on quantity, on the number of repetitions we accumulate in order to get the practice over with. It is not at all relevant to make it known that we are one of those amazing individuals who have completed five or ten sets of preliminaries. Some people practice with distracted minds, rushing through the motions as quickly as possible as though it was a mechanical chore. Their sessions are carried out looking right and left, without paying any attention to what they are doing. What is necessary is to focus body, speech, and mind one-pointedly on the practice—*that* is what purifies the negative karma and obscurations. This is the real thing, the authentic diamond as opposed to a mere roomful of glass beads.

My root guru, my uncle Samten Gyatso, did this himself. Throughout his entire life, he never missed a single day of doing 100 prostrations. He made the ngöndro part of his daily practice, even when he was old and very sick. He walked with the help of two canes, one in each hand, so that people used to say he walked on "four legs" like an animal. Yet, he still managed to do 100 prostrations each day. The ngöndro that he adhered to was the preliminary practices for *Chetsün Nyingtig*.

Samten Gyatso died when he was sixty-four. I do not know what he practiced as a little boy. But from the time I met my uncle and from what others could remember about him, he never, until the day he died, spent a single day without going through the preliminaries. My father, Chimey Dorje, did the ngöndro practices for both *Chetsün Nyingtig* and *Künzang Tuktig* every day. Even though the ngöndro preliminaries are extremely simple, they are, at the same time, also extremely profound. I suggest that you do the preliminary practices every day; this will be both excellent and very beneficial!

To reiterate, once you have taken the four mind-changings to heart, you will have formed a solid foundation and Dharma practice will not be at all difficult. If not, it is like trying to build a house without a foundation. The great masters of the past, especially those in the Kagyü lineage, have said, "Because they are the foundation, the preliminaries are more profound than the main part." Lay the solid foundation that results not merely from having "done" the preliminaries by going through the motions, but from having taken to heart the four reflections and the four or five times 100,000 preliminaries. Then you cannot help practicing in a genuine way. But simply having repeated the mantras and having the idea, "Okay, I did it," will not be the foundation for higher practices.

Whoever truly takes to heart the preliminaries is said to act like a wounded deer who flees to a place of solitude, not just "acting" like a practitioner in the eyes of others. Milarepa said, "I fled to the mountains to practice in solitude because I was frightened of death. Through practicing, I realized the nature that is beyond birth and death. Now I have captured the stronghold of fearlessness." That is how to practice.

If we undertake these preliminary practices in an authentic way so that we feel we cannot afford to waste a single moment, we will be able to practice like Milarepa. This is a solid foundation. Whatever is built upon it, such as the main practice of yidam deity, mantra, and completion stage, Trekchö and Tögal, will be like the stories of a building that will remain firmly grounded and stable. It's not enough to strive for the higher teachings and ignore the real substance of the Dharma, which is a change in attitude. Unless we can change our hearts at a profound level, the samsaric traits of our personality will all remain, and we will still be seduced by appearances. As long as our mind is fickle, it is easy to become carried away in the chase of power and wealth or the pursuit of beautiful objects, in concerns of business and politics, in intrigues and deceit. It is easy to become an insensitive practitioner who cannot be "cured" or changed by the Dharma. Although one may have great theoretical understanding, it does not penetrate to the core. That state is like a butter skin that is not made flexible by the butter inside, even though it holds the butter.

So, do not grab at the higher teachings of Trekchö and Tögal. They are like the impressive wolf-skin hats worn in Kham; they look very good, but what keeps your ears warm in the winter is the unimpressive collar of plain sheepskin! It's much more important to emphasize the preliminaries and lay a solid foundation: then whatever is built on top of that afterward will make sense. Otherwise, it will be empty talk.

Most important of all, more crucial than the extraordinary practices of Trekchö and Tögal, are the general and the specific preliminaries. Without having taken to heart these mind-changings, whatever practice you do will never lead anywhere. Nothing can be built when there is no foundation to build on. You may already know this very well; it may not be the first time you are hearing this. My words may be like trying to give the reading transmission of OM MANI PADME HUNG to Avalokiteshvara. Nonetheless, I wanted to say this to refresh your memory.

18

TAKING REFUGE

Padmasambhava

The master Padmakara of Uddiyana, who appeared as a nirmanakaya in person, was asked by Lady Tsogyal, the princess of Kharchen: Great Master, please be kind and teach the basis for all Dharma practice, the means by which to end birth and death, a little cause that has immense benefit, a method that is easy to apply and has little hardship.

The nirmanakaya master replied: Tsogyal, taking refuge is the basis for all Dharma practice. The Three Jewels are the support for all Dharma practice. The means that brings an end to birth and death is to take refuge along with its subsidiary aspects.

Lady Tsogyal asked: What is the essential meaning of taking refuge? What is its definition? When divided, how many types are there?

The master replied: The essential meaning of taking refuge is to accept the Buddha, Dharma, and Sangha as your teacher, path, and companions for practicing the path, and then to pledge that they are the fruition you will attain. Thus taking refuge means a pledge or acceptance. Why is such an acceptance called "taking refuge"? It is because

Adapted from Padmasambhava, *Dakini Teachings* (Boudhanath: Rangjung Yeshe Publications, 1999), "Refuge."

of accepting the Buddha, Dharma, and Sangha as the support, refuge, and protector or rescuer for being freed from the great fear of the sufferings and obscurations. That is the essential meaning of taking refuge.

The definition of taking refuge is to seek protection from the terrors of the three lower realms and from the inferior view of believing in a self within the transitory collection as is held by non-Buddhist philosophers.[13]

When divided, there are the three types: the outer way of taking refuge, the inner way of taking refuge, and the secret way of taking refuge.

The Outer Way of Taking Refuge

Lady Tsogyal asked: Concerning the outer way of taking refuge, what is the cause of wanting to take refuge? In what object does one take refuge? What kind of person takes refuge? What are the manners or methods through which one takes refuge? With what particular attitude does one take refuge?

Master Padma replied: The cause of wanting to take refuge is fear of the miseries of samsara, trusting in the Three Jewels as the place of refuge, and moreover, accepting the Three Jewels as the objects of refuge and the protectors of refuge. Through these three you give rise to the intention of taking refuge. In general, one wants to take refuge due to fear of death.

There are many people who do not even notice that half of their life has passed and who do not think of their future lives for even an instant. They have no refuge.

If you were not going to die or if you were certain of a human rebirth, you would not need to take refuge. However, after dying and transmigrating, there are the overwhelming miseries of the lower realms.

In what object does one take refuge? You should take refuge in the Three Jewels. Who can bring an end to birth and death? It is exclusively the omniscient Buddha who is free from all defects and who has perfected all virtues. Therefore, only the Dharma he has taught and the Sangha who uphold his doctrine are able to bring an end to the cycle of birth and death of self and others. Since these are the sole objects of refuge, you should take refuge in them.

In general, there are many people who consider the teachings of the truly and perfectly enlightened one as no more than the words of a fortune-teller, and who, when pressed, go to spirits for refuge. It is difficult for such people to have refuge.

What kind of person takes refuge? The one who possesses interest, devotion, and faith and who thinks of the virtues of the Three Jewels. One should possess these three particular attitudes:

> Since samsara is without beginning and end, I must turn away from it this very moment!
> The gods of the non-Buddhists and so forth are not my objects of refuge!
> The omniscient state of buddhahood alone is my true object of refuge!

This is how the special taking refuge takes place.

When taking refuge, mere lip service is useless. This is like empty muttering. It is uncertain where it will lead you.

What is the manner in which one takes refuge? You should take refuge with respectful body, speech, and mind. You should take refuge with three thoughts: fear of the lower realms and samsara, trust in the blessings of the Three Jewels, and steadfast faith and compassion.

The person who believes that this life is perfect and that the next one will also be perfect will simply die while still about to practice the Dharma. That is not enough.

In this context, you should know the rituals of taking refuge.

With what particular attitude does one take refuge? You should take refuge with a sense of responsibility for the welfare of others. You should take refuge with this attitude, as you will not attain the true and complete enlightenment simply by renouncing samsara and desiring the result of nirvana:

> In order to free all sentient beings from the miseries of samsara,
> I will take refuge until I and all the sentient beings of the three realms have achieved supreme enlightenment!

In general, all wishing is dualistic wishing. Taking refuge without being free from dualistic fixation is not sufficient.

Lady Tsogyal then asked the master: How many kinds of training does the outer way of taking refuge entail?

The master replied: As soon as you have taken refuge you must skillfully practice the eight trainings, in order to prevent your commitment from degenerating.

She asked: What are these eight trainings?

The master replied: First, there are the three special trainings: Having taken refuge in the Buddha, you should not bow down to other gods; having taken refuge in the Dharma, you should give up causing harm to sentient beings; having taken refuge in the Sangha, you should not associate with heretical people. These are the three special trainings.

To explain that further: First, having taken refuge in the Buddha, "not to bow down to other gods" means that if you bow down to mundane gods such as Mahadeva, Vishnu, Maheshvara, or others, your refuge vow is damaged. If you go to such gods for refuge, your refuge vow is destroyed.

Secondly, having taken refuge in the Dharma, to "give up causing harm to sentient beings" means that your refuge vow is definitely destroyed if you engage in killing. It is damaged even if you just beat other beings out of anger, enslave them, make holes in their noses, imprison them in a cattle shack, pluck out their hair, take their wool, and so forth.

Thirdly, having taken refuge in the Sangha, "to refrain from associating with heretical people" means that your vow is damaged if you keep company with people who hold the view and conduct of eternalism or nihilism. If your view and conduct are in conformity with theirs, your refuge vow is destroyed.

In any case, all Dharma practice is included within taking refuge. People with wrong views do not have this understanding.

These are the five general trainings.

1. When beginning your practice, make an extensive offering with a vast amount of the best kinds of food and drink. Present the offerings before the Precious Ones on the fourteenth day and beseech them to arrive for the offering. Following that, make offerings on the fifteenth day. These offerings are of four kinds: the offering of prostrations, the offering of material objects, the offering of praise, and the offering of practice.

First, the offering of prostration: Stand up straight and join your palms. Thinking of the virtues of the buddhas and bodhisattvas, imagine that you are touching their feet adorned with the design of the wheel as you make prostrations.

Next is the offering of material objects: Present offerings such as flowers that are entirely unowned by anyone and visualized offerings, as well as your own body.

Make praises with melodious tunes.

The offering of practice is to make the aspiration that the roots of your virtue resulting from having cultivated the bodhichitta of undivided emptiness and compassion may be for the attainment of enlightenment for the sake of all sentient beings.

Master Padma said: The Three Precious Ones have not even an atom of need for a bowl of water or respect. The purpose of making the offering is to enable you to receive the light rays of the buddhas.

Concerning the offering of the best kinds of food and drink, make three heaps of the best type of food, and utter OM AH HUNG three times. Imagine that your offerings thereby become an ocean of nectar. Following that, envision your yidam deity surrounded by an infinite gathering of the Three Precious Ones and imagine that you present this nectar offering, requesting them all to accept it. If you are unable to offer in that way, simply make an offering while saying, "Precious Ones, accept this!"

If you do not have anything to offer, you should at least present bowls of water every day. If you do not do that, your refuge vow will degenerate.

The Precious Ones do not need these offerings of material nourishment in the same way as sentient beings. The food torma is for you to gather the accumulations without noticing.

2. The second training is to not abandon the sublime Precious Ones even for the sake of your body, your life, or a valuable gift.

Regarding not abandoning the refuge even for the sake of your body: even if someone threatens to cut your eyes out, cut off your legs, your ears, your nose, or your arms, you should let him do so rather than abandoning the Precious Ones.

Regarding not abandoning the refuge even at the cost of your life: even if someone threatens to kill you, you should let him do so rather than abandoning the Precious Ones.

Regarding not abandoning the refuge for the sake of a valuable gift: even if you are promised the whole world filled with precious stones in return for giving up the refuge, you should not renounce the refuge.

3. The third training is that no matter what happens to you, whether you are sick, under hardship, at ease, happy, or sad, you should lay

out a mandala and the five kinds of offerings and offer them to the Three Jewels. Then take refuge and make this supplication:

> Sacred master, great vajra-holder, all buddhas and bodhisattvas, please listen to me! May all my sickness and whatever is caused by spirits and negative forces not occur. Please create peace, auspiciousness, and goodness.

Aside from this it is also appropriate to gather merit by reading the scriptures aloud, chanting, and offering tormas, since such practices belong to the basics for taking refuge. If nothing helps, do not give rise to wrong views, thinking, The Precious Ones have no blessings! The Dharma is untrue! Think instead, I shall feel better when my evil karma has become exhausted! Without pursuing other ways such as soothsaying and shamanistic rituals, engage only in taking refuge.

4. In whichever direction you travel, remember the buddhas and bodhisattvas, make offerings, and take refuge. For instance, if tomorrow you are going toward the east, lay out a mandala and make offerings today, taking refuge in the buddhas and bodhisattvas of that direction.

    Which supplication should you make? You should supplicate as follows before taking leave:

> Master, vajra holder, all buddhas and bodhisattvas, please listen to me! Please prevent obstacles caused by humans and non-humans and make everything auspicious from the time of leaving this place until I arrive at my destination.

If you do not do that the day before departure you should do it at the time of departure.

At the time of leaving, if you do not remember to take refuge within ten or seven steps of crossing your threshold, your refuge vow is damaged.

Once you entrust your mind to the refuge, it is impossible that you will be deceived.

5. Think of the good qualities of taking refuge and train in it again and again. Having taken refuge in the Three Precious Ones, regard them as your place of hope and look up to them as your place of trust.

Keep the Precious Ones as your only source of refuge and make supplications to them. Pray to the Precious Ones for blessings.

Think that your present representation of the Three Jewels, whether a cast image, a carved relief, a painting, a stupa, a volume of a book, or so forth, is the dharmakaya. It is possible that the essence of dharma-kaya will be suddenly realized when making prostrations, offerings, or supplications. Even if that does not happen, by prostrating and making offering to the Three Jewels and creating a karmic connection, one will become a disciple of a buddha in the future.

Master Padma said: No matter what arises in you such as the virtues and happiness of the enlightened ones, regard these to be the blessings of your master and the Precious Ones. By thinking in that way, you will receive the blessings. No matter what problems and misery you may meet, regard them as your own evil karma. That will bring an end to all your negative karmas. In general, if you do not entrust your mind to the Precious Ones, but hold the wrong view of thinking, The Precious Ones have no blessings!, it is possible that you will not escape from the lowest hells.

Lady Tsogyal asked the master: What good qualities result from taking refuge?

The master replied: Taking refuge has eight good qualities.

1. You enter the group of Buddhists. Having taken refuge in the Three Jewels, you are called a Buddhist. Without having taken refuge, you are not included among the Buddhist group, even though you may claim to be a holy person, a great meditator, or the Buddha in person.
2. You become a suitable vessel for all the vows such as the Individual Liberation. Correspondingly, if you lose your refuge vow, it is said that all the vows based thereon are also destroyed.

In order to restore them, restoring the refuge vow will be sufficient. That is to say, it is sufficient that you make an offering to the Three Jewels and take the vow in their presence.

You also need to have taken refuge prior to any vow; from the one-day precepts and so forth up to the vows of Secret Mantra. Taking refuge is therefore known as that which causes you to become a suitable basis for all types of vows.

3. The vow of taking refuge in the Three Jewels diminishes and brings to an end all karmic obscurations accumulated throughout all your past lives. That is to say, your obscurations will be totally exhausted through the special taking refuge, while through the general taking refuge the karmic obscurations will diminish.

Again, when a genuine feeling of taking refuge has arisen in your being, karmic obscurations are utterly brought to an end, while by the mere words of taking refuge they will diminish.

Furthermore, if you take refuge at all times, while walking, moving about, lying down, and sitting, the karmic obscurations will be completely exhausted, while by just taking refuge from time to time they will diminish.

4. You will possess vast merit. The mundane merits of long life, good health, splendor and majestic dignity, great wealth, and so forth result from taking refuge. The supramundane unexcelled enlightenment also results from taking refuge.
5. You will be immune to attack by humans and nonhumans, and immune to the obstacles of this life. It is said that as soon as the genuine taking refuge has arisen in your being, you cannot be harmed by human obstacles in this life. Also you cannot be harmed by nonhumans such as nagas and malicious spirits.
6. You will achieve the fulfillment of whatever you may wish for. When the genuine taking refuge has arisen in your being, it is impossible not to accomplish whatever you intend. In short, it is said that placing your trust in the objects of refuge, you will receive whatever you desire, just as when supplicating a wish-fulfilling gem.
7. You will not fall into the lower realms, evil destinies, or perverted paths. The "three lower realms" refers to the hell, hungry ghost, and animal realms. "Evil destinies" refers to being reborn in places devoid of the Dharma, such as among primitive border tribes. "Perverted paths" refers to non-Buddhist philosophies. So in order to avoid falling into these, it is said that one should simply take refuge.
8. The final benefit is that of swiftly attaining the true and complete enlightenment. What need is there to mention other benefits!

It is said in the Mahayana teachings of Secret Mantra that one can attain enlightenment within this single body and lifetime. This means that without a doubt you will swiftly attain enlightenment. So it is necessary to cut the misconception of thinking that it is enough to take refuge just once in a while. You should take refuge again and again both day and night. Then you will definitely swiftly attain true and complete enlightenment.

Master Padma said: If you exert yourself in taking refuge, you do not need to practice many other teachings. There is no doubt that you will attain the fruition of enlightenment.

Lady Tsogyal again asked the master: What is the actual practice of taking refuge?

The master replied: The actual application of taking refuge is as follows: First, form the aspiration of thinking:

> I will establish all sentient beings in complete enlightenment. In order to do that I will gather the accumulations, purify the obscurations, and clear away the hindrances. For this purpose I will take refuge from this very moment until reaching enlightenment!

Then, without being distracted, say three times:

In the supreme of all humans, all the buddhas of the ten directions, I and all the infinite sentient beings take refuge from this very moment until reaching supreme enlightenment.

In the supreme of all peace, devoid of attachment, the Dharma teachings of the ten directions, I and all the infinite sentient beings take refuge from this very moment until reaching supreme enlightenment.

In the supreme of all assemblies, the members of the noble Sangha who are beyond falling back and who dwell in the ten directions, I and all infinite sentient beings take refuge from this very moment until reaching supreme enlightenment.

Following that, repeat many times without being distracted:

I take refuge in the Buddha.
I take refuge in the Dharma.
I take refuge in the Sangha.

Then make this supplication three times:

Three Precious Ones, please protect me from the fears of this life.
Please protect me from the fears of the lower realms.
Please protect me from entering perverted paths!

When you are about to finish, say:

> Through this, my roots of virtue, may I attain buddhahood
> in order to benefit beings!

You should make the dedication in this way.

Lady Tsogyal asked the nirmanakaya master Padmakara: What is the method of taking the refuge vow?

The master replied: "One should prostrate to and circumambulate a master who possesses the refuge vow, present him with flowers, and say as follows.

> Master, please listen to me. Buddhas and bodhisattvas in the ten directions, please listen to me. From this very moment until attaining supreme enlightenment, I, ——,[14] take refuge in the supreme of all humans, the billion truly perfected dharmakaya buddhas.
>
> I take refuge in the supreme of all peace, devoid of attachment, the teachings of Mahayana.
>
> I take refuge in the supreme of all assemblies, the Sangha of noble bodhisattvas who are beyond falling back.

At the third repetition of this you will have obtained the vow. Make prostrations and scatter flowers. Then practice the trainings explained above and exert yourself in taking refuge.

This was the explanation of the outer way of taking refuge along with its application.

Lady Tsogyal asked the master: How is one protected by having taken refuge?

The master replied: Whoever practices the trainings correctly, having taken refuge as explained above, will definitely be protected by the Three Jewels. Since this is so, if you fear straying into an errant path and pray to meet a genuine path, you will surely meet it. You will definitely also be protected from the fears of this life.

When all the qualities of taking refuge have arisen in your being, you should not be content to stop. Increase more and more the qualities that have arisen within you. You should use all the qualities that arise in your mind to gather the accumulations and purify the obscurations. When such exertion is generated, the full measure of ability has been produced.

All people who do not feel inclined to give rise to profound qualities such as [insight into] emptiness or the mandala of deities within their being can still purify their obscurations and gather the accumulations simply by taking refuge.

You may then argue, If one is protected by taking refuge in such a way, does that mean that the buddhas appear and lead all sentient beings? The reply is that the buddhas cannot take all sentient beings out of samsara with their hands. If they were able to do that, the buddhas with their great compassion and skillful means would have already freed all beings without a single exception.

Well then, you may ask, by what is one protected? The answer is that one is protected by the [practice of the] Dharma.

When taking refuge has arisen within your being, you do not need to practice other teachings. It is impossible that you will not be protected by the compassion of the Three Jewels. It is similar to the fact that you will definitely be fearless when you have an excellent escort.

Thus Master Padma explained the outer way of taking refuge to Lady Tsogyal.

THE INNER WAY OF TAKING REFUGE

The nirmanakaya master Padmakara was asked by Lady Tsogyal, the princess of Kharchen: To which inner objects does one take refuge? What kind of person takes refuge? Through which manner or method does one take refuge? Which particular attitude and what duration of time does it entail? What particular circumstance is required? What is the purpose and what are the qualities?

The master replied: Regarding the objects of refuge, you should take refuge in the guru, yidam, and dakini.

The person who takes refuge should be someone who has entered the gate of Secret Mantra.

The manner or method is to take refuge with devoted and respectful body, speech, and mind.

Regarding the particular attitude of taking refuge, you should take refuge by perceiving the guru as a buddha, not abandoning the yidam even at the cost of your life, and continuously making offerings to the dakini.

Regarding the duration of time, you should take refuge from the time of having generated bodhichitta in the empowerment ceremony until attaining the state of a vajra holder.

Regarding the circumstance, you should take refuge by feeling devotion to the Secret Mantra.

As for the purpose or virtues of taking refuge, it has the purpose of making you a suitable vessel for the Secret Mantra and for receiving extraordinary blessings.

Lady Tsogyal asked the master: Concerning the inner way of taking refuge, which trainings does one need to practice?

The master replied: There are eight trainings. First there are the three special trainings.

1. Having taken refuge in the guru, you should not feel ill will toward him or even the intention to deride him.
2. Having taken refuge in the yidam, you should not interrupt the meditation of the yidam's form or its recitation.
3. Having taken refuge in the dakini, you should not break the periodical offering days.

The five general trainings are the following.

1. Consecrate as nectar the first part of whatever you eat or drink. Offer it, visualizing the guru above your head. Offer it, visualizing the yidam in your heart center and the dakini in your navel center. You should train in partaking of food in this way.
2. In whichever direction you go, supplicate the guru, yidam, and dakini. Visualize the guru above the crown of your head. Visualize yourself as the yidam, and visualize the dakini and the Dharma protectors as your escorts. This is the training in walking.
3. Even at the cost of your life or limb, you should train in regarding the guru to be as dear as your heart, the yidam as dear as your eyes, and the dakini as dear as your body.
4. No matter what happens, such as sickness, difficulty or ease, joy or sorrow, you should train in supplicating the guru, making offerings to the yidam, and giving feasts and torma to the dakini. Other than that, you should not pursue other means such as soothsaying and shamanistic rituals.
5. Recollecting the virtues of the guru, yidam, and dakini, you should take refuge again and again. By taking refuge in the guru, obstacles are cleared away. By taking refuge in the yidam, the body of Mahamudra[15] will be attained. By taking refuge in the dakini, you will receive the siddhis.

Lady Tsogyal asked Master Padma: With which virtues is the inner way of taking refuge endowed?

Master Padma replied: By taking refuge in the guru, you are protected from the fetters of conceptual mind. The hindrances of ignorance and stupidity are cleared away. The accumulation of insight and awareness is perfected, and you will receive the accomplishment of spontaneous realization.

By taking refuge in the yidam, you are protected from ordinary perception, the accumulation of self-existing wisdom will be gathered, and the accomplishment of Mahamudra will be attained.

By taking refuge in the dakini, you will be protected from obstacles and evil spirits. The impediment of the poverty of hungry ghosts is cleared away, the accumulation of detachment and freedom from clinging will be perfected, and the accomplishment of the sambhogakaya of great bliss will be attained.

Lady Tsogyal asked Master Padma: What is the actual practice of the inner way of taking refuge?

The master replied: You should first arouse the aspiration toward unexcelled enlightenment. Then visualize the guru, yidam, and dakini upon seats of sun, moon, and lotus in the sky before you and say three times:

> Root of the lineage, lord guru,
> Source of the siddhis, yidam deity,
> Bestower of excellent blessings, dakini,
> I pay homage to the three roots.

Following that, focus your mind undistractedly upon the guru, yidam, and dakini and repeatedly say:

> I take refuge in the guru, yidam, and dakini.

Then supplicate as follows:

> All gurus, yidams, and dakinis, please bestow upon me the blessings of your body, speech, and mind!
> Please confer the empowerments upon me! Please grant me the supreme and common siddhis! Please extend your kindness to me, your devoted child!

Following that, dissolve the guru into the top of your head, the yidam into your heart center, and the dakini into your navel center.

Lady Tsogyal asked the master: What is the method of taking the inner refuge vow?

The master replied: The ceremony of first taking the refuge vow is as follows. It is important to have received empowerment. Obtaining the empowerment itself is the receiving of refuge. If you do take refuge without receiving empowerment, then make prostrations to and circumambulate the guru, present him with flowers, and say:

> Master, please listen to me. Assembly of yidam deities, gathering of mandala deities, dakinis and retinue, please listen to me. From this very moment until attaining the supreme vidyadhara level of Mahamudra, I, ——, take refuge in the root of the lineage, all the sublime and holy gurus.
>
> I take refuge in the source of accomplishment, all the assemblies of yidam deities.
>
> I take refuge in the bestowers of excellent blessings, all the dakinis.

The refuge vow is obtained after repeating this three times.

That was the ceremony of taking the vow. I have explained the inner way of taking refuge.

THE SECRET WAY OF TAKING REFUGE

Lady Tsogyal, the Princess of Kharchen, asked the master: Concerning the secret way of taking refuge, in what object does one take refuge? What type of person takes refuge? Through which manner or method does one take refuge? With what particular attitude does one take refuge? For what duration of time does one take refuge? By which circumstance does one take refuge? What purpose or virtue is entailed?

The master replied: As to the objects of the secret way of taking refuge, you should take refuge in the view, meditation, and action.

The type of person who takes this refuge should be someone of the highest faculties who desires to attain enlightenment.

As to the manner or method, you should take refuge by means of the view, meditation, action, and fruition. That is to say, you take refuge with the view possessing confidence, the meditation possessing experience, and the action possessing equal taste.

As to the particular attitude, the view free from craving means not to desire either to attain buddhahood or to cast away samsara. The meditation free from fixation on concreteness and without falling into partiality cannot be described by any ordinary words. The conduct free from accepting and rejecting is devoid of falling into any category whatsoever.

The duration of time is to take refuge until attaining enlightenment.

The circumstance is to take refuge without desiring further rebirth.

The purpose or virtue is to attain complete enlightenment within this very lifetime.

Lady Tsogyal asked: Concerning the secret way of taking refuge, in which trainings does one need to practice?

Master Padma replied: First there are the three special trainings:

1. Concerning the view possessing realization: You should train in gaining the confidence that there is no buddhahood elsewhere to achieve, since all sentient beings and buddhas have the same basis. You should train in gaining the confidence that appearance and emptiness are inseparable, through realizing that appearances and mind are without difference.
2. Concerning training in the meditation possessing experience: Do not place your mind facing outward, do not concentrate it inward, but train in letting it rest naturally, freely, and free from reference point.
3. As to the action: Train in uninterrupted experience. Although at all times of walking, moving around, lying down, and sitting there is nothing to be meditated upon, train in not being distracted for even an instant.

The following are the seven general trainings.

1. Do not abandon your master even though you realize your mind to be the Buddha.
2. Do not interrupt conditioned roots of virtue even though you realize appearances to be mind.
3. Shun even the most subtle evil deed, even though you have no fear for the hells.
4. Do not denigrate any of the teachings, even though you do not entertain any hope for enlightenment.
5. Do not be conceited or boastful even though you realize superior samadhis.
6. Do not cease feeling compassion for sentient beings, even though you understand self and other to be nondual.

7. Train by practicing in retreat places, even though you realize samsara and nirvana to be nondual.

Lady Tsogyal asked the nirmanakaya master: Concerning the secret way of taking refuge, in what manner does it protect and with what virtues is it endowed?

Master Padma replied: Having taken refuge in the view, you are protected from both eternalism and nihilism. The hindrances of wrong views and fixation are cleared away, the accumulation of the luminous dharmata is perfected, and the unceasing siddhis of body, speech, and mind will be attained.

Having taken refuge in the meditation, the view will also protect the meditation. The obstacles of deep clinging and habitual tendencies are cleared away, the accumulation of nondual unity gathered, and the siddhis of confidence and primordial liberation will be attained.

Having taken refuge in the action, you are protected from perverted conduct and the view of nihilism. The obstacles of hypocrisy and foolishness are cleared away, the accumulation of nonattachment during bustle is perfected, and the siddhi of turning whatever is experienced into realization will be attained.

Lady Tsogyal asked Master Padma: What is the actual practice of the secret way of taking refuge?

The master replied: The view, in natural ease, should be free from craving and devoid of partiality and extremes.

The meditation should be free from fixating on concreteness and reference points. It cannot be expressed by any ordinary words whatsoever.

That is to say, do not place your mind facing outward, do not concentrate it inward, rest in naturalness free from reference point.

Rest undistractedly in the state of unceasing experience at the time of walking, moving around, lying, or sitting.

The feelings of fulfillment or exhilaration, feeling void, blissful, or clear, are all temporary experiences. They should never be regarded as marvelous.

When states of mind that are agitated, obscured, or drowsy occur, use these experiences as training. Whatever occurs, such as these, do not regard them as defects.

Lady Tsogyal asked: What is the method of taking the vow of the secret way of taking refuge?

The master replied: Prostrating to and circumambulating the master, present him with flowers. The disciple should assume the cross-legged posture and with compassion take the vow of cultivating bodhichitta for the benefit of self and others.

Then, placing the gaze firmly in the sky and without moving the eyeballs, rest your awareness—vivid, awake, bright, and all-pervasive—free from fixation on perceiver or the perceived. That itself is the view possessing confidence, the meditation possessing experience, and the action possessing companionship! Thus it should be pointed out. Meditate then as mentioned above.

This was the explanation of the secret way of taking refuge.

The nirmanakaya master Padma said: This was my oral instruction in which the outer, inner, and secret teachings, the higher and lower views, and the vehicles of mantra and philosophy[16] are condensed into a single root within the outer, inner, and secret way of taking refuge.

When you apply it accordingly, you will turn toward Dharma practice, your Dharma practice will become the path, and your path will ripen into fruition. Princess of Kharchen, you should understand this to be so.

This completes the teachings on practicing the taking of refuge as one's path.

Samaya. Seal, seal, seal.

19

THE INNERMOST REFUGE

Tulku Urgyen Rinpoche

Namo
In the empty essence, dharmakaya,
In the cognizant nature, sambhogakaya,
In the manifold expression, nirmanakaya,
I take refuge until enlightenment.

—PADMASAMBHAVA

Certain concepts in Buddhism are similar to the Western concept of an omniscient, omnipotent god. The closest thing to this "divinity" is the three kayas, dharmakaya, sambhogakaya, and nirmanakaya. Although we could call these three kayas "God," that is not really necessary. I will now explain what these three kayas are.

The first, dharmakaya, is all-pervasive like space; in actuality it is the unmistaken nature of our mind. Sambhogakaya is like the light of the sun, and is the cognizant quality of mind. Nirmanakaya is like the appearance of a rainbow in space, and acts for the welfare of all beings. Outwardly we can think of the three kayas as space, sunlight, and a rainbow, but the meaning of these symbols lies within our own mind.

Adapted from Tulku Urgyen Rinpoche, *Repeating the Words of the Buddha* (Boudhanath: Rangjung Yeshe Publications, 1996), "The Innermost Refuge."

The Dharma teachings are structured as two aspects: means and knowledge, known in Sanskrit as *upaya* and *prajña*. The aspect of "means" is to visualize the buddhas in front of oneself and engage in different practices. The "knowledge" aspect is to realize that the buddhas are contained within our buddha nature, the essence of our mind. The reason it is possible for us to reach enlightenment is because the enlightened essence is already present in ourselves. The real buddha is the nature of our mind, the knowledge aspect.

This in itself, however, is not enough, because the buddha nature is covered by obscurations. In order to remove the veils, we need the means, which provides a way to purify the obscurations and gather the two accumulations of merit and wisdom. A practice in which we think that the Buddha is outside ourselves, ignoring the buddha within, will by itself never bring complete enlightenment. If we expect the Buddha up there in the sky to give us all the common and supreme accomplishments, we are placing our hopes in an object external to ourselves. The ultimate deity is within our own mind. We attain enlightenment by recognizing our true nature and training in that recognition.

All Dharma teachings have two aspects: the relative or superficial and the ultimate or real. Visualizing the Buddha as being outside ourselves is superficial and is not enough for enlightenment. The basis for awakening to enlightenment is to experience the buddha in ourselves. But the recognition of the real is nevertheless dependent upon the superficial, because it is by making offerings, purifying obscurations, and gathering the accumulations with the support of a buddha imagined outside that we can remove the obscurations and realize the buddha within.

Taking refuge means to place our trust in the Buddha, the teacher. What he taught is called the Dharma, and the great practitioners who have followed those teachings are called the Sangha. If we look at ourselves right now, we can see that alone we lack the power to reach enlightenment. By placing our trust in the Three Jewels we receive blessings, which make it easier to realize accomplishment. But understand that the true basis for awakening to the state of enlightenment is found within ourselves.

This potential for enlightenment is present as the nature of our own mind. To recognize that fact is the knowledge aspect. Then, in order to fully facilitate this recognition we apply the means—visualizing the Buddha, making praises, and performing different types of conceptual practices. The true path of the buddhas is the unity of means and knowledge. It is not sufficient to simply apply the means, thinking that a superior being is outside oneself and making offerings and praises to that outer image. Only by combining the two aspects of means and knowledge do we attain enlightenment.

An ordinary example for the unity of means and knowledge is to bring together a person who knows how to make an airplane, the knowledge aspect, with all the materials for the airplane, the means. Having all the pieces of an airplane in itself is not enough. Neither is only having somebody who knows how to make one. It is only by combining the two that a plane that will actually fly can be made.

According to Vajrayana, one combines the means as the development stage with the knowledge aspect as the completion stage. The development stage entails visualization—creating the image of the divine being—praises, apologies, offerings, and the other sections of the *sadhana* practice. The completion stage involves recognizing the nature of mind by looking into *who* visualizes, thus bringing the buddha nature into practical experience. The development stage is necessary because right now we are normal beings, and a normal being is unenlightened, unstable in the realization of the buddha nature. By ourselves we do not have complete power, so we ask for help from the buddhas and bodhisattvas. By offering the seven branches, for instance, we purify our obscurations, removing that which prevents us from gaining true insight. The knowledge aspect is the nature of our mind. Both means and knowledge are necessary. Each aids the other. Only utilizing the method is like gathering the husk without getting the corncob—it is not enough.

Another example is when a person studies to become a Tibetan doctor. He starts with the knowledge aspect, learning how to identify different parts of the body, to diagnose diseases, what medicines to apply for a successful cure, and so forth. However, knowledge by itself is not sufficient to cure anybody; the doctor also needs the necessary medicines. So collecting the medicinal plants and blending the right concoctions is the means aspect. It is the combination of these two aspects, means and knowledge, that cures a sick person.

The equivalent of "God" or a supreme being in Buddhism is called Samantabhadra, meaning the Ever-excellent. He is the primordial dharmakaya buddha. When Samantabhadra manifests on the sambhogakaya level he is called Vajradhara, the Vajra Holder. His nirmanakaya form is called Vajrasattva. There is an incredible number of gods and deities in Buddhism, but their basic source, where they manifest from, is the dharmakaya buddha Samantabhadra, the sambhogakaya buddha Vajradhara, and the nirmanakaya buddha Vajrasattva. Deities are not related to one another like a family relationship, with some being parents and others the offspring. Their body is self-existing, while their mind is pure wisdom, innate wakefulness.

The self-existing body of dharmakaya is like space, totally beyond any constructs or concepts. The body of sambhogakaya is like rainbow light. The nirmanakaya, or tulku, manifests on a physical level in this world without departing from the state of the other two. One thousand nirmanakaya buddhas will appear during this world's present period, which is known as the Good Aeon. Buddha Shakyamuni is the fourth of these one thousand. The nirmanakaya buddhas are first emanated and then reabsorbed. In the instance of Buddha Shakyamuni there were one billion emanations, meaning one billion simultaneous Buddha Shakyamunis in different realms.

Everything appears out of the dharmakaya, out of Buddha Samantabhadra. The sambhogakaya itself is manifest from dharmakaya and is represented by the five buddha families. Out of sambhogakaya appear nirmanakayas, beings who manifest in order to benefit others. To benefit human beings, a buddha must appear in human form; therefore, the thousand buddhas of this aeon are human beings. Unless buddhas appear as human beings, how can we see them and receive teachings? We don't perceive the sambhogakaya level and, needless to say, ordinary people do not perceive the dharmakaya level either. Nirmanakayas appear as teachers in flesh-and-blood form, just like Buddha Shakyamuni. These beings communicate the teachings, the Buddha Dharma. Since people have different capacities, there are three or nine different levels of teachings, generally known as the nine vehicles.

These teachers are also called the tamers, while the various classes of beings—hell beings, hungry ghosts, animals, human beings, demigods, and gods—are called those to be tamed. Those who tame them are the emanations of the buddhas that appear in each of the six realms. A buddha is someone who has accomplished everything there is to accomplish for the benefit of himself. All his activity is aimed at accomplishing the welfare of others. A buddha appears only for others.

The buddhas manifest in all the six realms, not just the human world. In the realm of gods the Buddha is called Shakra, the king of gods. Among the demigods he is called Taksang, among humans he is called Shakyamuni, among animals he is called Steadfast Lion, among the hungry ghosts he is called Flaming Mouth, and among the hellbeings he is called Dharmaraja. Most beings only perceive these buddha emanations as kings or rulers of their various realms.

Nirmanakayas appear in four different ways. Created nirmanakayas are sacred images, like the three famous statues that were originally kept at the Bodh Gaya stupa, two of which are now in Lhasa. Then there is the supreme nirmanakaya, which, according to the sutras, is the Buddha Shakyamuni. The supreme nirmanakaya for the Vajrayana teachings is Padmasambhava, who manifested as one billion simultaneous Padma-sambhavas. There are also the incarnated nirmanakayas, the great masters who in the Tibetan tradition are called tulkus. Finally there are the variegated nirmanakayas, which appear in many different forms in order to influence or benefit beings according to their needs. These can appear in an incredible variety of forms, including bridges or ships. Buddhas can appear in every possible form, in a way that lies far beyond the domain of ordinary people.

Now I will explain the relationship between the three kayas. The dharmakaya is like space in that it accommodates the manifestations of the other two kayas. Space is all-encompassing: nothing appears or disappears outside of it; everything manifests and eventually disintegrates within infinite space. The sambhogakaya is like the sun, which appears in the sky and shines with unchanging brilliance. And the nirmanakaya is like the surface of water, which reflects the sun. One sun can simultaneously be reflected upon billions of surfaces of water; wherever there is water the reflection of the sun appears.

Nirmanakaya manifests in all different ways, including the supreme, created, incarnated, and variegated nirmanakayas, without leaving dharmakaya and sambhogakaya, and in accordance with what is required to benefit beings. *Nirmana* means magically created, like a magical apparition. Those who have total mastery over life and death are not like us normal people, who cannot voluntarily leave and enter incarnations. Our rebirth is decided by the force of our karmic actions, but nirmanakayas are not bound by the law of karma. They are like a reflection of the sun. The sambhogakaya, which is like the sun shining in the sky, cannot appear outside space or without space; the two cannot be separated. Similarly, the sun's reflection on the surface of water cannot appear without the sun. Although we give the three kayas three different names, they are in essence indivisible. This indivisibility of the three kayas is sometimes called the essence-kaya, the fourth kaya, which is the nature of our mind. The dharmakaya, sambhogakaya, and nirmanakaya depicted as being outside are merely symbols. What they refer to, the true meaning, is the nature of our own mind.

20

A GUIDED MEDITATION

Drubwang Tsoknyi Rinpoche

As a support for and an enhancement of the Dzogchen training, I would like to introduce the practice of taking refuge as well as a traditional guru yoga. As the starting point, keep the pure motivation of the bodhisattva resolve, sit with a straight back, let your breathing flow freely, and for a short while leave your mind without fabrication, utterly uncontrived. First of all we need to improve our motivation by thinking, "For the benefit of all sentient beings, I will practice this meditation session."

Now imagine a lotus tree in the sky before you, with one branch or stem in the center and one in each of the four directions. On the central branch sits Padmasambhava in the form known as Nangzi Silnön, meaning the "glorious subjugator of all that appears and exists," with his right hand holding a vajra. This is the most common way of depicting him. He is surrounded by all the masters of the Dzogchen lineage.

On the branch in front of them are all the yidams, headed by Yang-dag Heruka, and surrounded by all the deities of the Eight Sadhana Teachings. On the branch to his right is Buddha Shakyamuni, surrounded

Adapted from Tsoknyi Rinpoche, *Carefree Dignity* (Boudhanath: Rangjung Yeshe Publications, 1998), "A Guided Meditation."

by an immense gathering of buddhas of the past, present, and future. On the branch behind him, imagine the sacred Dharma in the form of scriptures, each resounding with vowels and consonants like a humming beehive. On the branch to his left is Avalokiteshvara surrounded by all the noble Sangha, the sublime beings of both Mahayana and Hinayana. In short, imagine that in the sky before you are all the gurus, the yidams, the dakas and dakinis, the buddhas, the teachings, the enlightened practitioners, and all the Dharma protectors in a vast gathering, like cloud banks assembled vividly in the sky before you.

Toward the external refuge, the Buddha, Dharma, and Sangha, make this supplication: "In this and in all future lives may I be under your protection; please grant your blessings that I may have the opportunity to reach liberation." Let devotion fill your mind, through a sense of deep longing. Then, recite aloud the prayer of going for refuge:

In the Buddha, the Dharma, and the supreme assembly,
I take refuge until enlightenment.
By the merit of generosity and so forth,
May I attain buddhahood for the welfare of all beings.

The visualization of the Dzogchen lineage over the head of Padmasambhava starts from above with Samantabhadra, then Vajrasattva, Garab Dorje, Vimalamitra, Guru Rinpoche, and so forth. The twenty-five disciples of Padmasambhava, the hundred major tertöns, and so forth are all vividly present around him, as are the yidams headed by Yangdag Heruka and all the other deities of the Eight Sadhana Teachings. In between, filling in all the spaces in the sky, are the dakas and dakinis. The gurus who are the sovereigns of all the buddha families, the yidam deities who are the source of accomplishments, and the dakinis who dispel all obstacles are vividly present as the inner objects of refuge.

Let your longing and devotion arise from deep within you. Let the sun of devotion rise in the sky, and as it shines on the snow mountain of your heart, the blessings of the lineages will stream down like a river. Devotion is like sunlight that melts the ice, allowing the river of blessings to stream forth. The blessings of the three kayas of Padmasambhava's essence and the blessings of the Three Roots are transferred into your own body, speech, and mind, where they pervade and transform your very being.

After reciting the refuge prayer, imagine that the whole field of refuge dissolves into light, first moving in from the outside, then in a clockwise manner. All the yidams dissolve into Yangdag Heruka, who dissolves into the buddhas; then the buddhas dissolve into Buddha Shakyamuni; he dissolves into the Dharma scriptures; which dissolve into Avalokiteshvara—and finally, all of them dissolve into Padmasambhava, the main figure present in the sky before you, who remains as a single figure.

Address yourself then to Padmasambhava, supplicating him as the single embodiment of the Three Jewels. In essence he is all the awakened ones of the past, all the buddhas of the future, and all the buddhas of the present. Thinking of him like this, supplicate him mentally.

Imagine now that from the forehead of Padmasambhava, the white letter OM radiates a brilliant white light that touches your own forehead. Imagine that through this you are conferred the vase empowerment, the empowerment for practicing the development stage of deity yoga. The obscurations and negative karma you created with your body are purified, and the seed for realizing the nirmanakaya level is planted in your being.

From the red letter AH in Padmasambhava's throat, rays of beautiful red light shine forth and touch your own throat. Through this you receive the secret empowerment. Your obscurations and the negative karma created by your voice are purified, and you are empowered to practice the completion stage involving the channels and energies. The seed for realizing the sambhogakaya level is planted in your being.

Now from the blue letter HUNG in Padmasambhava's heart center, azure blue light streams forth and dissolves into your own heart center, purifying all mental obscurations and negative karma from all past lives. You are thus conferred the third empowerment of wisdom knowledge, empowering you to practice consort yoga, follow the *phonya* path, and become invested with the fortune to realize the dharmakaya level.

From Padmasambhava's navel center, multicolored rays of light stream forth and dissolve into your previous three centers as well as your navel center. This light purifies the negative karma created through a combination of body, speech, and mind, especially the defilement of habitual tendencies. By being conferred this fourth or precious word empowerment, you're authorized to practice the path of Trekchö, the primordial purity of cutting through, and of Tögal, the spontaneous presence of the direct crossing. And you are given the fortune to realize the fourth kaya, the essence body.

Now imagine that Guru Rinpoche dissolves into light, which becomes indivisible from yourself so that your body, speech, and mind are indivisible from Guru Rinpoche's Body, Speech, and Mind.

The essence of your mind is empty, the dharmakaya nature. The cognizant quality of your nature is the sambhogakaya, while your unconfined capacity, the indivisibility of the previous two, is the nirmanakaya. By resting evenly in the state in which your very identity is indivisible from the three kayas of all the buddhas of the past, present, and future, you are inseparable from Guru Rinpoche himself. You take the innermost refuge, and again you repeat the refuge prayer.

At this point we should remain evenly for a short while in the very intent that is pointed out through the four empowerments, the awareness wisdom. When I ring the bell, let the mere hearing of this sound remind you of self-existing awareness, so that simultaneously with the hearing of the sound you simply lapse into the uninterrupted state of self-existing wakefulness. [Rinpoche rings the bell. Period of silence.]

You should have some sharpness of presence of awareness. [Rinpoche rings the bell again.]

[Period of silence.]

STUDENT: Don't we always have to take the support of a teacher to make sure that our practice is correct?

RINPOCHE: Of course we need to follow a spiritual teacher, and of course we need to receive instructions. Of course we need to put those instructions into practice. But if one spends one's whole life trying to follow spiritual teachers, something is wrong there also. We need to supplicate our root guru in order to discover the indivisible nature of his mind and our own mind. That is definitely necessary. But it's not good to think, "If I'm not with my teacher I won't know how to practice," or, "If I'm not with my teacher I can't deal with disturbing emotions," or, "If I'm not with my teacher, I am lost, I do not know what to do."

In the old days, people had more opportunities because they were more free, not so busy, not so much work. People had the opportunity to stay with the master for three years, or six years or nine years. These days it is not like that. The teachers themselves are really busy and often have no time, and the disciples have no time also. They may only have four or five days to stay together, like us!

During the days of our retreat together, we should try to understand as much as we can. Whatever we understood we should put into practice, put to actual use. When we leave here, we should leave together with the true teacher, the teacher who is our intrinsic nature. That teacher can be our constant companion.

You know, we are soon going our different ways—I am going to

Singapore and Malaysia; some of you are going back to your own countries or traveling to other places. Maybe we will meet again, maybe not—who knows? There is nothing sure in this world. Everything is impermanent; nothing is fixed or guaranteed. You should try your best to recognize the ground luminosity inside yourselves by means of the path of rigpa.

Somebody who hasn't asked anything?

STUDENT: How do we receive blessings? Is it through faith and devotion?

RINPOCHE: Devotion is the root of blessings, the basis for receiving blessings. Blessings definitely do exist, so we should know what they are and what the role of devotion is in receiving blessings. Otherwise, there is not much point in devotion.

Blessings are contagious, so to speak, and are transmitted in a fashion that is rather like catching a cold. If somebody has a cold and you are too close, you catch a cold too. Likewise, if you get close to a master who has blessings, they can be transmitted to you. Blessings here mean the sense of some power of realization or power of samadhi, some kind of atmosphere of realization that is naturally present. You move close to him, in the sense of opening yourself up through devotion and making sincere, heartfelt supplications. In other words, you lower your defenses, whatever doubts and suspicions that prevent you from being "infected" with the blessings. The moment you do that, you catch a cold as well. Devotion is a very deeply felt and sincere emotion, which comes from the bottom of one's heart. It is partly a sense of really rejoicing, rejoicing in the qualities that are embodied in the teacher. At the same time, there is a sense of gratitude for the teacher's incredible kindness. This combination of rejoicing and gratitude is what opens us up, what generates devotion.

Devotion can be toward the Buddha, the Dharma, the Sangha, in terms of truly rejoicing in and appreciating their amazing qualities, of knowledge and compassion, and so forth. To be open toward that and rejoice in those qualities is one aspect of devotion. At the same time, when we understand how it benefits ourselves to train in the recognition of our basic nature, we feel gratitude, an appreciation of the kindness.

Otherwise, there could be many kinds of devotion. There is the devotion that is simply love, love generated by the thought, "He was nice to me, so I like him." There is devotion that is an admiration, in that you feel in awe of a person or thing. Then there is devotion inspired by some kind of longing to emulate someone—you want to be like that as well. However, in the beginning, devotion is some kind of fabrication. We are trying to feel in a certain way, trying to open up. It is artificial, but it makes us grow closer to understanding the view, in the sense that devotion opens us up to realize emptiness, makes it easier. When some authentic experience of emptiness strengthens devotion even further, at that point it is no longer artificial or contrived. We may begin by trying to feel devotion, and then, later on, actual experience allows it to become totally uncontrived. Uncontrived devotion springs out of the experience of the view. Because when there is some seeing in actuality of what is called rigpa or ordinary mind, the natural mind that really solves or liberates disturbing emotions—when the conceptual frame of mind is opened up by this recognition—*then* we have a personal taste of the value and the worth of the practice. It is that real appreciation that is uncontrived devotion. In this way, devotion and the view of emptiness mutually strengthen one another.

21

THE EXCELLENCE OF BODHICHITTA

Shantideva

Homage to all buddhas and bodhisattvas.

1. To those who go in bliss,* the Dharma† they have mastered, and to all their heirs,‡

From Shantideva, *The Way of the Bodhisattva* (Boston: Shambhala Publications, 1997), "The Excellence of Bodhichitta."

* "Those who go in bliss" (Tib. bde gshegs; Skt. sugata): a title of the buddhas.

† The word *Dharma* is here a translation of the Tibetan *chos sku* (Skt. *dharma-kaya*), literally the "Dharma body." According to the commentarial tradition, two interpretations are possible. The term may be taken to mean simply "the body of the teachings" (which is the interpretation of Khenpo Kunpel and Khenpo Shenga), with the result that the first line of the poem consists of a salutation to the Three Jewels of Buddha, Dharma, and Sangha. On the other hand, it may be understood as referring to the dharmakaya or "truth body," the absolute aspect of a buddha, i.e., one of the three bodies of a buddha, along with the sambhogakaya, or "body of divine enjoyment," and the nirmanakaya, or "body of manifestation."

‡ The heirs of the buddhas are the bodhisattvas, those who aim to attain buddhahood for the sake of all beings. In this context, reference is actually being made to superior bodhisattvas, whose realization corresponds to the Mahayana path of seeing and beyond, in other words who are abiding on the bodhisattva bhumis or grounds, and who are therefore sublime objects of refuge.

To all who merit veneration, I bow down.
According to tradition, I shall now in brief describe
The entrance to the bodhisattva discipline.

2. What I have to say has all been said before,
    And I am destitute of learning and of skill with words.
    I therefore have no thought that this might be of benefit to others;
    I wrote it only to sustain my understanding.

3. My faith will thus be strengthened for a little while,
    That I might grow accustomed to this virtuous way.
    But others who now chance upon my words,
    May profit also, equal to myself in fortune.

4. So hard to find such ease and wealth*
    Whereby to render meaningful this human birth!
    If now I fail to turn it to my profit,
    How could such a chance be mine again?

5. As when a flash of lightning renders the night,
    And in its glare shows all the dark black clouds had hid,
    Likewise rarely, through the buddha's power,
    Virtuous thoughts rise, brief and transient, in the world.

6. Thus behold the utter frailty of goodness!
    Except for perfect bodhichitta,

---

* In order to progress toward enlightenment, it is necessary to possess eight forms of ease, or freedom, and ten forms of wealth. The former are: the freedom of not being born (1) in one of the hells, (2) as a preta or hungry ghost, (3) as an animal, (4) in the realms of the gods of measureless life span, (5) among barbarians who are ignorant of the teachings and practices of the Buddha Dharma, (6) as one with wrong views concerning karma and so forth, (7) in a time and place where a buddha has not appeared, and (8) as mentally and physically handicapped.

The ten forms of wealth or endowment are subdivided into five considered as intrinsic and five as extrinsic to the personality. The five intrinsic endowments are (1) to be born a human being, (2) to inhabit a "central land," i.e., where the Dharma is proclaimed, (3) to be in possession of normal faculties, (4) to be one who is not karmically inclined to great negativity, and (5) to have faith in the Dharma. The five extrinsic endowments are the facts that (1) a buddha has appeared in the universe in which one is living, and at an accessible time, (2) that he has expounded the Doctrine, (3) that his Doctrine still persists, (4) that it is practiced, and (5) that one has been accepted by a spiritual master.

There is nothing able to withstand
The great and overwhelming strength of evil.

7. The mighty buddhas, pondering for many ages,
   Have seen that this, and only this, will save
   The boundless multitudes,
   And bring them easily to supreme joy.

8. Those who wish to overcome the sorrows of their lives,
   And put to flight the pain and sufferings of beings,
   Those who wish to win such great beatitude,
   Should never turn their back on bodhichitta.

9. Should bodhichitta come to birth
   In one who suffers in the dungeons of samsara,
   In that instant he is called the buddhas' heir,
   Worshipful alike to gods and men.

10. For like the supreme substance of the alchemists,
    It takes the impure form of human flesh
    And makes of it the priceless body of a buddha.
    Such is bodhichitta: we should grasp it firmly!

11. If the perfect leaders of all migrant beings
    Have with boundless wisdom seen its priceless worth,
    We who wish to leave our nomad wandering
    Should hold well to this precious bodhichitta.

12. All other virtues, like the plantain tree,*
    Produce their fruit, but then their force is spent.
    Alone the marvelous tree of bodhichitta
    Will bear its fruit and grow unceasingly.

13. As though they pass through perils guarded by a hero,
    Even those weighed down with dreadful wickedness

---

* The Tibetan word *chu shing* ("water tree") denotes a hollow plant that dies after bearing fruit. Often, when the latter characteristic is being emphasized, the word is translated as "plantain," but when its hollowness is in question, the term is sometimes, as elsewhere in the present text, rendered as "banana tree."

Will instantly be freed through having bodhichitta.
Who then would not place his trust in it?

14. Just as by the fires at the end of time,
Great sins are utterly consumed by bodhichitta.
Thus its benefits are boundless,
As the Wise and Loving Lord explained to Sudhana.*

15. Bodhichitta, the awakening mind,
In brief is said to have two aspects:
First, aspiring, *bodhichitta in intention*;
Then, *active bodhichitta*, practical engagement.

16. Wishing to depart and setting out upon the road,
This is how the difference is conceived.
The wise and learned thus should understand
This difference, which is ordered and progressive.

17. *Bodhichitta in intention* bears rich fruit
For those still wandering in samsara.
And yet a ceaseless stream of merit does not flow from it;
For this will rise alone from *active bodhichitta*.

18. For when, with irreversible intent,
The mind embraces bodhichitta,
Willing to set free the endless multitudes of beings,
At that instant, from that moment on,

19. A great and unremitting stream,
A strength of wholesome merit,
Even during sleep and inattention,
Rises equal to the vastness of the sky.

20. This the Tathagata,†
In the sutra Subahu requested,‡

---

* The reference is to Maitreya, the buddha of the future, as recounted in the *Ganda-vyuha-sutra*.

† Tathagata (Tib. de bzhin gshegs pa): literally "one thus gone," a title of the Buddha.

‡ A reference to the *Subahu-paripriccha-sutra*, the *Sutra of the Questions of Subahu*. The Sanskrit original of this sutra has been lost, but is preserved in a Chinese translation.

Said with reasoned demonstration,
Teaching those inclined to lesser paths.

21. If with kindly generosity
One merely has the wish to soothe
The aching heads of other beings,
Such merit knows no bounds.

22. No need to speak, then, of the wish
To drive away the endless pain
Of each and every living being,
Bringing them unbounded virtues.

23. Could our fathers or our mothers
Ever have so generous a wish?
Do the very gods, the rishis,* even Brahma†
Harbor such benevolence as this?

24. For in the past they never,
Even in their dreams, conceived
Such profit even for themselves.
How could they have such aims for others' sake?

25. For beings do not wish their own true good,
So how could they intend such good for others' sake?
This state of mind so precious and so rare
Arises truly wondrous, never seen before.

26. The pain-dispelling draft,
This cause of joy for those who wander through the world—
This precious attitude, this jewel of mind,
How shall it be gauged or quantified?

27. For if the simple thought to be of help to others
Exceeds in worth the worship of the buddhas,

---

* According to Indian tradition, the rishis were sages who perceived the sound of the Vedas and transmitted them to the world. They form a class by themselves between gods and humans.

† Brahma, the creator of the universe according to the Vedas.

What need is there to speak of actual deeds
That bring about the weal and benefit of beings?

28. For beings long to free themselves from misery,
But misery itself they follow and pursue.
They long for joy, but in their ignorance
Destroy it, as they would a hated enemy.

29. But those who fill with bliss
All beings destitute of joy,
Who cut all pain and suffering away
From those weighed down with misery,

30. Who drive away the darkness of their ignorance—
What virtue could be matched with theirs?
What friend could be compared to them?
What merit is there similar to this?

31. If they who do some good, in thanks
For favors once received, are praised,
Why need we speak of bodhisattvas—
Those who freely benefit the world?

32. Those who, scornfully with condescension,
Give, just once, a single meal to others—
Feeding them for only half a day—
Are honored by the world as virtuous.

33. What need is there to speak of those
Who constantly bestow on boundless multitudes
The peerless joy of blissful buddhahood,
The ultimate fulfillment of their hopes?

34. And those who harbor evil in their minds
Against such lords of generosity, the Buddha's heirs,
Will stay in hell, the Mighty One has said,
For ages equal to the moments of their malice.

35. By contrast, good and virtuous thoughts
Will yield abundant fruits in greater measure.

Even in adversity, the bodhisattvas
Never bring forth evil—only an increasing stream of goodness.

36. To them in whom this precious sacred mind
    Is born—to them I bow!
    I go for refuge in that source of happiness
    That brings its very enemies to perfect bliss.

22

DEVOTION AND COMPASSION

Tulku Urgyen Rinpoche

> *The play of overwhelming compassion being unobstructed,*
> *In the moment of love the empty essence nakedly dawns.*
> *May we constantly practice, day and night,*
> *This supreme path of unity, devoid of errors.*

> —LORD KARMAPA RANGJUNG DORJE

The most perfect circumstance for realizing the correct view of emptiness is upwardly to generate devotion to all the enlightened ones and downwardly to cultivate compassion for all sentient beings. This is mentioned in *The Aspiration of Mahamudra* by the third Karmapa, Rangjung Dorje. This incredibly profound song of realization expounds teachings on the ground, path, and fruition, as well as all the key points for Mahamudra, Dzogchen, and Madhyamika. One of the lines is: "In the moment of love the empty essence nakedly dawns." "Love" here is to be understood as both devotion and compassion. In the moment of devotion we bring to mind the eminence of our master and lineage

---

Adapted from Tulku Urgyen Rinpoche, *Repeating the Words of the Buddha* (Boudhanath: Rangjung Yeshe Publications, 1996), "Devotion and Compassion," and *Rainbow Painting* (Boudhanath: Rangjung Yeshe Publications, 1995), "Devotion and Compassion."

gurs, doing this sincerely, not just superficially. We think of their great qualities with such genuine admiration and devotion that the hairs of our body stand on end and our eyes are filled with tears. This heartfelt appreciation should be genuine, because it is only through the kindness of the guru that the mind essence can possibly be understood. From this gratitude, strong devotion is felt, stripping our minds bare. That very moment, we unmistakenly and unerringly recognize the natural face of rigpa.

It is the same way when thinking with compassion of all sentient beings. Although they possess self-existing wisdom, they are unaware of it, remaining completely deluded life after life. Chasing after samsara's illusory experiences, they undergo tremendous suffering. It is not like we, as Buddhist practitioners, have an enlightened essence of rigpa and they don't. Everybody is totally equal; yet, not knowing their own nature, sentient beings suffer incessantly. Thinking in this way, we are overcome with great pity and compassion. At that instant of true compassion, as in the moment of true devotion, the empty essence dawns nakedly.

In the Kagyü and Nyingma traditions it is said that devotion is the panacea, the medicine that can cure all sicknesses. If we just focus on devotion we do not need to spend years studying debate, philosophy, grammar, art, and so forth. In the past, thousands of practitioners attained accomplishment through the path of devotion combined with the paths of Mahamudra and Dzogchen. To ignore compassion, devotion, and renunciation is like a bird trying to fly without wings: it's not possible. One should remember the famous statement: "Devotion is the head of meditation, revulsion is the foot of meditation, and nondistraction is the heart of meditation." To take a similar example, consider a person: if we call the view of emptiness the heart, devotion the head, and compassion the feet, how can he travel anywhere using only the heart of emptiness? How can he walk without legs?

Devotion and compassion are not mentioned here simply because we ought to feel them. There is a direct reason for cultivating them. The teachings mention that compassion and devotion should be unfabricated, but this doesn't happen automatically in the beginning. We need to cultivate them, to use some effort to produce these feelings. In other words, in the beginning, we must rely on conceptual thought to make it possible to have compassion and devotion.

Think of it this way: we wouldn't know any Dharma teachings or how to attain liberation if it weren't for the buddhas, their teachings, and their perfect followers. The buddhas are not like us; they have great qualities. Bringing this to mind naturally and unavoidably generates devotion. Similarly, to generate compassion, think of how it is a fact that all sentient beings have been our own parents. In that sense they are closely related to us. If we really think of how other beings suffer, what they go through, we cannot help but feel compassion. When we think of their suffering there is a real reason for pity.

Having slowly cultivated devotion and compassion, we can use them as an aid to genuinely recognize rigpa. Gradually, the sequence is reversed. The natural quality of recognizing the naked state of rigpa is an unfabricated devotion and compassion that doesn't need to be mustered.

Devotion and compassion are enhancements to the practice of emptiness, of the view. Once all misdeeds and obscurations are purified through conditioned virtue, the unconditioned virtue increases. At first devotion and compassion are necessary to produce. They are important stepping-stones to recognizing rigpa. Unfabricated and natural devotion and compassion are the expression of rigpa, but not for a beginner. In the context of Dzogchen, it is said that compassion and devotion naturally occur, without any effort. But frankly speaking, for a beginner it doesn't happen like that. At first we have to cultivate devotion and compassion, to put some effort into developing them. Later on, as we become more stable in awareness, they become effortless and unfabricated. It is this way in Mahamudra, Dzogchen, and Madhyamika.

The main practice of devotion is taking refuge, and the main practice of compassion is to generate bodhichitta. If we investigate, we will not find a single Vajrayana practice without those two, taking refuge and generating bodhichitta. Look at it this way: once we have a heavy investment in taking refuge and generating bodhichitta, we have the capital to be able to do the business of the higher practices and gain the profit of the development stage, the completion stage, and the three great practices—Mahamudra, Dzogchen, and Madhyamika. Without the capital, we won't be able to do any business at all. Devotion and compassion are the basic capital for Buddhist practice.

Unless we connect with the two types of precious bodhichitta, we will not approach enlightenment even in the slightest; this is certain. The two types of bodhichitta are relative bodhichitta, compassion, and ultimate bodhichitta, the insight into emptiness. Without these two, there is absolutely no way to take even one step closer toward buddhahood. Any Dharma practice devoid of these two kinds of bodhichitta will not bring the practitioner even one step toward enlightenment—I will swear to that.

If we want to quickly awaken to buddhahood, it is essential to unite means and knowledge. Whatever conceptual practice we do should ideally be combined with the recognition of mind essence. Devotion and compassion are the heart of conceptual Dharma practice.

The great masters of the Kagyü lineage state that it is delusion to count on any method for recognizing mind essence other than purifying obscurations, gathering the accumulations, and relying on the blessings of a realized master. This means that no matter how smart or strong we are, if we don't follow a master and instead stubbornly push ourselves through years of meditation training without developing compassion and devotion, purifying obscurations, and gathering the accumulations, we will remain deluded.

The essence of both devotion and compassion is actually the same: it is a kind of love. Whether that feeling is directed toward enlightened pure beings or ordinary impure beings, whether it is devotion or compassion, the essence remains the same: at the moment the mind is laid bare of thoughts, the empty essence dawns nakedly and can be directly perceived. In the Kagyü lineage, devotion is always said to be the main quality to focus on, and so the Kagyü lineage is called the lineage of devotion. But compassion or devotion are the same in facilitating the realization of mind essence.

Our training in devotion, compassion, purifying the obscurations, and gathering the accumulations should be combined with recognizing our mind essence. Otherwise, to reach enlightenment using means without knowledge takes a tremendously long time—three aeons, according to the Sutra path. The Vajrayana path is much more swift.

We attain complete enlightenment by unifying means and knowledge, prajña and upaya. The definitions of these two aspects vary according to the different vehicles. In the Sutra teachings, the means is compassion, while the knowledge is emptiness. By unifying compassion and emptiness, we attain true and complete enlightenment. Tantric teachings equate the means aspect with the development stage and the knowledge aspect with the completion stage. By unifying these two stages, we attain true and complete enlightenment.

According to the Mahamudra system, the means aspect is the Six Doctrines of Naropa, while the knowledge aspect is Mahamudra practice itself. These two are called the path of means and the path of liberation. By unifying means and liberation, we attain true and complete enlightenment. In the Madhyamika system, the Middle Way, the means aspect is relative truth; the knowledge aspect is ultimate truth.

It is by unifying these two truths that we attain true and complete enlightenment.

Finally, in the Dzogchen teachings, the means aspect is called "spontaneously present nature," while the knowledge aspect is called "primordially pure essence." By unifying primordial purity and spontaneous presence, Trekchö and Tögal, we attain true and complete enlightenment.

Previously, I mentioned that buddha nature has been present in all beings since beginningless time. It is not a new thing that we achieve through effort or meditation; rather, it is something that is primordially present as our very nature. This buddha nature has never for a single instant been apart from our mind. Only due to not acknowledging it have we strayed through samsaric existence. This straying about due to the ignorance of our nature has been going on not just for a few lifetimes but since beginningless time. Until now, our nature, the enlightened essence, has been veiled in thick layers of ignorance and disturbing emotions. Now we must recognize this nature as it is, free from all obscurations. But merely recognizing our nature is not enough. We must stabilize the recognition by applying it in practice, because if we do not familiarize ourselves with our buddha nature, we will inevitably fall under the power of disturbing emotions again and again. It is said, "You may recognize your essence, but if you do not grow familiar with it, your thoughts will arise as enemies and you will be as helpless as a baby on a battlefield."

Once more I think it is important to stress that apart from depending upon the gathering of the two accumulations and the blessings of a qualified guru, relying on other methods is delusion. The purpose of gathering the two accumulations is to purify our obscurations. And the method for realizing buddha nature requires devotion from the core of our hearts—not mere lip service or platitudes, but a true and genuine devotion to the Three Jewels. There is a lot of talk about emptiness in Buddhism. It is considered a very important and profound subject. However, unless we make it our personal experience and increasingly familiarize ourselves with it, our idea of emptiness may vary wildly from year to year, depending on our current intellectual fantasies, and we will not make much progress. So, how can we make genuine progress in our personal experience? Chiefly through devotion to the Three Jewels. The compassionate activity of the buddhas is like a hook that is just waiting to catch sentient beings who are ready and open and who are attuned to this compassion. If we have faith and devotion, we are like an iron ring that can be caught by the hook. But if we are closed and lack faith and devotion, we are like a solid iron ball. Not even the "hooks" of the buddhas can catch an iron ball.

It is not that the buddhas are without compassion or disregard certain sentient beings. Their compassion and activity are impartial and all-pervasive, like the sun shining in the sky. But if we are like a cave that faces north, the sunshine will never reach inside us. We need to have faith and devotion in order to connect with the compassionate power of the buddhas. If we do not possess these qualities, we cannot open ourselves to this connection, and there is no way that the buddhas can help us.

The state of enlightenment is totally beyond concepts. There is no joy or sorrow within it, such as being happy when one is pleased or feeling sad when one is treated badly. The state of buddhahood is beyond all these. Because of this, buddhas make no preferences between sentient beings; each one is like their only child. The compassionate "hook" of their enlightened activity is totally impartial and all-pervasive, like the sunshine radiating from the sun.

The compassion of the awakened state is beyond both partiality and distance. It is like sunshine in that it is totally unbiased. It is not that the sun shines on some countries and not on others; the sun has no concept that "I will shine on that spot and leave this one in darkness." The buddhas' compassion transcends all distance as well. Imagine that you have positioned a mirror facing the sun: the moment you do so, the sun's rays are instantly reflected. It is the same with the buddhas: the moment we think of them, they "gaze" on us; the rays of their compassion contact us.

The state of enlightenment lies beyond time and space. Its capacity is such that an instant as brief as a snap of the fingers can be transformed into an entire aeon, and an aeon can be transformed into a single moment. We are never excluded from the gaze of enlightened beings. We are never outside their vision. The enlightened state of all the buddhas, bodhisattvas, the dakas and dakinis, and so forth is the dharmadhatu itself. This state of realization is said to be of "one taste," identical in its essential pure nature. All the various buddhas are like different butter lamps lit in one room. The individual flames are separate and distinct, but the nature of the light itself is indivisible.

The state of mind of all the buddhas is dharmakaya itself. The nature of our mind is also dharmakaya. The fact that we have the same essence serves as a direct link between us and all awakened beings. Lacking faith and devotion, it is as though the dharmakaya nature of our mind is encased in obscurations. But the very moment we open up in devotion, we receive the blessings of the buddhas.

The dharmakaya of enlightened beings is like a butter lamp where the flame is burning brightly. The dharmakaya nature of a sentient being's mind is like a butter lamp where the wick has not yet been lit. Therefore, it is very important to allow the compassion and blessings of enlightened beings to enter us. The link between us and the state of enlightenment is faith and devotion. To simply think, "I will only worry about recognizing mind essence," while not engendering any trust in the authentic enlightened state will not help us progress very much.

To progress in the practice of recognizing mind essence, it's exceedingly important to generate faith and devotion toward enlightened beings and compassion toward those who are not enlightened. One reason for compassion is that all sentient beings, without a single exception, have been our mothers in past lives. Imagine that we could somehow roll the entire world up into small pellets and count them. The number of these pellets would still be less than the number of mothers that we have had in our past lives. Among all the six classes of sentient beings, there is not a single one who has not been our mother. This is why we always hear repeated in the teachings, "All sentient beings, my mothers, . . ." or "my mother sentient beings. . . ." Actually, all sentient beings are our mothers from past lives.

Why is a mother so special? When we are born, we are totally helpless and incapable of caring for ourselves. We are absolutely dependent upon our mother. She is the one who looks after us much more in the beginning than our father does. A father may of course be kind, but not in the same way as a mother. A mother gives constant, unconditional love and care to a baby—she pays more attention to it than to herself. In fact, a mother is continually saving her baby's life: if she just abandoned it, it would not remain alive. An infant is that helpless.

Some people are puzzled by the nature of compassion and want to know what is meant by the term. Here's an example: imagine that your mother is in front of you, surrounded by slaughterers who chop off her hands, legs, and arms. They pull out her eyes, cut off her ears and nose, and finally chop off her head. How would you feel seeing your mother chopped up into pieces? Wouldn't you feel desperately sad and grief-stricken? That emotion is compassion. Right now we may merely think of our present mother, but, in fact, all other sentient beings—no matter who they are, even animals—have been our mothers. Our present separation from them is only a matter of time and space. If we really take this to heart, how can we help feeling compassion for all sentient beings?

All sentient beings want only happiness. No one wants to suffer. But through attachment, anger, and delusion, beings only create negative karma for themselves, forging a path straight into the three lower realms. In the past, our mother sentient beings headed to these three unfortunate states; in the present moment, they are heading there again, and in the future they will continue on that same painful route. Contemplating this, how can we help but feel compassion? The emotion this evokes is what is meant by compassion. If we keep turning our backs and abandoning all our mothers for the sake of our own pleasure and benefit, thinking, "I will do a little meditation, attain enlightenment, and be happy," then what kind of people are we? Isn't that a totally heartless way to behave?

Without fertile soil a seed cannot grow into a flower. Compassion is like that fertile soil. The blessing of faith is like the rain that falls from above. When the seed of training in mind essence is planted in the fertile soil of compassion and is watered by the rain of blessings through our devotion, it will automatically grow.

A genuinely compassionate person is naturally honest and decent and will shy away from hurting others through evil deeds. Therefore, he or she will automatically progress and will engender many qualities. If we have compassion, we will naturally heed the cause and effect of our actions. We will be careful. Someone who lacks compassion can easily become a complete charlatan who does not care about anyone else. Such an impostor only takes advantage of others. He or she will definitely not progress.

To lack trust in enlightened beings is like planting a seed in dry soil. How will the seed grow? However, if the seed meets with fertile soil and rainwater, nothing can prevent it from sprouting and growing. Conversely, the seed lying on bare rock without fertile soil and moisture will remain the same from year to year, with no difference, no progress.

It is not enough to practice by merely sitting and saying, "Empty, empty. This mind is empty!" We want to genuinely progress: in order to do this, faith and devotion are essential, and compassion is indispensable. Without devotion and compassion, we are as hardened as someone who sees a buddha fly past in the sky and says, "So what!" Or we are like someone who watches another living creature being chopped up with their entrails hanging out who says, "I don't care!" Then our practice is no different from the seed lying on bare stone. It will never grow. When such a jaded and faithless person sees the buddhas fly by in the sky, he thinks, "They are probably just holding their breath or pulling some trick." Likewise, when he sees another person being cut up, he says, "That's their karma. It has nothing to do with me. I'm fine here. Their suffering is their business." With such an attitude there will never be any true progress in meditation.

Here is another example of someone who lacks faith. Let's say that we tell someone about how the American lifestyle is, about the beautiful houses and gadgets and so forth. That person might reply, "I don't believe you. I've never been there and seen them, so these things cannot exist. You're lying: whatever I haven't seen doesn't exist." This may sound absurd, but many, many people have said, "I don't see any buddhafields, so they don't exist. I don't see any hell realms, so there are no such places."

The reason I do not think this way is that I trust in my main teacher, Buddha Shakyamuni. He could clearly perceive the three times and see the six realms of sentient beings and all the buddhafields in every direction. Because of the depth of his wisdom, I consider everything he said to be utterly and flawlessly true. Between Buddha Shakyamuni and myself there has been a lineage of great masters in whom I also have total trust. This trust extends all the way to my root guru, in whom I have complete faith from the very core of my heart. I have total confidence in all these beings; I don't feel that any one of them ever told a lie.

Since Buddha Shakyamuni there have been countless other practitioners who have had that same trust and confidence in the teachings of the enlightened ones. Through these qualities they were able to attain great accomplishment. They could fly through the sky, pass through solid matter, and reach complete enlightenment in a single lifetime. If we disbelieve the statements of the buddhas because we can't experience such things through our own senses, we are like someone who, when he is told, "Behind this hill are some villages," replies "No, there aren't, because I haven't seen them." How does that sound? Doesn't it sound stupid?

These many practitioners of the past trusted the Buddha when he said, "There are buddhafields above and lower realms below; in between are the effects of our own karmic actions." They had confidence in the words of the enlightened one, the statements of the bodhisattvas, and the oral instructions of their own root gurus. Inspired by this trust, they put the teachings into practice, and through doing so they gained realization. In fact, they could not avoid attaining accomplishment; neither could they avoid benefiting countless other beings. This is not merely an old story from the past; this is still happening today.

If we rely only on our own personal and limited experience as the measure for everything, we can certainly say, "I don't see any buddha-fields, so there aren't any. I don't see any hell realms below, so there aren't any. If I do something negative right now, I don't suddenly end up in the lower realms. Nothing at all happens. Therefore, my actions have no effect." But fortunately we have more than our own limited knowledge to rely on when we evaluate such statements. We have the words of the perfectly enlightened one, as well as the lineage of great masters. There have been and indeed still are countless practitioners who have been able to attain accomplishment through their trust in the bud-dhas. This is the reason we *can* feel complete trust in those teachings.

I myself have never been to any buddhafields with this present body, so I could say that according to my own experience there are no buddha-fields. Similarly, in this very body, I have never been to the hells, so I could say that there are none. I could also say that my actions have no karmic consequences. I could certainly be in doubt about all these things, were it not for the three types of perfect measure. These are the words of the Buddha, the statements of the great bodhisattvas, and the oral instructions of our own root gurus. For these reasons I myself can say I do not have any doubt regarding these matters, but totally trust in these teachings. This kind of trust makes accomplishment through Dharma practice possible. Conversely, if we continue to hesitate and generate doubts about the teachings of the Buddha, accomplishment is not possible.

Take this example: in one hand I have a huge diamond, in the other a chunk of glass. I say, "One of these is a diamond: would you like to buy it for a very good price?" Now, you are not sure which is the dia-mond and which is just glass. Because of this doubt, you would have to say, "I don't know," and you would never be able to purchase the dia-mond no matter how much of a bargain it would be. That is how it is to be in doubt. Doubt hampers every activity we do in this world, no matter what.

To sum up, we need devotion to enlightened beings and compassion for those who are not. Possessing these two, what is then the main train-ing? It is maintaining nondistraction. When we forget mind essence and are carried away, the demon of distraction lies in ambush. But with devotion and compassion, the practice of recognizing mind essence will automatically progress. Many people come to me saying, "I've tried to meditate for years, but nothing happens; I'm not making any progress." This is because of not using the effective method, the right means. We may have the knowledge aspect of having recognized mind essence, but without combining it with means of trust and compassion, we will not make any headway. We may know how to assemble and drive a car, but if we do not have the necessary parts we will never be able to ride anywhere.

Please keep this teaching at the very core of your heart; not at the edge or to one side of your heart, but at the very center. Please think, "That old Tibetan man said devotion and compassion are essential. I'll keep that right in the center of my heart." I have wanted to say this for a long time, but I feel that now people are more willing to listen. It's because it's extremely important that I felt it should be said repeatedly.

I am telling you the truth here. I am being honest with you. I am not lying. If you practice the way I have described here, then each month and year will yield progress. And in the end, no one will be able to pull you back or prevent you from attaining enlightenment.

23

BODHICHITTA: THE TEACHINGS ON TAKING THE AROUSING OF BODHICHITTA AS THE PATH

Padmasambhava

The great master Padmakara is an emanation of Buddha Amitabha. Having trained his mind in the numerous Mahayana sutras, he loves all sentient beings as a mother loves her only child. Acting always for the welfare of others, he is the steersman who delivers all samsaric beings to nirvana. Without being asked he gives instruction to all those to be tamed. Endowed with great compassion, he is the king of all bodhisattvas.

When he was staying in the Lion Fortress Cave at Monkha, I, Lady Tsogyal of Kharchen, aroused bodhichitta, the mind set on supreme enlightenment. Having offered a mandala of precious substances to the great master, I made this petition: Emaho! Great master, you have taught that having cultivated love and compassion for all beings, the sole

From Padmasambhava, *Dakini Teachings* (Boudhanath: Rangjung Yeshe Publications, 1999), "Bodhichitta."

importance in the Mahayana teaching is to train in bodhichitta. This being so, how should we engage in the training of bodhichitta?

The master replied: Tsogyal, if, having entered the Mahayana, you do not train in bodhichitta, you will fall into the lower vehicles. Therefore it is essential to always arouse the mind set on supreme enlightenment and to exert yourself in the trainings of benefiting others.

Countless detailed explanations of that have been given in the sutras and tantras of the Mahayana. When bodhichitta is explained concisely in accordance with these teachings, it is divided into three sections: the outer training, the inner training, and the secret training.

THE OUTER TRAINING IN BODHICHITTA

Lady Tsogyal asked: What are the methods of the outer training?

The master replied: There are twelve points to the outer training:

1. The essence of training in bodhichitta
2. Its divisions
3. Its definition
4. The characteristics of the person
5. The object from whom you take the vow
6. The ceremony for taking it
7. The benefits of the training
8. The reasons for training
9. The shortcomings of not training
10. The precepts
11. The dividing line between losing and possessing it
12. The method for repairing it if damaged

She asked: How are these points you described?

1. The Essence

The master replied: The essence of arousing bodhichitta is the desire to attain unexcelled enlightenment together with the vow to do so in order to liberate all sentient beings from samsara.

2. The Divisions

The sutras describe many classifications of divisions, but in short, there are two kinds: aspiration and application. The aspiration is the wish to accomplish the welfare of beings, but that alone is not sufficient. It is important to actually engage in benefiting all sentient beings.

It seems to be quite difficult for prejudiced people who are not free from egotism to give rise to bodhichitta.

3. The Definition

The definition of bodhichitta is the arising in oneself of an altruistic attitude that has not previously arisen.

This attitude will not arise in beings who have not gathered the accumulations.

4. The Characteristics of the Person

The person who engages in the training of bodhichitta should possess certain characteristics. He should aspire toward the teaching of the Mahayana, unlike the shravakas and pratyekabuddhas. Due to great intelligence, he should be totally free from doubt. He should have taken refuge in a master and in the Three Jewels and should feel weary of incorrect or inferior teachings. He should be naturally peaceful and gentle.

The people of Tibet are hostile toward the Dharma, the ministers are evil-minded, the king is gullible; there are only a few who are suitable recipients for the Mahayana teachings. Tsogyal, be free from partiality toward friend and enemy.

5. The Object

The object from whom you take the bodhichitta vow should be a master, who has the Mahayana aspiration and whose mind is filled with love and compassion. He should be a teacher who does not act for the benefit of himself for even an instant and who observes his precepts without transgressions.

In this dark age, one will fall into the hands of Mara unless one follows a qualified master.

6. The Ceremony

The ceremony for taking the bodhichitta vow is as follows. Having arranged an extensive display of offerings before the Three Jewels on the fifteenth or the eighth of the waxing moon in an auspicious year and month, pay respect to the Sangha. Offer a *ganachakra* to the yidam. Make extensive *torma* offerings to the dakinis, Dharma protectors, and elemental spirits. Give away all your possessions and gather a vast amount of merit.

That same evening, offer the initiation fee to the master. With respect for the master, the disciple should gather the accumulations by means of the seven branches of purity.[17]

In particular, you should apologize for misdeeds as follows. Visualize the syllable AH at the crown of your head. By means of the light streaming forth from it, establish all sentient beings in the enlightenment of the buddhas and make offerings to all noble beings. By means of the light being absorbed back into the AH, absorb the nectar of the siddhis of all the noble ones, which then dissolves into your body, speech, and mind and burns away all of your misdeeds and obscurations. Imagining that, recite AH 108 times.

Imagine that the light radiating from the HUNG in the heart of the wisdom being in the master's heart center dissolves into your body, speech, and mind and thereby burns away all misdeeds. Thinking this, recite HUNG 108 times.

Then follows the verbal apology. Remembering all misdeeds accumulated since beginningless samsara, recite this apology three times with remorse.

> Vajra master and all vidyadharas, pay heed to me!
> Assembly of yidam deities together with your retinue of peaceful
>   and wrathful buddhas, pay heed to me!
> Victorious ones of the ten directions together with your sons, pay
>   heed to me!
> Mother dakinis guarding the teachings together with the Dharma
>   protectors, pay heed to me!

> In the presence of those who are worthy of veneration, I, ——, remorsefully apologize for all the evil karmic actions I have accumulated by the power of erroneous thinking by means of body, speech, and mind, through committing unvirtuous actions and misdeeds, causing others to commit them, or rejoicing in their doing so, since beginningless lifetimes to this very day.

Then resolve not to further proliferate misdeeds. Repeat the above supplication and then say three times:

Just as the tathagatas and their sons of the past, by means of the perfect life-examples of the paths and bhumis, turned away from unvirtuous actions and misdeeds, so will I, ——, from this very moment until reaching the essence of enlightenment, turn away from committing misdeeds through erroneous thinking. I vow to henceforth refrain from them.

THE ACTUAL AROUSING OF BODHICHITTA

This has two parts. The first is for the beginner to arouse the bodhichitta of aspiration.

From the core of his heart the disciple should arouse the genuine attitude of thinking: In order to save all the sentient beings of samsara from the ocean of suffering, I will attain unexcelled enlightenment!

At the end of repeating the above supplication he should say three times:

With the attitude of regarding all sentient beings as being my fathers and mothers, my brothers and sisters, my sons and daughters, or my teachers and Dharma friends, I, ——, from this very day until reaching the essence of enlightenment, will generate the firm intention of liberating all beings who have not been liberated. I will cross over the ones who have not crossed over, I will relieve the ones who are not relieved, and I will establish in the nondwelling state of enlightenment of the buddhas all beings who have not passed beyond suffering.[18]

Secondly, for arousing the bodhichitta of application, form the thought: From this very moment and for as long as samsara is not emptied, without being distracted for even a single moment, I will accomplish the welfare of beings in manifold ways. Repeat the above supplication, after which you should say three times:

From this very moment until samsara is emptied, I, ——, will persistently generate the firm intention to gradually train, carry out and perfect the *six paramitas* and *the four means of magnetizing*. Just as the buddhas of the past and all the bodhisattvas by means of the perfect life-examples of the paths and bhumis, were endowed with the root and branch vows, in that way I also will train, carry out, and perfect them. Please regard me as a bodhisattva.

The master then says, So be it! and the disciple, It is good! It is meaningful! After having repeated the above three times, one has obtained the vow.

In order to keep the vow unimpaired from that moment on, the master should instruct the disciple in the precepts. The disciple should then offer a gift and perform an extensive offering of thanksgiving.

From that moment on it is of the greatest importance to continuously exert oneself in arousing bodhichitta and in the trainings of bodhichitta, like the steady flow of a river.

7. The Benefits

The benefits of training in the bodhichitta you have thus developed are as follows. Elevated above the shravakas and pratyekabuddhas, you are included in the assembly of Mahayana practitioners. Your disturbing emotions, misdeeds, and obscurations are all annihilated from their very root. All the virtuous actions of your body, speech, and mind become causes for what is meaningful, and a vast gathering of merit will be perfected in your being. You will always be watched over by the buddhas and bodhisattvas and the great protectors of the Dharma. All sentient beings will love you as their own child and find you beautiful to behold. You will never be separated from the Mahayana teachings.

In short, you will quickly accomplish the superior qualities of buddhahood and awaken to true and complete enlightenment. Thus the qualities are inconceivable. Therefore be persistent in just this.

8. The Reasons for Training

It may be sufficient to attain liberation by yourself alone, so why should you liberate all sentient beings from samsara? Since all beings are your own parents, your debt of gratitude is inconceivably great, and so you need to train in order to repay their kindness.

Their kindness consists in forming the basis for your life and body; raising you from childhood with the best food and drink; undertaking all kinds of pain and difficulties for your benefit; cherishing you as higher than themselves, more important even than their own hearts.

Moreover, they have endowed you with wealth and possessions, educated you, connected you to the sacred Dharma, and so forth. Because of the inconceivably great kindness of these parents, you must liberate them all from samsara. Since all sentient beings have the basic cause, the essence of enlightenment, you are also connected with them and so you must liberate them all from samsara.

Tsogyal, if you desire happiness for yourself alone, you have no connection to perfect buddhahood.

9. *The Shortcomings of Not Training*

The defects of not training are as follows. Having fallen to the level of being a shravaka and pratyekabuddha, you are hindered in attaining the great enlightenment; all the actions you perform become futile; all the merit you have accumulated in the past will be exhausted; you will always be hampered by spirits; others will feel hostile and dislike you. In short, your wishes will never be fulfilled and so forth. Thus there are countless shortcomings.

Tsogyal, how silly it is to expect to be a Mahayana follower without possessing bodhichitta.

10. *The Precepts*

There are two types of precepts to observe. For the precept of the bodhichitta of aspiration you must train again and again in bodhichitta with the intention to never forsake sentient beings. The bodhichitta of aspiration is impaired if:

—preceded by the intention to reject another sentient being, you get angry or physically hit another person and allow one day to pass without applying an antidote.
—preceded by the intention to deceive your master, teacher, vajra friend, or anyone else worthy of respect, you deceive them and let one day pass without applying an antidote.
—you cause someone to regret a vast root of merit he has created, which is an object for rejoicing and not for feeling regret. This occurs when, preceded by the intention to make him feel remorse, you say, "There is something superior to this! This is not excellent!"
—motivated by anger, you utter a sentence of criticism to a bodhisattva who has developed bodhichitta.
—without compassion, you deceive another sentient being.

These deeds are called the five perverted actions if you allow one day to pass without counteracting them with an antidote. Give them up as they will cause you to lose your vow of aspiration.

Tsogyal, you can be ruined by taking many precepts that you do not keep.

There are, moreover, five actions to which you should adhere.

1. As an antidote to showing anger or beating sentient beings, you should always be peaceful and gentle and try to help them.
2. As an antidote to deceiving someone worthy of respect, you should be conscientious and never lie even at the cost of your life.
3. As an antidote to causing others to feel regret, establish all sentient beings in the virtue that leads to the great enlightenment of the buddhas.
4. As an antidote to criticizing others out of anger, you should praise all followers of the Mahayana while regarding them as your teachers.
5. As an antidote to deceiving sentient beings, you should take your own mind as witness and, with pure intention, follow those who are stable.

Adhere to these deeds and you will be a holder of the teachings of Shakyamuni even though you are born as a woman.

Secondly, the precepts of the bodhichitta of application will be explained under three points: (1) the ten nonvirtues to be abandoned, (2) the ten virtuous actions that are the antidotes, and (3) the ten paramitas that are to be engaged in.

THE TEN NONVIRTUES
Among the ten nonvirtues, there are first the three physical deeds: killing, taking what is not given, and engaging in sexual misconduct.

Killing. The essence of killing is to interrupt the continuation of life. There are three types enacted by the three poisons:

1. Killing out of desire means to slaughter animals due to desire for their meat, skin, and so forth.
2. Killing out of anger means, for example, to murder another with a vicious intention.
3. Killing out of delusion means to kill without intention, for example, when a child kills a bird or an ant dies by being trodden on.

Sentient beings who are not free from the three poisons have no happiness.

The act of killing is completed when committed by means of the following four aspects:

1. The preceding thought of intending "I will do such a misdeed!"
2. The deliberate engagement in the act and pursuing it with effort.
3. The actual deed of killing, experiencing the act.
4. The conclusion of rejoicing in the act without feeling regret.

The results of killing appear in three ways.

1. The result of ripening is that by killing out of desire you will mainly be reborn as a hungry ghost, by killing out of anger you will mostly be reborn in the hells, and by killing out of delusion you will mainly be reborn as an animal.
2. The result of the dominant action is that, dominated by the former unvirtuous action, you will have a short life span and much sickness even if you take rebirth as a human being.
3. The result corresponding to the cause is that you will take pleasure in the act of killing, due to your former habitual tendencies.

Tsogyal, therefore we should not commit these actions. The sutras teach that if you put effort into abandoning these actions you will turn away from the previous result of ripening, the result corresponding to the cause, and the dominant result. Then you will attain the abundant happiness of gods and men.

Taking What Is Not Given. The essence of the second physical nonvirtue, taking what is not given, is the act of making another person's possession your own.

This nonvirtue includes taking by force, for example, robbing in open daylight, taking by sneak such as stealing unnoticed, and taking by deceit, for example, dishonesty with weights and scales.

Tsogyal, people who have not turned away from desire possess no happiness.

Just as before, this action is consummated when four aspects are complete, and the results are again of three types:

1. The result of ripening is that you fall into the three lower realms according to whether the act is done to a greater, medium, or lesser degree. In particular, you will be reborn as a hungry ghost.
2. The dominant result will be that, even if you are reborn as a human being, you will have few possessions and encounter a lot of thievery and robbery.
3. The result corresponding to the cause is that, due to this unwholesome

habitual tendency being accumulated in the all-ground, you will delight in taking what is not given in future lives.

Tsogyal, if you give up committing such actions you will have three results. You will obtain the opposite of the previous three results, such as being reborn in the forms of gods and men, having much wealth, and so forth.

Sexual Misconduct. The essence of the third physical nonvirtue, sexual misconduct, is the act of engaging in intercourse with an object of desire with whom one has no authority to do so.

When divided, there are the following kinds:

1. It is unsuitable for a commoner to have intercourse with someone under the guardianship of a king, such as his queen.
2. It is unsuitable to have intercourse with someone prohibited by the law.
3. In India, it is unsuitable to have casual intercourse with someone under the guardianship of parents, since men and women not in their own household are protected by their parents.
4. It is unsuitable to have intercourse with someone protected by "civilized principles," which means someone with whom it is shameful, such as a mother or a sister.
5. It is unsuitable to have intercourse with someone under the guardianship of the sacred Dharma, such as the guru's consort, an ordained person, and so forth.

Lustful people do not enter the path of liberation. Tsogyal, apply the antidote.

There are also occasions on which it is unsuitable to have intercourse even with your rightful companion:

1. It is unsuitable to have intercourse at an inappropriate time such as on the full moon, the new moon, and the eighth day.
2. It is unsuitable to have intercourse in an inappropriate location, such as in the presence of a shrine for the Three Jewels.
3. It is unsuitable to have intercourse in an inappropriate orifice, such as engaging in the manner of animals.

Tsogyal, in general people who have not abandoned the life of householders are trapped in the prison of Mara.

As before, the act of sexual misconduct is consummated by means of the four completing aspects, and again there are three types of results:

1. Through the result of ripening you will be reborn in the three lower realms. Even if you do take rebirth in the higher realms, you will have fights with your spouse and so forth.
2. The dominant result is that even in future lives your helpers, spouse, and so forth will be unresponsive and show various acts of ingratitude.
3. The result corresponding to the cause is that your unwholesome habitual tendencies will cause you to take pleasure in sexual misconduct.

Tsogyal, if you give up these acts and refrain from engaging in them, you will obtain the opposites of their results, so abandoning them is of great importance.

Secondly, there are four types of verbal nonvirtues.

Telling Lies. The essence of the first, telling lies, is to verbally state that something untrue is true.

When divided, there are the following kinds:

1. There are lies that neither benefit nor harm, such as the lies of an old senile man.
2. There are lies that do benefit or harm, such as benefiting one person while harming another.
3. The "lie of having supreme human qualities" means that you claim to possess such qualities in your stream-of-being, such as higher perceptions, when you do not.

Tsogyal, do not utter a lot of thoughtless words.

As before, the act of telling lies is consummated by means of the four completing aspects, and again there are three types of result:

1. The result of ripening is that you fall into the lower realms.
2. The dominant result is that even if you are reborn as a human, your voice will hold no power.
3. The result corresponding to the cause is that in future lives you will again delight in telling lies.

Tsogyal, if you give up these acts you will obtain the opposites of their results, so abandoning them is of great importance.

Divisive Talk. The essence of the second verbal nonvirtue, divisive talk, is the act of separating people who are good friends.
When divided, there are the following types:

1. Public divisive talk by talking directly to someone's face.
2. Indirect divisive talk by talking in a roundabout way.
3. Private divisive talk by talking to others individually.

Tsogyal, people who cannot keep their lips tight will have no happiness.
The four completing aspects are just as before, and there are again three types of results:

1. The result of ripening is that you will fall into the three lower realms.
2. The dominant result is that, even if you take rebirth as a human being, you will have few friends and many arguments. You will always have many regrets and be disliked by everyone, and whatever you utter will be ineffective.
3. The result corresponding to the cause is that in future lives you will again take pleasure in divisive talk.

Tsogyal, if we abandon such acts we will attain the opposites of their results, so it is important to abandon them.

Idle Gossip. The essence of the third verbal nonvirtue, idle gossip, is to waste free time.
When divided, there are the following types:

1. Shamanistic incantations.
2. Storytelling and word games.
3. Bantering conversation.

Just as before, it is consummated by the four aspects and will have these three types of results:

1. The result of ripening is that you will fall into the three lower realms.
2. The dominant result is that, even if you are reborn as a human being, your words will be undignified, babbling, and unconnected.

3. The result corresponding to the cause is that in future lives you will again take pleasure in uttering idle gossip.

Tsogyal, if you give up these acts you will attain the opposite of their results, so do not be fond of pointless chatter.

Harsh Words. The essence of the fourth verbal nonvirtue, harsh words, is talk that hurts another person.

When divided, there are the following kinds:

1. Exposing someone's faults in public.
2. Hurting someone indirectly.
3. Uttering in private something that will hurt another person.

Tsogyal, the fire of harsh words burns the heart of both yourself and others. The weapon of harsh words kills the life force of liberation.

This act is consummated by the four completing aspects, and has the following three types of results:

1. The result of ripening is to be reborn in the three lower realms.
2. The dominant result is that, even if you take rebirth as a human being, whatever you say will be offensive to others and you will always appear to aggravate them.
3. The result corresponding to the cause is that you will be fond of speaking harsh words.

Tsogyal, if you abandon these actions you will attain the results of their opposites. The sentient beings of the dark age have no happiness.

Thirdly, there are three mental nonvirtues.

Covetousness. The essence of the first, covetousness, is attachment to something excellent.

When divided, there are the following types:

1. Refraining from giving away your own possessions.
2. Desiring to make others' possessions belong to yourself.
3. Attachment to something excellent that belongs to neither oneself nor others.

Tsogyal, do not hold on to ownership of material things. Dharma practitioners with no understanding of impermanence have no happiness.

This action is consummated by the four aspects and has the following three results:

1. The result of ripening is rebirth in the three lower realms.
2. The dominant result is that, even if you take rebirth as a human being, you will always live in an unpleasant area where there is hunger and thirst.
3. The result corresponding to the cause is that in future lives you will take pleasure in covetousness.

Tsogyal, it is therefore essential to abandon these actions.

Ill Will. The essence of the second mental nonvirtue, ill will, is an attitude of hostility.

When divided, there are the following types:

1. Ill will resulting from anger.
2. Ill will resulting from resentment.
3. Ill will resulting from jealousy.

Tsogyal, do not commit mental actions that hurt yourself and harm others.

This act is consummated by the four aspects and has the following three types of results:

1. The result of ripening is to take rebirth in the lower realms.
2. The dominant result is that, even if you are reborn as a human, others are unjustifiably hostile toward you and constantly you meet with enmity and lawsuits.
3. The result corresponding to the cause is that you will develop a malicious frame of mind.

Tsogyal, if you do not give up ill will you can practice neither Hinayana nor Mahayana.

Wrong Views. The essence of the third mental nonvirtue, wrong views, is to exaggerate or denigrate.

When divided, there are the following kinds:

1. The wrong view of holding the non-Buddhist beliefs of eternalism or nihilism.

2. The wrong view of holding a rule or ritual to be paramount, such as "asceticism of dogs and chickens."[19]
3. The wrong view of holding the belief of the "transitory collection."[20]

Tsogyal, there are few who understand the difference between Dharma and non-Dharma.

These actions are consummated by the four aspects and produce the following three results:

1. The result of ripening is to take rebirth in the three lower realms.
2. The dominant result is that, even if you are reborn as a human being, you will take birth in a place such as in an uncivilized border tribe, where you will not even hear the name of the Three Jewels.
3. The result corresponding to the cause is that the habitual tendencies of holding wrong views will solidify in your all-ground, after which you will be fond of holding wrong views.

Tsogyal, all noble beings denounce these ten nonvirtues. They are renounced by all learned people. They are not to be committed even by those who seek to attain the special splendor and wealth of gods and humans, so give them up.

There are many people who do not recognize good from evil, but those who do have entered the Buddha's teachings. To commit nonvirtue while knowing well the cause and effect of virtuous actions and misdeeds is to be no different from an animal.

Lady Tsogyal asked: When abandoning these actions, what are the results one will attain?

The master replied: As the result of ripening you will be reborn among gods and humans. Like Brahma your voice will be melodious, like Indra your body will more beautiful than that of others, and like a universal monarch you will have great wealth.

As the dominant result you will hold great learning, you will be very intelligent, and you will meet with the Dharma of the Buddha's teachings. Ultimately you will attain the three levels of enlightenment.

As the result corresponding to the cause you will, in all future lifetimes, exert yourself in abandoning the ten nonvirtues.

Lady Tsogyal asked: Concerning these ten nonvirtues, is there any difference in the severity of evil?

The master replied: Yes, there are differences. In general, there is the division in terms of the disturbing emotions.

1. Through committing the ten nonvirtues out of anger, you will be reborn as a hell-being.
2. When the nonvirtues are committed out of desire, you will be reborn as a hungry ghost.
3. When the nonvirtues are committed out of delusion, you will be reborn as an animal.

There is also a difference in severity in terms of the object:

1. By committing the ten nonvirtues toward a special object, you will be reborn as a hell-being.
2. By committing them toward an ordinary object, you will be reborn as a hungry ghost.
3. By committing them toward an inferior object, you will be reborn as an animal.

In particular, among the different types of killing, the most severe evil ripening stems from taking the life of a bodhisattva who has developed bodhichitta.

Among the different types of taking what is not given, the greatest misdeed is to steal that which belongs to the Three Jewels.

Among the different types of sexual misconduct, the greatest misdeed is to have forced intercourse with an arhat.

Among the different types of telling lies, the greatest misdeed is to deceive a master or a venerable member of the Sangha.

Among the different types of divisive talk, the greatest misdeed is to cause a schism in the Sangha.

Among the different types of harsh words, the greatest misdeed is to speak unpleasantly to a member of the Sangha.

Among the different types of idle gossip, the greatest misdeed is to disturb the mind of a monk or someone practicing the nature of nondual meditation.

Among the different types of covetousness, the greatest misdeed is to crave the funds donated to the Three Jewels.

Among the different types of ill will, the greatest misdeed is to plan committing the "five deeds with immediate result."

Among the different types of wrong views, the greatest misdeed is to disparage the true meaning.

Tsogyal, you should not commit any of these actions even at the cost of your life.

Generally speaking, there are also differences among the ten nonvirtues:

1. Through killing, divisive talk, harsh words, and ill will, you will be reborn as a hell-being.
2. Through sexual misconduct, taking what is not given, and covetousness, you will be reborn as a hungry ghost.
3. Through telling lies, idle gossip, and holding wrong views, you will be reborn as an animal.

THE TEN VIRTUES

Lady Tsogyal asked the master: How should one practice the ten virtues, the antidotes that are to be adopted?

The master replied: The ten virtues have four topics:

1. The essence is a pure action of body, speech, or mind that produces the truly high.[21]
2. The definition of *virtuous action* is that action which, when correctly committed by a person who has obtained the freedoms and riches, yields the result of a desired happiness.
3. The divisions are the virtues that are the opposites of the ten nonvirtues: to save lives, to be tremendously generous, to abide in pure living, to speak truthfully, to reconcile strife, to speak gently and with discipline, to speak meaningfully, to be loving toward all beings, to be unattached, and to be free from doubt about the results of actions and the definitive meaning.
4. The following are the ten supports that cause the virtues to remain in your stream-of-being: to have faith in the true teachings, to keep self-respect and pure conscience, to refrain from gambling and quarreling, to refrain from watching market gatherings, to always act conscientiously, to cast away laziness, to not associate with immoral friends, to train in the pliancy of body, speech, and mind, to cultivate the *fourfold spheres of perception*, and in particular to focus your mind on the path of noble beings.

Tsogyal, by acting in these ways, there is no doubt that you will attain the results of the truly high.

THE TEN PARAMITAS

Thirdly, for engaging in the actions of the ten paramitas, there are five topics.

1. The general essence is that which has the nature of the path for accomplishing unexcelled enlightenment.

2. The definition of *paramita* is that which causes you to reach (*ita*) to the great nirvana, the other shore (*param*) of the ocean of samsara.

3. The function is to perfect the two accumulations and accomplish the welfare of sentient beings.

4. There are two kinds of divisions: general and specific. The general division is the six paramitas of generosity, discipline, patience, diligence, concentration, and discriminating knowledge.

Specifically, generosity has three types: the giving of Dharma teachings, the giving of material things, and the giving of protection against fear.

Discipline also has three types: the discipline of refraining from misdeeds, the discipline of gathering virtuous qualities, and the discipline of benefiting sentient beings. In other words, these disciplines are observed by refraining from the ten nonvirtues, by the six paramitas, and by the four means of magnetizing.

Patience also has three types: the patience of being unconcerned about undergoing suffering when renouncing samsara, the patience of undertaking hardship in order to benefit beings, and the patience of keeping confidence in the Dharma, which means to refrain from fearing the profound nature.

Diligence also has three types: the diligence of applying the Mahayana teachings, the armorlike diligence of repelling adversity, and the relentless diligence of accomplishing the buddhahood of perfect omniscience.

Meditation also has three types: the meditation that focuses on the correct mundane path, the meditation that focuses on the supramundane path, and the general meditation that takes both as focus.

Knowledge again has three types: the knowledge that realizes conditioned things to be beyond focus, the knowledge that realizes the innate nature to be beyond focus, and the knowledge that realizes that all phenomena are beyond duality and transcend words, thought, and description.

You should know that in order to assimilate each method within your stream-of-being, you must have four paramitas complete:

To vanquish stinginess and poverty through the generosity of not expecting a reward is the paramita of strength.

To give while being free from the intentions of ordinary people and the Hinayana is the paramita of method.

To give with the thought, May I interrupt the poverty of myself and all sentient beings! is the paramita of aspiration.

To give with the total purity of the three spheres is the paramita of wisdom.[22]

Similarly, to vanquish nonvirtue with the discipline of not desiring samsaric results is the paramita of strength.

To observe your vows while being free from the eight worldly concerns is the paramita of method.

To wish, May the immoral behavior of all sentient beings be interrupted! while not desiring the states of gods and men for yourself alone is the paramita of aspiration.

To embrace that with the *nonconceptualization of the three spheres* is the paramita of wisdom.

To vanquish anger by behaving equally to everyone is the paramita of strength.

Not to hold a worldly purpose such as deceit and hypocrisy is the paramita of method.

Not to desire rebirth in a beautiful body of gods or humans for yourself alone, but to wish, May the ugliness of all sentient beings be pacified! is the paramita of aspiration.

To embrace that with the nonconceptualization of the three spheres is the paramita of wisdom.

To vanquish laziness with the diligence of keeping the faults and qualities in mind is the paramita of strength.

Not to hold a worldly purpose such as expecting to be held in faith by others is the paramita of method.

To wish, May all beings bring an end to laziness and exert themselves on the true path! is the paramita of aspiration.

To embrace that with the nonconceptualization of the three spheres is the paramita of wisdom.

To vanquish distraction through the concentration that has transcended the formless realms is the paramita of strength.

To practice for the sake of accomplishing the qualities of unexcelled enlightenment, with no desire for the states of gods or men, is the paramita of method.

To wish, May the distraction of all sentient beings be interrupted! is the paramita of aspiration.

To refrain from conceptualizing the three spheres is the paramita of wisdom.

To vanquish the constructs of distinguishing attributes with the knowledge of emptiness endowed with the nature of compassion is the paramita of strength.

To be inseparable from that throughout the three times is the paramita of method.

To wish, May I and all other beings realize the true meaning! is the paramita of aspiration.

To recognize the fact that, since the beginning, your mind essence has the nature of this knowledge is the paramita of wisdom.

Tsogyal, practice in this way undistractedly.

5. The result of practicing the ten paramitas is that you will be liberated from the lower realms and, attaining the special level of gods or men, you will perfect the paths and swiftly attain buddhahood after which you will become a great guide liberating sentient beings from samsara.

11. The Dividing Line between Losing and Possessing the Vow

The moment of obtaining the bodhichitta vow is as follows. Having gathered a vast accumulation of merit, when you give rise to the thought that you must accomplish the genuine welfare of beings through fully purifying your mind, you obtain the bodhichitta vow at the end of the third utterance of the complete ritual.

The moment of losing the bodhichitta vow is when you give rise to wrong views or denounce the Three Jewels, thus violating the trainings. It is therefore essential to exert yourself while keeping mindfulness and conscientiousness on guard.

12. The Method for Repairing When Damaged

If you damage the root precepts, you must retake the vow as instructed before. If you have damaged the branch precepts, you must apologize for that in the presence of the master or the Three Jewels.

THE INNER BODHICHITTA

Lady Tsogyal asked the master: How should one train when arousing bodhichitta in the inner way?

The master replied: For this there are also twelve points of training.

1. The Essence

The essence is to arouse the intention to help those beings who do not realize that the innate nature, the true meaning, is devoid of constructs.

2. The Definition

Without being dependent upon "outer" actions of body or speech, it is called "inner" because it is developed exclusively by your mind.

3. The Divisions

There are two divisions: aspiration and application.

The aspiration is to wish that sentient beings who have not realized this nature may realize it. Just to sit and mutter this is not enough; you must exert yourself in the means for making all sentient beings realize it.

Tsogyal, as long as you are not free from dualistic fixation the application is rather difficult.

4. The Characteristics of the Practitioner

In addition to earlier explanations, the characteristic of the person who engages in this training is to have only a minor degree of conceptual constructs.

Tsogyal, let your mind take some rest!

5. The Object from Whom It Is Taken

You should receive it from a master who has realized the nature of the twofold selflessness through training in the three types of knowledge, and is thus free from the eight worldly concerns.

Tsogyal, a master is essential for entering the gate of the Mahayana teachings.

6. The Ceremony for Receiving

Free yourself from the three spheres of concepts, give up concerns for all worldly activities, and thus request the true oral instructions.

7. The Benefits of the Training

You will rise far above the Hinayana and erroneous paths. Thus it has the effect of abandoning all thoughts of selfishness and dualistic fixation, and of realizing the nature of selflessness.

8. The Reason for the Training

The reason for training in this inner way of arousing bodhichitta is to establish all sentient beings on the true path, the nature of the twofold selflessness.

9. The Shortcomings of Not Training

The defect of not training is that you will stray from the nature of selflessness.

For ordinary people whose minds have not been changed by a philosophical school and for non-Buddhists who have entered an incorrect philosophical school, the self of the individual is regarded as being that which controls and experiences the conditioned five aggregates, *twelve sense-bases*, and *eighteen constituents*. Moreover, regarding this self as being permanent and concrete, they fixate on it as being friend and enemy, self and other.

Tsogyal, you must pull up this stake of fixation.

The danger of conceptualizing such an individual self is that by apprehending an ego and a self-entity, objects will appear as "something other." By apprehending this duality, you will regard that which benefits the "self" as friend and that which harms the "self" as enemy. Thus the experiences of attachment and aversion will cause you to commit various kinds of unvirtuous actions. Through these actions you will wander in the lower realms and the whole of samsara.

Tsogyal, unless you expel this evil spirit you will find no happiness.

What type of person denounces this self? In general it is denounced by all Buddhists. In particular, the shravakas specifically denounce it. Needless to say, we who have entered the gate of the Mahayana also denounce fixation on the individual self.

It is claimed that the shravakas partially realize the self of phenomena, and that also the pratyekabuddhas do not realize it fully. That is to say, the shravakas mistakenly assert the existence of matter instead of understanding the self of phenomena, and the pratyekabuddhas dwell in the state of fixating on the empty mind-essence instead of understanding the correct meaning.

Tsogyal, as long as you are not free from the beliefs of the lower philosophical schools you will not perceive the true meaning.

The danger of conceptualizing the self of phenomena is that by such assertion and fixation you will give rise to disturbing emotions. These will cause you to wander in samsara. That is pointless effort even if you were to exert yourself for aeons.

What type of person denounces the self of phenomena? In general all Mahayana followers denounce it. In particular, it would be a bad sign if we who have entered the gate of Secret Mantra fixate on partiality, as the followers of the Middle Way also denounce it.

10. The Points to Be Observed

You should train yourself in the meaning of selflessness of which there are two kinds, aspiration and application.

The three important points of aspiration to be observed are as follows.

1. To continually form the aspiration of thinking, May all sentient beings always realize the meaning of selflessness!
2. To train yourself three times a day and three times a night in rejoicing in others who meditate on the meaning of selflessness.
3. To always train yourself assiduously in not straying from the meaning of selflessness.

Secondly, the two points of application to be observed are the outer and the inner.

The four outer points are as follows:

1. Not to separate yourself from the master or spiritual friend who teaches the meaning of selflessness until you have realized it.
2. To give up partiality concerning dwelling place, country and area, caste, enemy, and friend.
3. To study, reflect and meditate upon the teachings that demonstrate selflessness and emptiness.
4. Not to fixate on yourself as being a name, family, or body.

The four inner trainings are as follows:

1. Not to apprehend names as being things, since all labels and names of outer things have no existence in your mind.
2. To acknowledge that everything that comprises the world and the beings within it has no self-nature, although it appears, just like dreams and magic.
3. To seek out three times a day and three times a night this mind that fixates on various objects, although nothing whatsoever exists.
4. Not to stray from the meaning that is nameless and devoid of extremes. Even though you search your mind, it is not found to be anything whatsoever.

It is of utmost importance to train yourself diligently in this way. Through exerting yourself in this way, you will annihilate the evil spirit and turn away from samsara.

11. The Dividing Line between Losing and Possessing the Vow

The moment of obtaining the inner bodhichitta vow is when you receive the oral instructions from your master.

The moment of losing it is when you pursue ordinary dualistic fixation without understanding the nonexistence of a self-nature. Since it is lost at that moment, be sure to apply the antidote!

12. The Method for Repairing When Damaged

Train in remaining undistracted from the meaning just explained and you will automatically untie the knot of dualistic fixation.

THE SECRET TRAINING

Lady Tsogyal asked the master: How should one train in the secret arousing of bodhichitta?

The master replied: This has eleven points.

1. The Essence

The essence of the secret arousing of bodhichitta is to recognize that which is beyond effort since the beginning, the primordial purity of non-arising free from the limitations of thought and description.

2. The Definition

It is naturally secret from all the lower vehicles since it lies beyond that which can be indicated by words or thought of by the mind.

3. The Divisions

When divided, there are two positions: asserting the universal purity to be nonmeditation and asserting the spontaneously present nature to be primordially perfected as nonmeditation. You should be free from any partiality concerning this.[23]

4. The Characteristic of the Practitioner

The characteristic of the person who engages in this is that he should be of the highest capacity with a mind weary of concrete phenomena.

Tsogyal, this can only be a person who possesses former training.

5. The Object from Whom One Receives

The object from whom you receive it should be one who has realized the single circle of dharmakaya and therefore remains in the state of the effortless great expanse.

Tsogyal, this can only be a master who has realized the meaning of the Great Perfection.

6. The Ceremony for Receiving

The ritual for receiving is the empowerment of awareness-display.

Abandon your impure mundane physical activities as well as your pure virtuous actions. Remain like a person who has completed his deeds.

Abandon your impure unwholesome verbal utterances as well as your chanting and recitations and remain like a mute tasting sugar.

Abandon your impure samsaric thought activity as well as your pure nirvanic thought activity and remain like a person whose heart has been torn out.

By your master's mere indication you will thus perceive the primordial dharmakaya of your mind beyond the reach of words and description.

Tsogyal, this oral instruction of mine is a teaching of liberation simultaneous with understanding.

7. The Effect of Training

The purpose of training in this is that without abandoning samsara it is liberated in itself after which the disturbing emotions are spontaneously perfected as wisdoms. Thus it has the quality of bringing enlightenment in the present moment.

8. The Reason for Training

The reason for training in this way is that you must possess the nature free from bias and partiality.

9. The Shortcoming of Not Training

The danger of not training yourself is that you will fall into the partiality of philosophical schools and have the defect of being intrinsically fettered.

Tsogyal, if your practice falls into partiality it is not the Great Perfection.

10. The Points to Be Observed

1. View as a mere convention that the root of all phenomena is contained within your own bodhichitta awareness, the primordial purity of nonarising.
2. View that this bodhichitta awareness is primordially enlightened, since it does not possess any constructs such as a watcher or an object to be watched.
3. Recognize that whatever type of thought or fixation arises within the state of this awareness is primordially empty and luminous awareness itself.
4. Recognize that whatever outer appearances may arise do not possess any identity whatsoever from the very moment they are experienced, and therefore do not transcend being the display of dharmata.
5. Experience the nonduality of objects and mind as the innate great bliss, free from accepting and rejecting, affirming or denying.

6. In particular, experience all disturbing emotions and suffering as the sacred path of enlightenment.
7. Realize that sentient beings, from the moment they are experienced, do not possess any true existence and therefore that samsara is the primordial purity of nonarising and does not have to be abandoned.
8. Realize that everything experienced as kayas and wisdoms is contained within your mind and therefore that buddhahood is beyond being accomplished.

Do this and you will become the successor of Glorious Samantabhadra.

11. *The Dividing Line between Losing and Possessing and the Method of Repairing When Damaged*

Here, there are no such efforts since you are primordially never separated from this throughout the three times.

EPILOGUE

Tsogyal, I have condensed the meaning of all the sutras, tantras, scriptures, and oral instructions into these outer, inner, and secret ways of arousing bodhichitta.
Put them into practice!
Bring them into the path!
Take them to heart!
Be in harmony with their meaning!
They are the root of the Mahayana teachings.

Thus he spoke.

This was the Mahayana training of bodhichitta entitled "The Teachings on Taking the Arousing of Bodhichitta as the Path." It was written down in Mönkha Senge Dzong.[24]
Completed.
Treasure seal.
Concealment seal.
Entrustment seal.

24

THE BODHISATTVA VOW

Chögyam Trungpa Rinpoche

Before we commit ourselves to walking the bodhisattva path, we must first walk the Hinayana or narrow path. This path begins formally with the student taking refuge in the Buddha, the Dharma, and the Sangha—that is, in the lineage of teachers, the teachings, and the community of fellow pilgrims. We expose our neurosis to our teacher, accept the teachings as the path, and humbly share our confusion with our fellow sentient beings. Symbolically, we leave our homeland, our property, and our friends. We give up the familiar ground that supports our ego, admit the helplessness of ego to control its world and secure itself. We give up our clingings to superiority and self-preservation. But taking refuge does not mean becoming dependent upon our teacher or the community or the scriptures. It means giving up searching for a home, becoming a refugee, a lonely person who must depend upon himself. A teacher or fellow traveler or the scriptures might show us where we are on a map and where we might go from there, but we have to make the journey ourselves. Fundamentally, no one can help us. If we seek to relieve our

From Chögyam Trungpa, *The Myth of Freedom* (Boston: Shambhala Publications, 1976), "The Bodhisattva Vow."

loneliness, we will be distracted from the path. Instead, we must make a relationship with loneliness until it becomes aloneness.

In the Hinayana the emphasis is on acknowledging our confusion. In the Mahayana we acknowledge that we are a buddha, an awakened one, and act accordingly, even though all kinds of doubts and problems might arise. In the scriptures, taking the bodhisattva vow and walking on the bodhisattva path is described as being the act of awakening *bodhi*, or "basic intelligence." Becoming "awake" involves seeing our confusion more clearly. We can hardly face the embarrassment of seeing our hidden hopes and fears, our frivolousness and neurosis. It is such an overcrowded world. And yet it is a very rich display. The basic idea is that, if we are going to relate with the sun, we must also relate with the clouds that obscure the sun. So the bodhisattva relates positively to both the naked sun and the clouds hiding it. But at first the clouds, the confusion, that hide the sun are more prominent. When we try to disentangle ourselves, the first thing we experience is entanglement.

The stepping-stone, the starting point in becoming awake, in joining the family of buddhas, is the taking of the bodhisattva vow. Traditionally, this vow is taken in the presence of a spiritual teacher and images of the buddhas and the scriptures in order to symbolize the presence of the lineage, the family of Buddha. One vows that from today until the attainment of enlightenment I devote my life to work with sentient beings and renounce my own attainment of enlightenment. Actually we cannot attain enlightenment until we give up the notion of "me" personally attaining it. As long as the enlightenment drama has a central character, "me," who has certain attributes, there is no hope of attaining enlightenment because it is nobody's project; it is an extraordinarily strenuous project but nobody is pushing it. Nobody is supervising it or appreciating its unfolding. We cannot pour our being from our dirty old vessel into a new clean one. If we examine our old vessel, we discover that it is not a solid thing at all. And such a realization of egolessness can only come through the practice of meditation, relating with discursive thoughts and gradually working back through the five *skandhas*. When meditation becomes a habitual way of relating with daily life, a person can take the bodhisattva vow. At that point discipline has become ingrown rather than enforced. It is like becoming involved in an interesting project upon which we automatically spend a great deal of time and effort. No one needs to encourage or threaten us; we just find ourselves intuitively doing it. Identifying with buddha nature is working with our intuition, with our ingrown discipline.

The bodhisattva vow acknowledges confusion and chaos—aggression, passion, frustration, frivolousness—as part of the path. The path is like a busy, broad highway, complete with roadblocks, accidents, construction work, and police. It is quite terrifying. Nevertheless it is majestic; it is the great path. "From today onward until the attainment of enlightenment I am willing to live with my chaos and confusion as well as with that of all other sentient beings. I am willing to share our mutual confusion." So no one is playing a one-upmanship game. The bodhisattva is a very humble pilgrim who works in the soil of samsara to dig out the jewel embedded in it.

25

THE TWO TRUTHS

Thinley Norbu Rinpoche

The space of appearance, or dharmadhatu, is free from all conceptualization, so there is no basis to the "two truths" (b.Den.pa gnyis). However, not all beings recognize this state which is free from conceptualization. In order to help beings recognize it, the Buddha distinguished between those with deluded and undeluded minds by explaining the two truths: relative truth (Kun.rdzob bden.pa)* and absolute truth (Don.-dam bden.pa).†

In order to accommodate the differences in the minds of individuals, the Buddha explained the two truths according to different systems.

According to the general Hinayana, relative truth is all phenomena, including the gross phenomena of the five skandhas. Absolute truth is the realization which comes from examining the five skandhas to find where the self or ego dwells. By examining, one realizes that this ego

---

From Thinley Norbu, *The Small Golden Key* (Boston: Shambhala Publications, 1993), "The Two Truths."

* *Kun*: all; *rdzob*: deceive or conceal; *Kun.rdzob*: conditional or relative; *bden.pa*: truth.

† *Don*: purpose, meaning; *dam.pa*: undeceived; *bden.pa*: truth

does not dwell anywhere, that it does not exist, and that the mind and all phenomena are composed of instantaneous indivisible particles. This is absolute truth according to the general Hinayana.

According to the Sautrantika (mDo.sde. pa) school of the Hinayana, relative truth is that objects do not function. Absolute truth is the essence of the functioning of phenomena.

According to the Yogacara (Sems.tsam.pa) school of the Mahayana, relative truth is parikalpita (Kun.brtag) and paratantra (gZhan.dbang). Absolute truth is parinispanna (Yongs.grub).

According to Patrül Rinpoche, relative truth is deluded mind and its objects, and absolute truth is that which is beyond the body, speech, and mind.

According to Mipham Rinpoche, within relative truth, the body can function, speech can be spoken, and the mind can understand. Within absolute truth, bodies are beyond function, speech is beyond expression, and the mind is beyond cognitive thought.

There are many other explanations of the two truths which will not be given here. One should examine the various systems carefully and decide which of them one wishes to follow.

The following is a brief explanation of the two truths of the Mahayana according to general Madhyamika and higher Madhyamika, and also according to the Vajrayana.

1. GENERAL MADHYAMIKA

The essence of relative truth according to general Madhyamika is the deluded mind and all phenomena which are the objects of deluded mind; it is whatever is true for the deluded mind.

According to this system, there are two divisions of relative truth: "inverted relative truth" (Log.pa'i kun.rdzob), which does not function, like the reflection of the moon in water, and "actual relative truth" (Yang. dag kun.rdzob), which is like the moon in the sky, which can shine and illuminate the darkness.

According to general Madhyamika, actual relative truth has four characteristics. It is:

Collectively perceived (mThun.par snang.ba): For example, water, fire, sun, and moon are perceived similarly by everyone;

Capable of effect or function (Don.byed nus.pa): For example, the earth can support all human beings;

Produced by root cause and condition (rGyu.rkyen gyis skyes.pa): For example, when a seed, which is the root cause, and water, warmth, and air, which are the contributing circumstances, come together, a plant grows; and

Nonexistent when examined (brTag na dben.pa).

The absolute according to the lower Svatantrika school (Rang.rgyud 'og.ma) of general Madhyamika is "self-awareness wisdom" (rang.rig. pa'i ye.shes). This is the realization that there is neither subject nor object. All is beyond thought or speech; all is just like a mirage.

2. HIGHER MADHYAMIKA

Inverted relative truth according to higher Madhyamika is all individual viewpoints and the conceptual doctrines of nihilists and substantialists. These are inverted relative truth because they do not function for the abandonment of samsara and the attainment of nirvana.

According to this view, all personal phenomena are inverted relative truth. For example, when a person doing devotional practice is in an unrealized state, all phenomena arise as inverted relative truth. But from the attainment of the first state of bodhisattvahood onward, during both actual meditation and after-meditation's phenomena, all arises as actual relative truth because all is unobstructed and is realized as illusion.

According to higher Madhyamika, actual relative truth also has four characteristics. It is:

Collectively perceived, like the eight examples of maya: magic, a dream, a bubble, a rainbow, lightning, the moon reflected in water, a mirage, and a city of celestial musicians (gandharvas);

Capable of effect or function, because with the realization that all phenomena are like the eight examples of maya, samsara can be abandoned and nirvana can be attained;

Produced by root cause and conditions because of the realization of the illusory nature of phenomena. The root cause of this realization is the two accumulations of merit and wisdom. The contributing circumstance, or necessary condition, is the teachings of the precious teacher; and

Nonexistent when examined because actually there is not even illusion; all phenomena, existence, nonexistence, truth, and untruth are great emptiness.

According to this view, the essence of absolute truth (Don.dam bden.pa)* is the dharmadhatu which is beyond all activity. Within absolute truth there are no distinctions because absolute truth is free from all mental activity. Sublime beings have the true realization that the essential characteristic of absolute truth is freedom from all mental activity, while ordinary philosophers and people who do not have this realization only guess at the meaning of absolute truth. For this reason, the Buddha taught two systems of absolute truth:

The *absolute truth of enumeration* (rNam.grangs don.dam bden.pa). According to the higher Svantantrika school (Rang.rgyud gong.ma), absolute truth is not explained by saying that all is just like mirage. Although there is really no truth to relative truth because absolute truth does not exist anywhere, in this system absolute truth can still be explained in relative terms as the absolute truth of enumeration by listing things as being great emptiness. For example: "Form is great emptiness, great emptiness is form, great emptiness is not different from form, form is not different from great emptiness." In the same way that form is is explained, the other skandhas of feeling, perception, intention, and consciousness are explained. All together, these are called the "sixteen great emptinesses."

The *absolute truth without enumeration* (rNam.grangs ma.yin.pa'i don.dam bden.pa). This system explains that the basis of understanding the nature of all phenomena is that it is separate from all activity, and that the wisdom of the Buddha is free from all enumeration.

According to the Prasangika (Thal.'gyur.ba) school of highest Madhyamika, in actual meditation, the absolute truth which is free from all mental activity is neither "absolute truth of enumeration" nor "absolute truth without enumeration"; there is no promise that absolute truth is anything.

Briefly, relative truth and absolute truth can be explained as follows.

Inverted relative truth. This is the ordinary state of the individual who maintains with attachment the point of view that all phenomena are real, not illusory. For example the mirage of a beautiful actress created by a magician, to which the onlookers become attached, believing it is real, is like the phenomena which arise in one's mind to which one

---

* The literal meaning of absolute truth (Don.dam bden.pa) is as follows. *Don* means purpose; the purpose is the attainment of liberation. *Dam.pa* means undeceived; with a good understanding of the nature of the mind, one is never deceived. *bDen.pa* means truth; the mind which is not mistaken, the natural mind which is undeluded and unchanging, is always true.

becomes attached, believing they are real. This is an example of the view of the ordinary individual.

Actual relative truth. This is the sublime state of the realization of the illusory nature of all phenomena. With this realization, all attachment to phenomena as being real vanishes, but in one's practice, there is still some attachment to this illusion because of previous habit. As one's practice becomes higher, even though there is still illusion, one's attachment to this illusion becomes less and less. For example, as the magician in a magic show is not attached to the beautiful actress whom he creates, so even if phenomena arise in the mind of a sublime being, there is no attachment to these phenomena as being real. This is the example of the view of the sublime being.

Absolute truth. This is the state of buddhahood in which there are neither phenomena nor absence of phenomena; neither conception of attachment nor of nonattachment. For example, one who is not affected by the apparitions, mirages, or mantras of the magician is like a buddha for whom there is neither attachment nor nonattachment. This is the example of the stage of buddhahood.

To summarize, absolute truth is the firm realization of the basic condition of the dharmata, the realization that all phenomena are beyond existing and not existing, eternalism and nihilism, being true or false, beyond all activity, and are free from the two extremes of knowing and not knowing.

The Prajñaparamita, the two truths of higher Madhyamika, and so on, all teach that relative truth is inseparable from absolute truth and absolute truth is inseparable from relative truth; in reality, there is only one truth.

For the Buddha's wisdom mind, there is no difference between object and subject, but because the wisdom mind of ordinary individuals is obscured, we must practice systematically. We must understand that the basic condition of all phenomena is illusion. We must realize that actually it neither exists nor does not exist, but is like the sky. The understanding that ultimately the two truths are inseparable is the relative truth which is understood by the sublime mind.

The self-nature of the mind which understands relative truth is absolute truth, because if we examine the nature of the thoughts which arise in the mind, we will see that they do not exist anywhere: they neither exist nor do not exist, they are unobstructed, unborn, unceasing, not permanent, not coming, not going, their meanings are not distinct or separate, their meanings are not indistinct or nonseparate: they are completely beyond all activity. This is the dharmata, and this dharmata is the absolute truth. Outside, inside, shape, color, and so on, do not exist anywhere; all is like the sky.

Whoever realizes actual relative truth also realizes absolute truth, because actual relative truth and absolute truth are inseparable. Ultimately, there are not two truths, because in Dharmadhatu there is no basis for expression of the two truths. Buddhahood is Wisdom Mind within which there is no dualistic mind. Where there is no dualistic mind, there are no two truths. When we remain in natural Wisdom Mind or awareness of inseparable great emptiness and luminosity, there are not two truths, because this is Dharmadhatu.

3. VAJRAYANA

According to the higher Vajrayana, inverted relative truth is attachment to all phenomena as being ordinary reality. Actual relative truth is seeing all phenomena as transformed into wisdom deities and their purelands by visualizing or meditating. Thus, all phenomena cannot go beyond the great empty expanse of the Dharmadhatu: this is absolute truth.

26

THE SUTRA OF THE HEART OF
TRANSCENDENT KNOWLEDGE

Thus have I heard. Once the Blessed One was dwelling in Rajagriha at
Vulture Peak mountain, together with a great gathering of the Sangha
of monks and a great gathering of the Sangha of bodhisattvas. At that
time, the Blessed One entered the samadhi that expresses the Dharma
called "profound illumination," and at the same time noble Avalokiteshvara, the bodhisattva mahasattva, while practicing the profound Prajñaparamita, saw in this way: he saw the five skandhas to be empty of
nature.

Then, through the power of the Buddha, venerable Shariputra said
to noble Avalokiteshvara, the bodhisattva mahasattva, "How should a
son or daughter of noble family train, who wishes to practice the profound Prajñaparamita?"

Addressed in this way, noble Avalokiteshvara, the bodhisattva mahasattva, said to venerable Shariputra, "O Shariputra, a son or daughter
of noble family who wishes to practice the profound Prajñaparamita
should see in this way: seeing the five skandhas to be empty of nature.

From the Prajñaparamita literature, translated by Chögyam Trungpa Rinpoche and
the Nalanda Translation Committee.

Form is emptiness; emptiness also is form. Emptiness is no other than form; form is no other than emptiness. In the same way, feeling, perception, formation, and consciousness are emptiness. Thus, Shariputra, all dharmas are emptiness. There are no characteristics. There is no birth and no cessation. There is no impurity and no purity. There is no decrease and no increase. Therefore, Shariputra, in emptiness, there is no form, no feeling, no perception, no formation, no consciousness; no eye, no ear, no nose, no tongue, no body, no mind; no appearance, no sound, no smell, no taste, no touch, no dharmas; no eye dhatu up to no mind dhatu, no dhatu of dharmas, no mind consciousness dhatu; no ignorance, no end of ignorance up to no old age and death, no end of old age and death; no suffering, no origin of suffering, no cessation of suffering, no path, no wisdom, no attainment, and no nonattainment. Therefore, Shariputra, since the bodhisattvas have no attainment, they abide by means of Prajñaparamita. Since there is no obscuration of mind, there is no fear. They transcend falsity and attain complete nirvana. All the buddhas of the three times, by means of Prajñaparamita, fully awaken to unsurpassable, true, complete enlightenment. Therefore, the great mantra of Prajñaparamita, the mantra of great insight, the unsurpassed mantra, the unequaled mantra, the mantra that calms all suffering, should be known as truth, since there is no deception. The Prajñaparamita mantra is said in this way:

OM GATE GATE PARAGATE PARASAMGATE BODHI SVAHA

Thus, Shariputra, the bodhisattva mahasattva should train in the profound Prajñaparamita."

Then the Blessed One arose from that samadhi and praised noble Avalokiteshvara, the bodhisattva mahasattva, saying, "Good, good, O son of noble family; thus it is, O son of noble family, thus it is. One should practice the profound Prajñaparamita just as you have taught and all the tathagatas will rejoice."

When the Blessed One had said this, venerable Shariputra and noble Avalokiteshvara, the bodhisattva mahasattva, that whole assembly and the world with its gods, humans, asuras, and gandharvas rejoiced and praised the words of the Blessed One.

27

SHUNYATA

Chögyam Trungpa Rinpoche

Cutting through our conceptualized versions of the world with the sword of prajña, we discover shunyata—nothingness, emptiness, voidness, the absence of duality and conceptualization. The best known of the Buddha's teachings on this subject are presented in the *Prajñaparamita-hridaya*, also called the *Heart Sutra*; but interestingly in this sutra the Buddha hardly speaks a word at all. At the end of the discourse he merely says, "Well said, well said," and smiles. He created a situation in which the teaching of shunyata was set forth by others, rather than himself being the actual spokesman. He did not impose his communication but created the situation in which teaching could occur, in which his disciples were inspired to discover and experience shunyata. There are twelve styles of presenting the Dharma and this is one of them.

This sutra tells of Avalokiteshvara, the bodhisattva who represents compassion and skillful means, and Shariputra, the great arhat who represents prajña, knowledge. There are certain differences between the Tibetan and Japanese translations and the Sanskrit original, but all

---

From Chögyam Trungpa, *Cutting Through Spiritual Materialism* (Boston: Shambhala Publications, 1973), "Shunyata."

versions make the point that Avalokiteshvara was compelled to awaken to shunyata by the overwhelming force of prajña. Then Avalokiteshvara spoke with Shariputra, who represents the scientific-minded person or precise knowledge. The teachings of the Buddha were put under Shariputra's microscope, which is to say that these teachings were not accepted on blind faith but were examined, practiced, tried, and proved.

Avalokiteshvara said: "O Shariputra, form is empty, emptiness is form; form is no other than emptiness, emptiness is no other than form." We need not go into the details of their discourse, but we can examine this statement about form and emptiness, which is the main point of the sutra. And so we should be very clear and precise about the meaning of the term "form."

Form is that which *is* before we project our concepts onto it. It is the original state of "what is here," the colorful, vivid, impressive, dramatic, aesthetic qualities that exist in every situation. Form could be a maple leaf falling from a tree and landing on a mountain river; it could be full moonlight, a gutter in the street, or a garbage pile. These things are "what is," and they are all in one sense the same: they are all forms, they are all objects, they are just what is. Evaluations regarding them are only created later in our minds. If we really look at these things as they are, they are just forms.

So form is empty. But empty of what? Form is empty of our preconceptions, empty of our judgments. If we do not evaluate and categorize the maple leaf falling and landing on the stream as opposed to the garbage heap in New York, then they are *there*, what *is*. They are empty of preconception. They are precisely what they are, of course! Garbage is garbage, a maple leaf is a maple leaf, "what is" is "what is." Form is empty if we see it in the absence of our own personal interpretations of it.

But emptiness is also form. That is a very outrageous remark. We thought we had managed to sort everything out, we thought we had managed to see that everything is the "same" if we take out our preconceptions. That made a beautiful picture: everything bad and everything good that we see are both good. Fine. Very smooth. But the next point is that emptiness is also form, so we have to re-examine. The emptiness of the maple leaf is also form; it is not really empty. The emptiness of the garbage heap is also form. To try to see these things as empty is also to clothe them in concept. Form comes back. It was too easy, taking away all concept, to conclude that everything simply is what is. That could be an escape, another way of comforting ourselves. We have to actually *feel* things as they are, the qualities of the garbage heap*ness* and the qualities of the maple leaf*ness,* the *isness* of things. We have to feel them properly, not just trying to put a veil of emptiness over them. That does not help at all. We have to see the "isness" of what is there, the raw and rugged qualities of things precisely as they are. This is a very accurate way of seeing the world. So first we wipe away all our heavy preconceptions, and then we even wipe away the subtleties of such words as "empty," leaving us nowhere, completely with what is.

Finally we come to the conclusion that form is just form and emptiness is just emptiness, which has been described in the sutra as seeing that form is no other than emptiness, emptiness is no other than form; they are indivisible. We see that looking for beauty or philosophical meaning to life is merely a way of justifying ourselves, saying that things are not so bad as we think. Things *are* as bad as we think! Form is form, emptiness is emptiness, things are just what they are, and we do not have to try to see them in the light of some sort of profundity. Finally we come down to earth, we see things as they are. This does not mean having an inspired mystical vision with archangels, cherubs, and sweet music playing. But things are seen as they *are,* in their *own* qualities. So shunyata in this case is the complete absence of concepts or filters of any kind, the absence even of the "form is empty" and the "emptiness is form" conceptualization. It is a question of seeing the world in a direct way without desiring "higher" consciousness or significance or profundity. It is just directly perceiving things literally, as they are in their own right.

We might ask how we could apply this teaching to everyday life. There is a story that when the Buddha gave his first discourse on shunyata, some of the arhats had heart attacks and died from the impact of the teaching. In sitting meditation these arhats had experienced absorption in space, but they were still dwelling upon space. Inasmuch as they were still dwelling upon something, there was still an experience and an experiencer. The shunyata principle involves not dwelling upon anything, not distinguishing between this and that, being suspended nowhere.

If we see things as they are, then we do not have to interpret or analyze them further; we do not need to try to understand things by imposing spiritual experience or philosophical ideas upon them. As a famous Zen master said: "When I eat, I eat; when I sleep, I sleep." Just do what you do, completely, fully. To do so is to be a *rishi,* an honest, truthful person, a straightforward person who never distinguishes between this and that. He does things literally, directly, as they are. He eats whenever he wants to eat; he sleeps whenever he wants to sleep. Sometimes the Buddha is described as the Maharishi, the Great Rishi who was not trying to be truthful but simply was true in his open state.

The interpretation of shunyata which we have been discussing is the view of the *Madhyamika* or "Middle Way" philosophical school founded by Nagarjuna. It is a description of an experiential reality that can never be accurately described because words simply are not the experience. Words or concepts only *point* to partial aspects of experience. In fact, it is dubious that one can even speak of "experiencing" reality, since this would imply a separation between the experiencer and the experience. And finally, it is questionable whether one can even speak of "reality" because this would imply the existence of some objective knower outside and separate from it, as though reality were a nameable thing with set limits and boundaries. Thus the Madhyamika school simply speaks of the *tathata*, "as it is." Nagarjuna much preferred to approach truth by taking the arguments of other philosophical schools on their own terms and logically reducing them *ad absurdum*, rather than by himself offering any definitions of reality.

There are several other major philosophical approaches to the problems of truth and reality which preceded and influenced the development of the Madhyamika school. These lines of thought find their expression not only in the earlier Buddhist philosophical schools but also in the approaches of theistic Hinduism, Vedantism, Islam, Christianity, and most other religious and philosophical traditions. From the point of view of the Madhyamika school, these other approaches can be grouped together into three categories: the eternalists, the nihilists, and the atomists. The Madhyamikas viewed the first two of these approaches as being false, and the third as being only partially true.

The first and most obvious of these three "misconceptions of the nature of reality" is eternalism, an approach that is often that of the more naive versions of theism. Eternalistic doctrines view phenomena as containing some sort of eternal essence. Things are born and die, yet they contain an essence that does not perish. The quality of eternal existence must adhere to some *thing*, so the holders of this doctrine usually subscribe to belief in God, a soul, an atman, an ineffable self. Thus the believer asserts that something does exist as solid, ongoing, and eternal. It is reassuring to have something solid to hang on to, to dwell upon, a fixed way of understanding the world and one's relationship to it.

However, eventually the believer in eternalistic doctrines may become disillusioned with a God he has never met, a soul or essence he cannot find. Which brings us to the next and somewhat more sophisticated misconception of reality: nihilism. This view holds that everything is generated out of nothingness, mystery. Sometimes this approach appears as both theistic and atheistic assertions that the Godhead is unknowable. The sun shines, throws light upon the earth, helps life to grow, provides heat and light. But we can find no origin to life; there is no logical starting point from which the universe began. Life and the world are merely the dance of maya, illusion. Things are simply generated spontaneously out of nowhere. So nothingness seems important in this approach: an unknowable reality somehow beyond apparent phenomena. The universe takes place mysteriously; there is no real explanation at all. Possibly a nihilist would say that the human mind cannot comprehend such mystery. Thus, in this view of reality, mystery is treated as a *thing*. The idea that there is no answer is relied upon and dwelt upon as the answer.

The nihilistic approach evokes the psychological attitude of fatalism. You understand logically that if you do something, things happen in reaction to it. You see a continuity of cause and effect, a chain reaction over which you have no control. This chain-reactive process springs from the mystery of "nothingness." Therefore, if you murder someone, it was your karma to murder and was inevitable, foreordained. For that matter if you do a good deed, it has nothing to do with whether or not you are awake. Everything springs from this mysterious "nothingness" which is the nihilistic approach to reality. It is a very naive view: one leaves everything to mystery. Whenever we are not quite certain of things that are beyond the scope of our conceptualized ideas, then we begin to panic. We are afraid of our own uncertainty, and we attempt to fill the gap with something else. The something else is usually a philosophical belief—in this case, the belief in mystery. We very eagerly, very hungrily search for nothingness, surveying every dark corner in our attempts to find it. But we find only the crumbs. We find nothing more than that. It is very mysterious. As long as we continue to look for a conceptual answer there will always be areas of mystery, which mystery is itself another concept.

Whether we are eternalists or nihilists or atomists, we constantly assume that there is a "mystery," something that we do not know: the meaning of life, the origin of the universe, the key to happiness. We struggle after this mystery, trying to become a person who knows or possesses it, naming it "God," the "soul," "atman," "Brahman," "shunyata," and so on. Certainly this is not the Madhyamika approach to reality, though the early Hinayana schools of Buddhism to some extent fell into this trap, which is why their approach is considered only a partial truth.

The Hinayana approach to reality sees impermanence as the great mystery: that which is born must change and die. However, one cannot see impermanence itself but only its manifestation in form. Thus the Hinayanists describe the universe in terms of atoms existing in space and moments existing in time. As such, they are atomistic pluralists. The Hinayana equivalent of shunyata is the understanding of the transitory and insubstantial nature of form, so Hinayana meditation practice is twofold: contemplation of the many aspects of impermanence—the processes of birth, growth, decay, and death, and their elaborations; and mindfulness practice that sees the impermanence of mental events. The arhat views mental events and material objects and begins to see them as momentary and atomistic happenings. Thus he discovers that there is no permanent substance or solid thing as such. This approach errs in conceptualizing the existence of entities relative to each other, the existence of "this" relative to "that."

We can see the three elements of eternalism, nihilism, and atomistic pluralism in different combinations in almost all the major philosophies and religions of the world. From the Madhyamika point of view, these three misconceptions of reality are virtually inescapable as long as one searches for an answer to an assumed question, as long as one seeks to probe the so-called mystery of life. Belief in anything is simply a way of labeling the mystery. Yogachara, a Mahayana philosophical school, attempted to eliminate this mystery by finding a union of mystery and the phenomenal world.

The main thrust of the Yogachara school is epistemological. For this school the mystery is intelligence, that which knows. The Yogacharyans solved the mystery by positing the indivisible union of intelligence and phenomena. Thus there is no *individual* knower; rather everything is "self-known." There is only "one mind," which the Yogacharyans called "self-luminous cognition," and both thoughts and emotions and people and trees are aspects of it. Thus this school is also referred to in the traditional literature as the *citta-matra* or "Mind Only" school.

The Yogachara school was the first school of Buddhist thought to transcend the division between the knower and the known. Thus its adherents explain confusion and suffering as springing from the mistaken belief in an individual knower. If a person believes that he knows the world, then the one mind appears to be split, though actually its clear surface is only muddied. The confused person feels that he has thoughts about and reactions to external phenomena and so is caught in a constant action and reaction situation. The enlightened person realizes that thoughts and emotions on the one hand, and the so-called external world on the other, are *both* the "play of the mind." Thus the enlightened person is not caught in the dualism of subject and object, internal and external, knower and known, I and other. Everything is *self*-known.

However, Nagarjuna contested the Yogacharin "mind-only" proposition and, in fact, questioned the very existence of "mind" altogether. He studied the twelve volumes of the Prajñaparamita scriptures, which came out of the second turning of the Wheel of Doctrine by the Buddha, the teaching of the middle portion of his life. Nagarjuna's conclusions are summed up in the principle of "nondwelling," the main principle of the Madhyamika school. He said that any philosophical view could be refuted, that one must not dwell upon any answer or description of reality, whether extreme or moderate, including the notion of "one mind." Even to say that nondwelling is the answer is delusory, for one must not dwell upon nondwelling. Nagarjuna's way was one of nonphilosophy, which was not simply another philosophy at all. He said, "The wise should not dwell in the middle either."

Madhyamika philosophy is a critical view of the Yogacharin theory that everything is an aspect of mind. The Madhyamika argument runs: "In order to say that mind exists or that everything is the play of the one mind, there must be someone watching mind, the knower of mind who vouches for its existence." Thus the whole of Yogachara is necessarily a theory on the part of this watcher. But according to the Yogacharyans' own philosophy of self-luminous cognition, subjective thoughts *about* an object are delusive, there being no subject or object but only the one mind of which the watcher is a part. Therefore, it is impossible to state that the one mind exists. Like the physical eye, self-luminous cognition cannot see itself, just as a razor cannot cut itself. By the Yogacharyans' own admission, there is no one to know that the one mind exists.

Then what can we say about mind or reality? Since there is no one to perceive a mind or reality, the notion of existence in terms of "things" and "form" is delusory; there is no reality, no perceiver of reality, and no thoughts derived from perception of reality. Once we have taken away this preconception of the existence of mind and reality, then situations emerge clearly, as they are. There is no one to watch, no one to know anything. Reality just *is,* and this is what is meant by the term "shunyata." Through this insight the watcher that separates us from the world is removed.

How then does belief in an "I" and the whole neurotic process begin? Roughly, according to the Madhyamikas, whenever a perception of form occurs, there is an immediate reaction of fascination and uncertainty on the part of an implied perceiver of the form. This reaction is almost instantaneous. It takes only a fraction of a fraction of a second. And as soon as we have established recognition of what the thing is, our next response is to give it a name. With the name of course comes concept. We tend to conceptualize the object, which means that at this point we are no longer able to perceive things as they actually are. We have created a kind of padding, a filter or veil between ourselves and the object. This is what prevents the maintenance of continual awareness both during and after meditation practice. This veil removes us from panoramic awareness and the presence of the meditative state, because again and again we are unable to see things as they are. We feel compelled to name, to translate, to think discursively, and this activity takes us further away from direct and accurate perception. So shunyata is not merely awareness of what we are and how we are in relation to such and such an object, but rather it is clarity that transcends conceptual padding and unnecessary confusions. One is no longer fascinated by the object nor involved as a subject. It is freedom from *this* and *that*. What remains is open space, the absence of the this-and-that dichotomy. This is what is meant by the Middle Way or Madhyamika.

The experience of shunyata cannot be developed without first having worked through the narrow path of discipline and technique. Technique is necessary to start with, but it is also necessary at some stage for the technique to fall away. From the ultimate point of view the whole process of learning and practice is quite unnecessary. We could perceive the absence of ego at a single glance. But we would not accept such a simple truth. In other words, we have to learn in order to unlearn. The whole process is that of undoing the ego. We start by learning to deal with neurotic thoughts and emotions. Then false concepts are removed through the understanding of emptiness, of openness. This is the experience of shunyata. Shunyata in Sanskrit means literally "void" or "emptiness," that is to say, "space," the absence of all conceptualized attitudes. Thus Nagarjuna says in his *Commentary on Madhyamika*: "Just as the sun dispels darkness, the perfect sage has conquered the false habits of mind. He does not see the mind or thought derived from the mind."

The *Heart Sutra* ends with "the great spell" or mantra. It says in the

Tibetan version: "Therefore the mantra of transcendent knowledge, the mantra of deep insight, the unsurpassed mantra, the unequaled mantra, the mantra that calms all suffering should be known as truth, for there is no deception." The potency of this mantra comes not from some imagined mystical or magical power of the words but from their meaning. It is interesting that after discussing shunyata—form is empty, emptiness is form, form is no other than emptiness, emptiness is identical with form, and so on—the sutra goes on to discuss mantra. At the beginning it speaks in terms of the meditative state, and finally it speaks of mantra or words. This is because in the beginning we must develop a confidence in our understanding, clearing out all preconceptions; nihilism, eternalism, all beliefs have to be cut through, transcended. And when a person is completely exposed, fully unclothed, fully unmasked, completely naked, completely opened—at that very moment he sees the power of the word. When the basic, absolute, ultimate hypocrisy has been unmasked, then one really begins to see the jewel shining in its brightness: the energetic, living quality of openness, the living quality of surrender, the living quality of renunciation.

Renunciation in this instance is not just throwing away, but, having thrown everything away, we begin to feel the living quality of peace. And this particular peace is not feeble peace, feeble openness, but it has a strong character, an invincible quality, an unshakable quality, because it admits no gaps of hypocrisy. It is complete peace in all directions, so that not even a speck of a dark corner exists for doubt and hypocrisy. Complete openness is complete victory because we do not fear, we do not try to defend ourselves at all. Therefore this is a great mantra. One would have thought that instead of saying, *Om gate gate paragate parasamgate bodhi svaha,* this mantra would say something about shunyata—*Om shunyata mahashunyata*—or something of the sort. Instead it says, *Gate gate*—"gone, gone, gone beyond, completely gone." This is much stronger than saying "shunyata," because the word *shunyata* might imply a philosophical interpretation. Instead of formulating something philosophical, this mantra exposes that which lies beyond philosophy. Therefore it is *gate gate*—"gone, given up, got rid of, opened." The first *gate* is "rid of the veil of conflicting emotions." The second *gate* represents the veil of primitive beliefs about reality. That is, the first *gate* represents the idea that "form is empty," and the second *gate* refers to "emptiness is form." Then the next word of the mantra is *paragate*—"gone beyond, completely exposed." Now form is form—*paragate*—and it is not only that form but emptiness is emptiness, *parasamgate*—

"completely gone beyond." *Bodhi*. *Bodhi* here means "completely awake." The meaning is "given up, completely unmasked, naked, completely open." *Svaha* is a traditional ending for mantras which means, "So be it." "Gone, gone, gone beyond, completely exposed, awake, so be it."

28

EGOLESSNESS

Chögyam Trungpa Rinpoche

The effort to secure our happiness, to maintain ourselves in relation to something else, is the process of ego. But this effort is futile because there are continual gaps in our seemingly solid world, continual cycles of death and rebirth, constant change. The sense of continuity and solidity of self is an illusion. There is really no such thing as ego, soul, or *atman*. It is a succession of confusions that create ego. The process that is ego actually consists of a flicker of confusion, a flicker of aggression, a flicker of grasping—all of which exist only in the moment. Since we cannot hold on to the present moment, we cannot hold on to me and mine and make them solid things.

The experience of oneself relating to other things is actually a momentary discrimination, a fleeting thought. If we generate these fleeting thoughts fast enough, we can create the illusion of continuity and solidity. It is like watching a movie; the individual film frames are played so quickly that they generate the illusion of continual movement. So we build up an idea, a preconception, that self and other are solid and

From Chögyam Trungpa, *The Myth of Freedom* (Boston: Shambhala Publications, 1976), "Egolessness."

continuous. And once we have this idea, we manipulate our thoughts to confirm it and are afraid of any contrary evidence. It is this fear of exposure, this denial of impermanence that imprisons us. It is only by acknowledging impermanence that there is the chance to die and the space to be reborn and the possibility of appreciating life as a creative process.

There are two stages to understanding egolessness. In the first stage we perceive that ego does not exist as a solid entity, that it is impermanent, constantly changing, that it was our concepts that made it seem solid. So we conclude that ego does not exist. But we still have formulated a subtle concept of egolessness. There is still a watcher of the egolessness, a watcher to identify with it and maintain his existence. The second stage is seeing through this subtle concept and dropping the watcher. So true egolessness is the absence of the concept of egolessness. In the first stage there is a sense of someone perceiving egolessness. In the second, even the perceiver does not exist. In the first, we perceive that there is no fixed entity because everything is relative to something else. In the second stage there is the understanding that the notion of relativity needs a watcher to perceive it, to confirm it, which introduces another relative notion, the watcher and the watched.

To say that egolessness does exist because things are constantly changing is quite feeble, since we still hold on to change as something solid. Egolessness is not simply the idea that since there is discontinuity, therefore there is nothing to hang on to. True egolessness involves the nonexistence of the discontinuity as well. We cannot hang on to the idea of discontinuity either. In fact, discontinuity really does not operate. Our perception of discontinuity is the product of insecurity; it is concept. So too is any idea about the oneness behind or within phenomena.

The idea of egolessness has often been used to obscure the reality of birth, suffering, and death. The problem is that once we have a notion of egolessness and a notion of pain, birth, and death, then we can easily entertain or justify ourselves by saying that pain does not exist because there is no ego to experience it, that birth and death do not exist because there is no one to witness them. This is just cheap escapism. The philosophy of shunyata has often been distorted by the presentation of the idea that: "There is no one to suffer, so who cares? If you suffer, it must be your illusion." This is pure opinion, speculation. We can read about it, we can think about it, but when we actually suffer, can we remain indifferent? Of course not; suffering is stronger than our petty opinions. A true understanding of egolessness cuts through opinion. The absence of a notion of egolessness allows us to fully experience pain, birth, and death because then there are no philosophical paddings.

The whole idea is that we must drop all reference points, all concepts of what is or what should be. Then it is possible to experience the uniqueness and vividness of phenomena directly. There is tremendous room to experience things, to allow experience to occur and pass away. Movement happens within vast space. Whatever happens, pleasure and pain, birth and death and so forth, are not interfered with but are experienced in their fullest flavor. Whether they are sweet or sour, they are experienced completely, without philosophical overlays or emotional attitudes to make things seem lovable or presentable.

We are never trapped in life, because there are constant opportunities for creativity, challenges for improvisation. Ironically, by seeing clearly and acknowledging our egolessness, we may discover that suffering contains bliss, impermanence contains continuity or eternity, and egolessness contains the earth quality of solid being. But this transcendental bliss, continuity, and beingness is not based on fantasies, ideas, or fears.

29

THE NATURE OF THE
MAHAMUDRA OF PERCEPTION

Khenchen Thrangu Rinpoche

Lord Buddha taught the Dharma in a way that was adapted to the mental capacity of his listeners. He taught beginners how to practice in a gradual fashion so that they could start at whatever level they happened to be at and progress step by step. When the Buddha turned the Wheel of the first set of teachings, he focused on the *Four Noble Truths*. The first Noble Truth is the truth of suffering, which we should all be able to easily understand. The second is that suffering has a cause, which is karmic actions and disturbing emotions. The third Noble Truth is that suffering can be brought to an end; and the fourth describes the way that leads to the cessation of suffering, called the path. In order to help beginners actually apply the teachings, the Lord Buddha began by introducing egolessness, the absence of the individual self.

It is a fact that ordinary sentient beings do suffer. They have problems and troubles, hardships and grief. Most of this suffering takes place in the realm of thought. The most difficult and troublesome thoughts

Adapted from Thrangu Rinpoche, *Songs of Naropa* (Boudhanath: Rangjung Yeshe Publications, 1997).

are disturbing emotions. One of the main disturbing emotions is anger, or a hostile frame of mind. Out of this anger, we may use harsh words or act out physically, throwing or breaking something or hitting someone. Sometimes our negative actions are motivated by attachment or greed. Other times they come from ignorance, indecision, or being unclear, stupid, or deluded. Sometimes we feel conceited or proud, sometimes jealous or competitive. So, do you understand the sequence of events? First, disturbing emotions occupy our minds, making us unsettled. Next, we express them through words, complicating matters. The worst situation is when we physically act out these unhealthy thought patterns. Disturbing emotions create a tremendous amount of problems, for ourselves and others. All of these disturbing emotions are based on ego-clinging—the feeling "Me, I am the most important." Once we understand this point clearly, we may decide to consciously do the opposite, saying to ourselves: "I will no longer consider myself important." Unfortunately, this doesn't solve the problem. Merely thinking "I shouldn't behave like that" is not in itself a direct remedy against ego-clinging. A thought cannot eliminate the concept of self.

Relative bodhichitta is a way to reduce disturbing emotions. By our shifting our attitude away from selfishness and aspiring to help others, disturbing emotions can be reduced. This type of training diminishes their strength, but it doesn't totally uproot them. That is why that type of bodhichitta is called "relative" or superficial. It only decreases disturbing emotions, but does not bring them to an end.

Ultimate bodhichitta, on the other hand, brings disturbing emotions to a permanent end. If we are introduced to and become certain about the nature of our mind, we can fully understand that there is no such thing as a self. Without carefully investigating, however, we tend to believe in the existence of a self. We're not very clear on exactly what constitutes "myself," assigning that term to all sorts of different things—our body, our consciousness, or some unclear mixture of these factors. We must practice to the point that we become clear of the fact that whatever the word *me* refers to, this object is not to be found anywhere at all. First we must learn to look for this "me." Next, we need to become completely certain that there is no such thing as an I or a self. At that point, the very basis for disturbing emotions and selfishness is totally eliminated from the very root.

This is why the Buddha taught in his very first set of teachings how we can cultivate insight into egolessness. In the second set of teachings, the Buddha went even further. He taught that it is not only the individual self that is nonexistent. Everything, all phenomena, all objects, as well as consciousness itself, is devoid of any true identity. All things have the nature of emptiness. Discovering this for ourselves changes our perspective. When we fully actualize emptiness, we are no longer obstructed by anything. Our minds are able to remain at great peace, at total ease. This is a wider or more expansive insight than that of simply realizing egolessness.

The understanding that all things are emptiness is entirely correct. However, we might misconstrue the meaning of emptiness to mean nothingness, a complete voidness. This misunderstanding fixates on the thought that all things are a blank, nothing whatsoever, which is not correct. To remedy this, the Buddha taught that not only is the identity of all things utterly empty; it is emptiness itself. This emptiness, by nature, has the capacity to know, to experience, to cognize. That is the wakeful wisdom quality that is indivisible from emptiness itself. This is the intent of the third set of teachings, the final turning of the Wheel of Dharma.

Among the teachings given by the great master Naropa is one that expresses the view of Mahamudra under three headings. I will explain the first one, called "Stating the nature of the Mahamudra of perception."

Concerning what is called Mahamudra:
All things are your own mind.
Seeing objects as external is a mistaken concept;
Like a dream, they are empty of concreteness.

What does it mean when we use the word *Mahamudra*? What is it that we are talking about? What does this term refer to? What is Mahamudra about? This verse introduces the nature of the Mahamudra of perception. Actually, what is it that we as sentient beings perceive? Through what is called the eye consciousness, we perceive visual objects and see sights. Because we have the capacity to hear through our ears, the ear consciousness, we hear sounds. We have the capacity to taste with our tongues, which is called the tongue consciousness. Through our nose consciousness we can experience smell, and through our body consciousness we can touch. In general Buddhist terminology these are labeled the five sense consciousnesses, or the five sense cognitions. The mind experiences the world through these five senses. However, our mind consciousness itself does not experience sights, smells, sounds, tastes, or textures directly. What is being perceived is a mental impression of these experiences. Based on that mental image, we create secondary thoughts about past, present, and future. We determine what we like and don't like, what should be accepted or rejected. That activity is named the sixth consciousness. Sometimes it is called the ideational consciousness, other times simply mind consciousness. Thus there are six consciousnesses altogether.

The term "all things" refers not only to mental objects but to the objects of all six consciousnesses—sights, sounds, smells, tastes, and textures, as well as mental objects. What is normally being experienced is an impression or an image that takes place in the mind. Not knowing this, we tend to believe, for example, that when the object of the eye consciousness is presented to the mind, this perceived object is somewhere outside. It is apprehended as being outside of ourselves; and the perceiver, the mind, is considered to be somewhere inside. Likewise, whatever quality we attach to these perceived objects as being either pleasant or unpleasant, good or bad, is similarly apprehended as a "real" entity that exists outside of ourselves.

This is how it seems to be, in that this is how we normally perceive. But is this the real state of things? No, it isn't, because it only seems like what we see is outside. Actually, what we experience is an impression that arises in or exists in our own mind. Whether it's something that is seen, heard, smelled, tasted, or felt physically, all these impressions or perceptions take place within our mind. All perceptions, be they the objects of the six consciousnesses or all the different thoughts and emotional reactions that might arise, are not external to ourselves; they are mental occurrences that take place in our own mind. Therefore, all things are your own mind. Believing objects to be external is a mistaken concept. To believe that what is being experienced is other than our own perception, some object that exists by itself, apart from and separate from our experience of it, is a deluded idea.

The great masters give all sorts of different teachings to help us understand how things actually are. They may ask us to use our own intelligence to figure out whether the normal way of experiencing is true or not. For example, look at a pillar in a room. The pillar appears to us through our seeing, our visual cognition, and in our minds the image of the pillar is perceived. Based on that we form the thought "There is a pillar in the room." The real proof of whether this is or isn't true is our own experience. The great Buddhist logicians Chandrakirti and Dignaga explained that we use our personal impressions as the final authentication of reality. They state that the sole evidence beings have that things are perceived as being outside is because we say, "I see them; therefore they exist." There is no other way to validate a perception. That is called the proof of clearly knowing. Based on this reasoning, there is no reason to believe that things exist outside our own experience or are separate from their being known.

Mahamudra is the catalyst that changes our normal comprehension. The starting point in the tradition is proof through experience. The belief that things are outside of ourselves is nothing other than a mental perception. When examined, it becomes apparent that this mere presence has no reality to it. It is likewise with the perceiving mind, in that it does not possess any concrete existence. When mind is pointed out and recognized, it is possible to realize that both perceptions and the perceiver are nonexistent.

We can discover this through intellectual reasoning or through direct experience. The end result is the same. The Buddha and many great masters used the analogy of a dream to facilitate the understanding of the essential unreality of all things. Whatever we perceive during the daytime, we also can experience at night in dreams. We can see and vividly experience mountains, houses, people, and all sorts of different things. Do they really exist because we see them in our dreams? Are there actually mountains and houses while we dream? No, it only seems like there are. While they don't really exist, still, for the dreamer it feels as if they do. That is why it is said that all things are like a dream— because, just as in a dream, all impressions of external objects in our waking experience appear only in the mind. Therefore, they're empty of concreteness. This point covered the nature of the Mahamudra of perception.

30

WISDOM THROUGH MEDITATION

Patrül Rinpoche

Through meditation, as you gain practical experience of what you have understood intellectually, the true realization of the natural state develops in you without any mistake. Certainty is born from within. Liberated from confining doubts and hesitations, you see the very face of the natural state.

Having first eliminated all your doubts through hearing and reflection, you come to the practical experience of meditation and see everything as empty forms without any substantiality, as in the eight similes of illusion:

As in a dream, all the external objects perceived with the five senses are not there, but appear through delusion.

As in a magic show, things are made to appear by a temporary conjunction of causes, circumstances, and connections.

As in a visual aberration, things appear to be there, yet there is nothing.

As in a mirage, things appear but are not real.

From Patrül Rinpoche, *The Words of My Perfect Teacher* (Boston: Shambhala Publications, 1998, and San Francisco: HarperSanFrancisco, 1994), "Wisdom through Meditation."

As in an echo, things can be perceived but there is nothing there, either outside or inside.

As in a city of gandharvas, there is neither a dwelling nor anyone to dwell.

As in a reflection, things appear but have no reality of their own.

As in a city created by magic, there are all sorts of appearances but they are not really there.

Seeing all the objects of your perception in this way, you come to understand that all these appearances are false by their very nature. When you look into the nature of the subject that perceives them—the mind—those objects that appear to it do not stop appearing, but the concepts that take them as having any true existence subside. To leave the mind in the realization of the nature of reality, empty yet clear like the sky, is transcendent wisdom.

To explain the six transcendent perfections in detail, each one is divided into three, making a total of eighteen sections. The category of material generosity has three sections of its own, making twenty sections altogether. If we add transcendent means, that makes twenty-one; transcendent strength, twenty-two; transcendent aspiration, twenty-three; and transcendent primal wisdom, twenty-four.*

Going into even more detail, each of the six transcendent perfections can be divided into six, making thirty-six sections. We can see how this works by examining the section on the giving of Dharma in transcendent generosity.

When the teacher who teaches, the Dharma to be taught, and the disciple to whom the teaching is to be transmitted come together, explaining the teaching is transcendent *generosity*. That the teacher does not seek gain or honor for teaching the Dharma, and does not contaminate what he is doing either with self-aggrandizement, resentment of the position of others, or any other negative emotion, is transcendent *discipline*. That he repeats the meaning of a phrase over and over again and ignores all difficulty and fatigue is transcendent *patience*. That he teaches at the appointed time without giving way to laziness and procrastination is transcendent *diligence*. That he explains his subject without letting his mind get distracted from the words and their meaning,

---

* The transcendent perfections of means (*thabs*), strength (*stobs*), aspiration (*smon lam*), and primal wisdom (*ye shes*) are added to the usual six to make what are called the ten transcendent perfections.

without making any errors, and without adding or omitting anything is transcendent *concentration*. That while teaching he remains imbued with wisdom free of all concepts of subject, object, and action is transcendent *wisdom*. All of the transcendent perfections are therefore present.

Now look at material giving—offering food or drink to a beggar, for example. When the gift, the giver, and the recipient are all brought together and the action is actually accomplished, that is *generosity*. Giving from what you would eat or drink yourself, rather than giving bad or spoiled food, is *discipline*. Never getting irritated, even when asked over and over again for alms, is *patience*. Giving readily, without ever thinking how tiring or difficult it is, is *diligence*. Not letting yourself be distracted by other thoughts is *concentration*. Knowing that the three elements of subject, object, and action have no intrinsic reality is *wisdom*. Here again all the six transcendent perfections are included. The same subdivisions can be defined for discipline, patience, and so on.

Summing up the essence of the transcendent perfections, Jetsun Mila says:

> Perfectly give up belief in any true existence,
> There is no other generosity than this.
> Perfectly give up guile and deceit,
> There is no other discipline.
> Perfectly transcend all fear of the true meaning,
> There is no other patience.
> Perfectly remain inseparable from the practice,
> There is no other diligence.
> Perfectly stay in the natural flow,
> There is no other concentration.
> Perfectly realize the natural state,
> There is no other wisdom.
> Perfectly praise Dharma in everything you do,
> There are no other means.
> Perfectly conquer the four demons,
> There is no other strength.
> Perfectly accomplish the twofold goal,
> There is no further aspiration.
> Recognize the very source of negative emotions,
> There is no other primal wisdom.

When Khu, Ngok, and Drom* once asked him what were the best of all the elements of the path, Atisha replied:

> The best scholar is one who has realized the meaning of the absence
>   of any true existence.
> The best monk is one who has tamed his own mind.
> The best quality is a great desire to benefit others.
> The best instruction is always to watch the mind.
> The best remedy is to know that nothing has any inherent reality.
> The best way of life is one that does not fit with worldly ways.
> The best accomplishment is a steady lessening of negative emotions.
> The best sign of practice is a steady decrease of desires.
> The best generosity is nonattachment.
> The best discipline is to pacify the mind.
> The best patience is to keep a humble position.
> The best diligence is to give up activities.
> The best concentration is not to alter the mind.†
> The best wisdom is not to take anything at all as truly existing.

And Rigdzin Jigme Lingpa says:

> Transcendent generosity is found in contentment;
> Its essence is simply letting go.
> Discipline is not to displease the Three Jewels.‡
> The best patience is unfailing mindfulness and awareness.
> Diligence is needed to sustain all the other perfections.
> Concentration is to experience as deities all the appearances to
>   which one clings.§
> Wisdom is the self-liberation of grasping and clinging;
> In it there is neither thinking nor a thinker.

---

* Atisha's three main disciples.

† This means neither suppressing thoughts nor following them, nor deliberately trying to alter the state of one's mind or achieve a specific state of meditation. All deluded thoughts are in a sense alterations of the natural flow of awareness.

‡ That is, having nothing to be ashamed of in front of the Three Jewels.

§ Concentration is the absence of distractions. The source of distraction is taking appearances as real. To meditate on appearances as deities (which means as pure wisdom manifestations with no concrete reality) is to be concentrated.

It is not ordinary. It is free from fixed convictions.*
It is beyond suffering. It is supreme peace.
Do not tell this to everyone—
Keep it sacred within your own mind.

To put in a nutshell the whole vast path of the bodhisattva teachings, including the six transcendent perfections, it could be summarized in its entirety as "emptiness of which compassion is the very essence." Saraha says in his *Dohas:*

Without compassion, the view of emptiness
Will never lead you to the sublime path.
Yet meditating solely on compassion, you remain
Within samsara; so how could you be free?
But he who comes to possess both of these
Will neither in samsara nor in nirvana dwell.

To dwell neither in samsara nor in nirvana is the "nondwelling nirvana" of the level of total buddhahood. As Lord Nagarjuna says:

Emptiness of which compassion is the very essence
Is only for those who want enlightenment.

Drom Tonpa once asked Atisha what was the ultimate of all teachings.

"Of all teachings, the ultimate is emptiness of which compassion is the very essence," replied the Master. "It is like a very powerful medicine, a panacea that can cure every disease in the world. And just like that very powerful medicine, realization of the truth of emptiness, the nature of reality, is the remedy for all the different negative emotions."

"Why is it, then," Drom Tonpa went on, "that so many people who claim to have realized emptiness have no less attachment and hatred?"

"Because their realization is only words," Atisha replied. "Had they really grasped the true meaning of emptiness, their thoughts, words, and deeds would be as soft as stepping on cotton wool or as *tsampa* soup laced with butter. The Master Aryadeva said that even to wonder whether or not all things were empty by nature would make samsara

---

* *nges shes,* lit. "certainties," is used here to mean extreme views, such as eternalism and nihilism, which state that phenomena definitively do or do not exist.

fall apart.* True realization of emptiness, therefore, is the ultimate panacea which includes all the elements of the path."

"How can every element of the path be included within the realization of emptiness?" Drom Tonpa asked.

"All the elements of the path are contained in the six transcendent perfections. Now, if you truly realize emptiness, you become free from attachment. As you feel no craving, grasping, or desire for anything within or without, you always have transcendent generosity. Being free from grasping and attachment, you are never defiled by negative actions, so you always have transcendent discipline. Without any concepts of 'I' and 'mine' you have no anger, so you always have transcendent patience. Your mind made truly joyful by the realization of emptiness, you always have transcendent diligence. Being free from distraction, which comes from grasping at things as solid, you always have transcendent concentration. As you do not conceptualize anything whatsoever in terms of subject, object, and action, you always have transcendent wisdom."

"Do those who have realized the truth become buddhas simply through the view of emptiness and meditation?" Drom Tonpa asked.

"Of all that we perceive as forms and sounds there is nothing that does not arise from the mind. To realize that the mind is awareness indivisible from emptiness is the *view*. Keeping this realization in mind at all times, and never being distracted from it, is *meditation*. To practice the two accumulations as a magical illusion from within that state is *action*. If you make a living experience of this practice, it will continue in your dreams. If it comes in the dream state, it will come at the moment of death. And if it comes at the moment of death it will come in the intermediate state. If it is present in the intermediate state you may be certain of attaining supreme accomplishment."

The 84,000 doors to the Dharma that the Conqueror taught are thus all skillful means to cause the bodhichitta—emptiness of which compassion is the very essence—to arise in us.

Without bodhichitta, teachings on the view and meditation, however profound they may seem, will be no use at all for attaining perfect buddhahood. Tantric practices like the generation phase, the perfection phase, and so on, practiced within the context of bodhichitta, lead to complete buddhahood in one lifetime. But without bodhichitta they are no different from the methods of the tirthikas. Tirthikas also have many

---

* "Here *srid pa* (samsaric existence) refers to anything that one believes to be real and to which one is attached." [DILGO KHYENTSE RINPOCHE]

practices involving meditating on deities, reciting mantras, and working with the channels and energies; they too behave in accordance with the principle of cause and effect. But it is solely because they do not take refuge or arouse bodhichitta that they are unable to achieve liberation from the realms of samsara. This is why Geshe Kharak Gomchung said:

> It is no use taking all the vows, from those of refuge up to the tantric samayas, unless you turn your mind away from the things of this world.
> It is no use constantly preaching the Dharma to others unless you can pacify your own pride.
> It is no use making progress if you relegate the refuge precepts to the last place.
> It is no use practicing day and night unless you combine this with bodhichitta.

Unless you first create the proper foundation with the refuge and bodhichitta, however intensively you might seem to be studying, reflecting, and meditating, it will all be no more use than building a nine-story mansion on a frozen lake in winter and painting frescoes on its plastered walls. Ultimately it makes no sense at all.

Never undervalue the refuge and bodhichitta practices, assuming that they are inferior or just for beginners. Complete them in full, within the framework of preparation, main practice, and conclusion that applies to any path. It is most important for everyone, good or bad, high or low, to concentrate their sincerest efforts on these practices.

In the particular case of lamas and monks who take donations from the faithful, who receive funds on behalf of the dead, or who do ceremonies to guide the dead, it is absolutely indispensable that they have sincere bodhichitta. Without it, none of their rituals and purifications will be of the slightest use to either the living or the dead. For others, they might appear to be helping, but deep down that help will always be mixed with selfish motives. For themselves, they will be defiled by accepting those offerings, and will engender endless faults that can only lead them to lower realms in their next life.

Even someone who can fly like a bird, travel under the earth like a mouse, pass through rocks unimpeded, leave imprints of his hands and feet on rocks, someone who has unlimited clairvoyance and can perform all kinds of miracles—if such a person has no bodhichitta, he can only be a tirthika or possessed by some powerful demon. He might, at first, attract some naïve innocents who will be impressed and bring offerings. But in the long run he will only bring ruin upon himself and others. On the other hand, a person who possesses true bodhichitta, even without having any other quality, will benefit whoever comes into contact with him or her.

You never know where there might be a bodhisattva. It is said that many bodhisattvas, using their skillful methods, are to be found even among slaughterers of animals and prostitutes. It is difficult to tell whether someone has bodhichitta or not. The Buddha said:

> Apart from myself and those like me, no one can judge another person.

So just consider anyone who arouses bodhichitta in you as being a real buddha, whether a deity, teacher, spiritual companion, or anyone else.

Whenever you feel that you have acquired certain qualities as signs of progress on the path, whatever they may be—realization of the natural state, clairvoyance, concentration, visions of the yidam, and so on—you can be certain that they really are true qualities if, as a result, the love and compassion of bodhichitta steadily continue to increase. However, if the effect of such experiences is only to decrease the love and compassion of bodhichitta, you can be equally sure that what looks like a sign of success on the path is in fact either a demonic obstacle or an indication that you are following the wrong path.

In particular, the authentic realization of the natural state cannot but be accompanied by extraordinary faith and pure perception toward those spiritually more mature than yourself, and extraordinary love and compassion for those who are less so.

The peerless Dagpo Rinpoche once asked Jetsun Mila, "When will I be ready to guide others?"

"One day," the Jetsun replied, "you will have an extraordinarily clear vision of the nature of your mind, quite different from the one you have now, and free from any kind of doubt. At that time, in a way that is not at all ordinary, you will perceive me, your old father, as a real buddha, and you will inevitably feel natural love and compassion for all beings. That is when you should start to teach."

Study, reflect, and meditate on the Dharma, therefore, without dissociating one from the other, on the firm basis of the love and compassion of bodhichitta. Without first eliminating doubts through study, you will never be able to practice. It is said:

To meditate without having studied
Is like climbing a rock when you have no arms.

Eliminating doubts through study does not mean that you have to know all the vast and innumerable subjects that there are to be known. In this degenerate era, that would never be possible within a short lifetime. What it does mean is that whatever teachings you are going to put into practice, you should know exactly how to do so from beginning to end without a single mistake. Any hesitations you might have, you should clear away by reflecting on those teachings.

When Atisha was at Nyethang, Nachung Tonpa of Shang, Kyung Tonpa, and Lhangtsang Tonpa asked him to teach them about the different systems of logic.

Atisha replied, "The non-Buddhist tirthikas and the Buddhists themselves have many systems, but they are all just chains of discursive thought. There is no need for all those innumerable ideas: life is too short to go through them all. Now is the time to reduce these things to their essence."

"How does one reduce them to their essence?" Nachung Tonpa of Shang asked.

"By training in bodhichitta with love and compassion for all living creatures throughout space. By making strenuous efforts in the two accumulations for the benefit of all those beings. By dedicating all the sources of future good thus created to the perfect enlightenment of each and every being. And, finally, by recognizing that all these things are empty by nature, like dreams or magical illusions."

If you do not know how to reduce any practice to its essence, no amount of information, knowledge, and intellectual understanding will be of any use to you at all.

When Atisha came to Tibet, he was invited to visit the great translator Rinchen Zangpo. He questioned the translator about which teachings he knew, naming a long list, one after another. It turned out that there were none that Rinchen Zangpo did not know. Atisha was extremely pleased.

"Wonderful!" he said. "The fact that someone as learned as yourself already lives in Tibet means my visit is quite superfluous. And how do you combine all these teachings when you sit down to practice?"

"I practice each one as it is explained in its own text," said Rinchen Zangpo.

"Rotten translator!" cried Atisha in disappointment. "Then my coming to Tibet was necessary after all!"

"But what should I do instead?" asked the translator.

"You should find the essential point common to all the teachings and practice that way," Atisha told him.

It is indispensable to seek the vital point of the practice, based on the teacher's pith instructions. Once you know the essential point, you must put it into practice, or it will be utterly useless. Jetsun Mila said:

> The hungry are not satisfied by hearing about food; what they need is to eat. In the same way, just to know about Dharma is useless; it has to be practiced.

The purpose of practice is to be an antidote for negative emotions and ego-clinging. Jetsun Mila again:

> It is said that you can tell whether someone has just eaten by how red his face is. Similarly, you can tell whether people know and practice the Dharma by whether it works as a remedy for their negative emotions and ego-clinging.

Potowa asked Geshe Tonpa what was the dividing line between Dharma and non-Dharma. The geshe answered:

> If it counteracts negative emotions, it is Dharma. If it doesn't, it is non-Dharma.
> If it doesn't fit with worldly ways, it is Dharma. If it fits, it is non-Dharma.
> If it fits with the scriptures and your instructions, it is Dharma. If it doesn't fit, it is non-Dharma.
> If it leaves a positive imprint, it is Dharma. If it leaves a negative imprint, it is non-Dharma.

Master Chegom says:

> To believe in the effects of actions is the right view for those of ordinary faculties. To realize all inner and outer phenomena as the union both of appearance and emptiness, and of awareness and emptiness, is the right view for those of higher faculties. To realize that the view, the one who holds it, and realization itself are indivisible* is the right view for those of the highest faculties.

---

* Since the view is the realization of emptiness, the realizer, what is realized, and the process of realization are recognized as being without any intrinsic reality. They only appear as the illusory magical display of awareness, empty and naturally radiant.

To keep the mind totally concentrated on its object is the correct meditation for those of ordinary faculties. To rest concentrated on the four unions* is the right meditation for those of higher faculties. A state of nonconceptualization in which there is no object of meditation, no meditator, and no meditative experience is the right meditation for those of the highest faculties.

To be as wary about the effects of actions as one is careful to protect one's eyes is the right action for those of ordinary faculties. To act while experiencing everything as a dream and an illusion is the right action for those of higher faculties. Total nonaction† is the right action for those of the highest faculties.

The progressive diminution of ego-clinging, negative emotions, and thoughts is the sign of "warmth" for all practitioners, be they of ordinary, higher, or the highest faculties.

Similar words are to be found in *The Precious Supreme Path* by the peerless Dagpo.

When studying Dharma, therefore, you should know how to get at the essence of it. The great Longchenpa says:

Knowledge is as infinite as the stars in the sky;
There is no end to all the subjects one could study.
It is better to grasp straight away their very essence—
The unchanging fortress of the dharmakaya.

Then, as you reflect on Dharma, you should rid yourself of any doubts. Padampa Sangye says:

Seek the teacher's instructions like a mother falcon seeking her prey.
Listen to the teachings like a deer listening to music;
Meditate on them like a dumb person savoring food;
Contemplate them like a northern nomad shearing sheep;
Reach their result, like the sun coming out from behind the clouds.

Hearing the Dharma, reflecting on it, and meditating upon it should go hand in hand. The peerless Dagpo says:

---

* The union of appearances and emptiness, awareness and emptiness, bliss and emptiness, and clarity and emptiness.

† This means acting without conceptualizing, in the realization that the actor, the action, and the object acted upon are all without intrinsic reality.

To churn together study, reflection and meditation on the Dharma
is an infallible essential point.

The result of study, reflection, and meditation should be a steady and
real increase in the love and compassion of bodhichitta, together with a
steady and real diminution of ego-clinging and negative emotions.

This instruction on how to arouse bodhichitta is the quintessence of
all Dharma teachings and the essential element of all paths. It is the
indispensable teaching, to have which is definitely enough by itself but
to lack which is sure to render everything else futile. Do not be content
just with hearing and understanding it. Put it into practice from the very
depth of your heart!

*I claim to be arousing bodhichitta, but still it has not arisen in
me.*
*I have trained in the path of the six perfections, but have
remained selfish.*
Bless me and small-minded beings like me,
That we may train in the sublime bodhichitta.

3 1

THE SONG OF REALIZATION

Milarepa

Namo Guru.

Jetsün Milarepa then went from Kyirong in Mang-Yül to Nyanang, and his former benefactors were overjoyed. "Please stay always here in Nyanang," they begged. There was a cave below a belly-shaped boulder between some old trees, and while he resided there, the monk-teacher Shakya Guna and some laypeople of Nyanang came before him.

"While elsewhere in meditation in mountain retreats, please tell us about the progress you reached and the confidence that you attained," they asked. In reply, the Jetsün sang this song.

I bow at the feet of Marpa the Translator.
While meditating at other mountain retreats,
I found a confidence in nonarising.
My clinging to former and future lives as two has dissolved.

The six types of experiences have turned to lies.
Doubts about birth and death are now cleared.

Translated from *Mila Gurbum* by Erik Pema Kunsang, 2001.

I found a confidence in equality.
My clinging to pleasure and pain as two has dissolved.

The experience of feelings has turned to lies.
Doubts about what to accept and reject are now cleared.
I found a confidence in indivisibility.
My clinging to samsara and nirvana as two has dissolved.

Training in the paths and levels has turned to lies.
Doubts about hope and fear are now cleared.

The laypeople then said, "What other realization arose in you?"
Milarepa replied, "I realized the way to go about spiritual practice that
accords with the understanding of common people." He then sang this
song.

When from outside arose the causal conditions of parents,
When from within arose the all-ground consciousness,
And in between, when having attained the perfect human body,
Today I have avoided a rebirth in the three lower realms.

When from outside arose the experiences of birth and death,
When from within arose revulsion and faith,
And in between, when thinking of the sacred Dharma,
Today I have escaped the foe of family and home.

When from outside arose the circumstance of the father guru,
When from within arose the intelligence of former training,
And in between, when having gained a confident understanding,
I have no feeling of doubt about the Dharma.

When from outside arose the six classes of beings,
When from within arose impartial compassion,
And in between, when remembering the meditation experience,
My compassion avoids being mere selfish ambition.

When from outside arose the self-liberated three realms,
When from within arose self-existing wakefulness,
And in between, when possessing the confidence of realization,
I have avoided the dread of evil.

When from outside arose the fivefold sense pleasures,
When from within arose the insight of no clinging,

And in between, when engaged in the conduct of equal taste,
I avoid clinging to the duality of pleasure and pain.

When from outside arose the vanishing of conceptual practice,
When from within arose the absence of hope and fear,
And in between, when free from the disease of deliberate effort,
I escape the clinging to good and evil as two.

The monk-teacher Shakya Guna then said, "The Jetsün's realization has always been excellent! Though I met the Jetsün in the past, I have not received an instruction in which I can trust and rely. Now please be kind enough to bestow empowerment and pith instructions upon me!"

After having given him empowerment and instruction, the Jetsün sent him to practice meditation. The monk-teacher gained some experience and related it to the Jetsün.

"If these perceptions and samsara do not exist, then there seems to be no need for practice. If the mind does not exist, then there seems to be no doer. If there is no master, then one does not know how to practice. Please clarify these and also give me the pointing-out instruction to the nature of mind."

In response, Jetsün Milarepa sang this song.

The nature of perceptions is nonarising.
If something arises, it is your clinging to its reality.
The nature of samsara is groundless and rootless.
If something has ground and root, it is your thought.

The nature of mind is unity.
If there is partiality, it is your attachment.
The nature of a master is to possess a lineage.
If you invent your own, you are deluded.

While the mind itself is like the sky,
It becomes obscured by thoughts, like the clouds from the south.
The pith instructions of the qualified guru
Are like gusts of strong wind.

Thought as well is luminous wakefulness.
Experience shines like the sun and moon.
Vivid beyond the ten directions and three times,
Intangible, it is beyond words.

Its certainty shines like the planets and stars.
Whatever arises is great bliss.
Its nature is the simplicity of dharmakaya.
The six sense impressions are the continuity of emptiness.

Effortless, spontaneous, unconditioned,
In this state, beyond self and others,[25]
I remain continuously in nonclinging wakefulness,
Without any separation from the three kayas, amazing!

"Monk-teacher, do not cling to the fame and happiness of this life.
Do not pursue words of sophistry. Equalize your life with practice! Since
this is the way to be practiced by everyone, you should practice the
meaning of these words."

Then Milarepa sang this song:

Fortunate and noble people,
Don't you know that the things of this life are beguiling?
Don't you know that enjoyments are magical displays?
Don't you know that samsara is in fact nirvana?

Don't you know that pleasures are just a dream?
Don't you know that that praise and blame are just echoes?
Don't you know that perceptions are just your mind?
Don't you know that your mind is the Buddha?

Don't you know that the Buddha is dharmakaya?
Don't you know that dharmakaya is your innate nature?
When you realize this, all that you experience is included within
    mind.

Day and night, look into this mind.
When looking into this mind, it is not a thing to be seen.
Let be in this state of not seeing.
I do not feel that Mahamudra's nature
Can in any way be matched.
So, I remain in the state of nonclinging mind.

Meditation and postmeditation are indivisible,
So I no longer have meditation stages.
Whatever is experienced is empty in essence,
So there is nothing for mindfulness to hold or lose.

I have tasted the flavor of nonarising,
And likewise realized its practice.
The training in karma mudra,
The practice of the nadis, pranas, and bindus,
Reciting mantras and visualizing the deity,
Contemplating the four Brahma abodes, and so forth —
These are all ways to enter this Supreme Vehicle.

Even if you were to meditate on them specifically,
It will not suffice to give up desire and anger.
Perceptions are your own mind,
So understand that this mind is empty.

When you no longer part from the experience of realization,
The keeping of discipline, making offerings, and so forth
Are all contained within that.

After hearing this, the monk-teacher Shakya Guna only practiced and attained an extraordinary level of experience and realization. The monk-meditator Töngom became one of the close disciples.

This was the story of accepting the monk-teacher Shakya Guna in the Belly Cave at Nyanang.

32

ROOT OF MAHAYANA

Padmasambhava

Sit on a comfortable seat, straighten your body, and expel the stale
  breath.
Supplicate the Three Jewels and generate devotion to your guru.
Apply mindfulness and reflect in the following way.

This bodily support adorned with the perfect freedoms and riches,
Like the udumbara flower, is extremely hard to find.
If you skillfully take advantage of it,
Then this find has great value, exceeding that of a wish-fulfilling
  gem.

Therefore follow spiritual guides and virtuous friends
At all times and on all occasions.
Giving up concerns for this life, and for the sake of the future,
Exert yourself to quickly take advantage of it, for if you don't, [it
  will not last].

From the Root Verses of *Lamrim Yeshe Nyingpo*, translated by Erik Pema Kunsang. Padmasambhava and Jamgön Kongtrül, *The Light of Wisdom*, Volume I (Boudhanath: Rangjung Yeshe Publications, 1999), "Root Text."

Like the rising and setting of the sun and moon, composite things
    are impermanent.
The time of death lies uncertain, like a flash of lightning in the sky.
At the time of death nondharmic things are of no help at all,
So practice the sacred and sublime Dharma correctly.

The root of practicing the sacred Dharma is the law of karma.
Through evil deeds and nonvirtues you will go to the three lower
    realms.
By virtuous actions you achieve the higher realms and liberation.
Therefore apologize for evil deeds and make the wholehearted vow
    to refrain from them.

Diligently take up the roots of virtue.
Prostrations and circumambulations purify the wrongdoings of your
    body.
Reciting and reading the Buddha's words purify the obscurations of
    your speech,
And supplicating the Three Jewels pacifies the faults of your mind.
Always train correctly in being mindful, careful, and conscientious.

In particular, for accomplishing the state of emancipation,
With the recognition and remembrance that all of samsara
Is like a fiery pit, a garden of razors, or a forest of swords,
Arouse again and again the intense and genuine attitude
Of desiring to be quickly freed from the three sufferings.

At some point, when you understand that all samsaric grandeur
Is impermanent, inconstant, and illusive,
Fascination with even the splendor of Brahma and Indra
Will have no occasion to arise for as much as an instant.

While truly perceiving the Three Precious Ones, the Roots, and the
    guardians of the Dharma
To be the unfailing and permanent protection,
Regard them respectfully as your refuge until enlightenment
In order to free yourself and others from the terrors of samsara.

Using your own experience as a measure,
Arouse the bodhichitta of aspiration
Through the four immeasurables of love, compassion, joy, and
    impartiality
In order that your mothers, all beings, may have happiness and be
    free from suffering.

With the intent of pursuing complete enlightenment solely for the
sake of others,
Give away, like grass, your body and possessions,
And give the relief of protection to those disturbed by dangers.
Practice the Dharma yourself and establish others in it.

With the intention of renouncing, a thoroughly delighted frame of
mind,
Constrain yourself from committing the negative misdeeds of your
three doors.
Practice as much as you can the conditioned and unconditioned
virtues,
And motivate yourself to carry out all your deeds for the sake of
sentient beings.

In order never to be overcome by harm-doers,
Cultivate patience through mindfulness of the demerits of anger.
Joyfully undertake hardships for the sake of the Dharma,
And be unafraid of the profound emptiness.

By awakening a courageous fortitude for what is virtuous,
Don the armor of tirelessly engaging in bodhisattva deeds.
Exert yourself without distraction throughout day and night,
And cast away weariness when achieving the welfare of others.

With the thorough intention to calm your mind,
Take the mundane *dhyanas* as the foundation.
Through fully accomplishing samadhi with vipashyana,
Enter the domain of experience of the *tathagatas*.

By means of the intelligence that fully discerns phenomena,
First comprehend the words of all teachings through learning.
Next seek an understanding of their meaning through reflection,
And finally realize the meaning through meditation.

Having ripened your own being, gather followers through
generosity,
Delight them with pleasing words, and comfort them by being
consistent.
Through counseling them in meaningful conduct, fully establish
them, temporarily and ultimately,
In the splendor of benefit and well-being.

As the essential point, take upon yourself the burden
Of all the miseries of sentient beings.

Give away your happiness and virtue to the six classes of beings,
And train in compassion and bodhichitta without being carried
    away by difficulties.

In particular, external objects grasped by fixation
Are all unreal and appear like an illusion,
Not permanent, yet their transiency is able to function.
They are not singular since a variety emerges and changes.

They are not independent but follow the karmic deeds.
They are not particles since partless atoms do not exist.
If they did exist, gross things could not be assembled.
If they had parts, this would contradict the assertion of partlessness.

They are nothing but a nonexistent and false appearance, an
    interdependence,
Like dreams, magical illusions, and the reflection of the moon in
    water.
Regard them as a city of gandharvas and as a rainbow.
The mind that observes is also devoid of an ego or a self-entity.

It is seen neither as something different from the aggregates
Nor as identical with these five aggregates.

If the first were true, there would exist some other substance.
This is not the case, so were the second to be true,
That would contradict a permanent self, since the aggregates are
    impermanent.
Therefore, based on the five aggregates,
The self is a mere imputation by the power of ego-clinging.

As to that which imputes, the past thought has vanished and is
    nonexistent.
The future thought has not occurred, and the present thought does
    not withstand scrutiny.
In short, understand the twofold self, the perceiver and the
    perceived,
To be totally quiescent like the sky and devoid of arising,
And also that this nonarising is beyond the domain of conceptual
    mind.

Since even the Omniscient Ones find no words for this,
This absence of mental constructs is called the Middle Way.
Having realized this, rest in equanimity,

Free from conceptual activity, in the state devoid of fixation.

Thoughts then subside and the natural state of the essence is seen.
Hereby you accomplish the virtues such as the eyes,
    superknowledges, and *dharani-recall*.
The causal vehicle of the paramitas
Is to gradually attain the paths and bhumis.

On the path of fruition, you should still regard
The practice of unified emptiness and compassion as the basis of the
    path.

33

THE MEDITATION OF ULTIMATE BODHICHITTA AND ITS RESULT

Jamgön Kongtrül

PRACTICING BY MEANS OF THE MEDITATION

The *Lamrim Yeshe Nyingpo* root text says:

Having realized this, rest in equanimity,
Free from conceptual activity, in the state devoid of fixation.

When you have fully understood this view, the natural state devoid of constructs, and through the reasoning of analyzing the ultimate you have not found any constructed attributes whatsoever, you should then rest in the continuity of discriminating knowledge that has attained a penetrating certainty of the fact of the absence of extremes—free from all kinds of concepts of adhering to extremes without clinging to anything whatsoever. Rest naturally, devoid of any corrective action by the

From *The Light of Wisdom*, Volume I (Boudhanath: Rangjung Yeshe Publications, 1999).

inferential mind's reasoning, such as clinging to the emptiness of refuting a true or concrete existence, or the like—just as the fire produced from the rubbing stick as well as its base naturally vanishes after consuming both pieces of wood. *The Treasury of the Nonarising Jewel* advises:

> Do not conceptualize and do not think of anything.
> Nonfabrication is itself the treasury of nonarising.

The Eight Thousand Verses also states:

> This cultivation of transcendent knowledge is to cultivate no concept whatsoever.

Both *The Ornament of the Sutras* and *The Ornament of Realization* state harmoniously:

> From this there is nothing whatsoever to remove,
> Nor even the slightest to add.
> Look truly into the true.
> To see the true is the total freedom.[26]

Thus one should continuously rest in equanimity. Concerning the postmeditation state, *The Compendium* says:

> I have no such pretense as settling in equanimity or emerging from it.
> And why, because of fully realizing the nature of phenomena.[27]

Accordingly, by having gathered the accumulation of merit to the best of one's ability with the taste of understanding all phenomena to be illusory, you will, when perfecting the highest stage of acquaintance, attain stability in the samadhis.

LINKING UP BY EXPLAINING THE RESULT

The *Lamrim Yeshe Nyingpo* root text says:

> Thoughts then subside and the natural state of the essence is seen.
> Hereby you accomplish the virtues such as the eyes,
> superknowledges, and dharani-recall.

The causal vehicle of the paramitas
Is to gradually attain the paths and bhumis.
On the path of fruition, you should still regard
The practice of unified emptiness and compassion as the basis of the
    path.

Having grown accustomed to the meditation in this way, all of the
turmoil of conceptual thinking calms down and you are able to remain
in your innate nature for as long as you desire, and thus your body and
mind become pliable. In the manner of not seeing you then clearly see
and cognize the essence of perfect wakefulness.[28] *The Compendium* says:

Sentient beings exclaim, "I see the sky!"
But examine the meaning of exactly how the sky is seen.
This is how the tathagata describes the way we see phenomena.

The Short Truth of the Middle Way says:

The extremely profound sutras state
That not seeing is the true seeing.[29]

This path of the unity of means and knowledge annihilates the two
obscurations. Thus you gradually accomplish all the temporary and ultimate qualities including the five eyes, the six superknowledges, unforget-
ting recall, unimpeded courageous eloquence, the miraculous power of
mastery over wind and mind, and the samadhi of the stream of Dharma.
Successively journeying through all the five paths and the ten bhumis,
you will attain all their qualities.[30]

In other words, the path of accumulation is to gather the accumulation of virtue conducive to liberation by endeavoring in the two accumulations such as generosity from the beginning of arousing bodhichitta up
until attaining the wisdom of heat. Of the three levels (of the path of
accumulation), one chiefly cultivates the four applications of mindfulness on the lesser path of accumulation, the four right endeavors on the
middling, and the four legs of miraculous action on the greater path of
accumulation.

Having fully completed the path of accumulation, you experience
the four aspects of ascertainment—mundane wisdom resulting from
meditation that corresponds to realization of the four truths. Thus, be-

cause this path "joins" you to the correct realization of the truths, it is called the path of joining.

The four aspects of ascertainment are the following four stages: the heat that is the omen for perceiving the truths, the summit of mundane samadhi, the acceptance of the profound Dharma, and the stage of supreme mundane attribute. The former two are endowed with the five ruling faculties and the latter two with the five powers. Each of these four can be divided into a greater, middling, and lesser stage so that they then are renowned as the twelve aspects of ascertainment.

At the end of the stage of supreme mundane attribute, you experience the wisdom endowed with the nature of sixteen moments, arrived at by dividing each of the four truths by the cognition, ensuing cognition, acceptance, and ensuing acceptance of the Dharma.

Thus, you relinquish all that is to be discarded through the path of seeing comprised of the three realms, and see in actuality with the supramundane discriminating knowledge the nature that has not been seen before, the truths of noble beings. This is therefore called the path of seeing, and it is endowed with the seven bodhi-factors.[31]

Beginning from that point, the path of cultivation is so called because one repeatedly makes oneself grow accustomed to the thatness that was previously realized. This path has the three aspects of higher, middling, and lesser and is endowed with the eightfold path of noble beings.

In this way, when you have perfected the thirty-seven factors conducive to enlightenment comprised of the paths of training, the ultimate wisdom of realization after reaching the end of the path of cultivation and having relinquished all the most subtle discards without exception by means of the vajralike samadhi, that is the path beyond training, also called the path of consummation, and thus you have realized the ten qualities of the stage beyond training.

There is the definite number of ten special levels of complete training in terms of defining "level," or *bhumi*, as the basis for the qualities of each of these stages as well as from the aspect of developing the bhumis above. On the path of seeing, one has attained the first bhumi of the Joyous; one is free from the five kinds of fear and has acquired the twelve times one hundred qualities.

On the three parts of the path of cultivation, journeying from the second to the tenth bhumi, the special qualities of abandonment and realization are increased to a higher and higher degree until they are multiplied one thousand times one billion. On the eighth bhumi you attain the ten masteries, on the ninth the four right discriminations, and on the tenth you receive the empowerment of the great rays of light. Thus you abide in buddhahood, the eleventh bhumi of Universal Illumination.

Each of these bhumis is explained in terms of nine special qualities as elucidated in the root text *Ornament of the Sutras* and elsewhere.

In this way, having summarized the meaning taught in the paramita vehicle of taking the causes as the path, "bodhichitta of emptiness with a core of compassion" is the root of all the teachings. Consequently, also in the Vajra Vehicles of taking the result as the path, you must practice the emptiness of knowledge as united with the great compassion of means as the basis or foundation of the path. For this reason, I will here first of all explain this unity. According to *The Five Stages*:

> The one who understands how to engage
> In knowledge and compassion as one—
> That stage, explained as "unity,"
> Is the domain of the buddhas' experience.

The Vajra Dome agrees:

> The one who fully trains his mind
> In emptiness inseparable from compassion,
> Will demonstrate the buddhahood
> As well as the Dharma and Sangha.

Moreover, *The Lamp for the Path of Enlightenment* states:

> Knowledge devoid of means as well as means devoid of knowledge,
> Is in all cases taught to be a fetter; therefore do not abandon either
>   of the two.

At this point, *Eliminating the Two Extremes* explains the meaning of the causal and resultant vehicles:

> Having fully turned the Dharma Wheel
> Of the causal teachings on applying the cause,
> [The Buddha prophesied] the short path of the resultant vehicle.[32]

In general, it is well known that the causal vehicles are so called because of "being led along by means of this," while the resultant vehicles are so called because of "being led right here."[33] Thus these terms are defined in the following way according to the view of the omniscient Longchenpa:

> The causal vehicles are so called because of accepting a sequence of cause and effect, asserting that buddhahood is attained by increasing the qualities of the nature of the sugata essence, which is merely present as a seed, through the circumstance of the two accumulations. The resultant vehicles are so called because of asserting that the basis for purification is the [sugata] essence endowed with qualities that are spontaneously present as a natural possession in sentient beings, just as the sun is endowed with rays of light; that the objects of purification are the temporary defilements of the eight collections,[34] like the sky being [temporarily] obscured by clouds; and that one realizes the result of purification, the primordially present nature, by means of that which purifies, the paths of ripening and liberation. Besides this, there is no difference in sequence or quality.[35]

The Two Segments also asserts:

> All sentient beings are buddhas themselves.
> However, they are obscured by the temporary stains.
> When these are cleared away, they are enlightened.

The Torch of the Three Ways describes the difference between the two:

> Though of identical purpose, it is undeluded,
> It has many means and minor hardships,
> And is to be mastered by those of sharp faculties;
> Thus is the vehicle of Mantra especially eminent.

Although these two vehicles, the causal and the resultant, have the identical purpose of ultimate fruition, the Secret Mantra is especially exalted in four ways in traversing the path. The former is deluded by engaging in the outer paramitas and therefore obstructed by not reaching the ultimate even after a long duration. Mantrayana, on the other hand, is undeluded because of being capable of swiftly facilitating perfection by means of the inner samadhi of united means and knowledge. The former must for a long time rely on partial and less profound means such as hardships and vows in order to purify a single disturbing emotion or to accomplish a single goal. Mantrayana, however, has methods that are both profound and manifold. One easily accomplishes the purpose even by each of the numerous types of development and completion along with their subsidiary practices.[36]

Through the former you must gain accomplishment with great difficulties because the means for accomplishing the results in accordance with the intellectual capacities are scarce; whereas through Mantrayana the means corresponding to the special qualities of objects, time, situation, and mental faculties are easy and even fetters can be transformed into something liberating. Since it is capable of easily causing attainment of the results, it is free from hardships.[37]

The followers of the lesser vehicles are of dull faculties due to not knowing the means, and the paramita followers are of medium faculties because of mistaking the means. Whereas through Mantrayana one is capable of transforming into enlightenment, by special means, even a karmic deed the engagement in which would otherwise cause rebirth in the lower realms.

In addition, through the former one engages exclusively in dualistic thinking, accepting and rejecting; while through Mantrayana one recognizes the world and the beings to be great purity and equality, the superior indivisibility of the two truths, without a perceiver and the perceived, and without accepting and rejecting one can bring whatever is experienced into the path. For this reason, it is exalted by being for those of sharper faculties. Moreover, many other ways of being exalted such as the six, seven, or twelve ways are also explained.

The reason for entering this path is as follows. The victorious ones, considering the remedies, have taught the 84,000 Dharma sections. They can be condensed into the twelve aspects of excellent speech or into the nine gradual vehicles. If they are again condensed, they can be included within the three or four Collections and so forth. In this way, regardless of the number of teachings given, all are steps for the paths of entering into this Unexcelled Yoga.

That is to say, even all the shravakas and pratyekabuddhas who have reached perfection must, due to the great rays of light of the buddhas, at some point emerge from their state of cessation and then enter the Greater Vehicle. Also those who have journeyed to the stage of Great Regent on the tenth bhumi through the bodhisattva vehicle and the Three Outer Tantras of Secret Mantra still must, for their attainment of the great enlightenment, relinquish from their very root not only the subtle conceptualization that ties one to samsara, but also the tendencies of the three experiences also known as the habitual tendency of transference.[38] The remedy for relinquishing these tendencies is exactly the self-cognizant wakefulness of the path of the fourth empowerment, the unchanging great bliss of unity, which has not been taught anywhere else than in the Unexcelled Yoga.[39]

Consequently, not only must you eventually enter the path of the Unexcelled Yoga no matter which vehicle-door you have entered, but also, the meaning of each lower vehicle is included within the following one. This vehicle of the Unexcelled Yoga is therefore the most eminent, the pinnacle of all the teachings and of all the gradual vehicles. According to the *Guhyagarbha Tantra*:

> This natural essence of secrets
> Has been definitively resolved as being the source
> Of all the Collections (Pitakas) and all the tantras.

Moreover, the *Exposition Tantra* states:

> As for this king of self-cognizance, the realization of the nature of
> equality,
> Just as all rivers flow into the great ocean,
> All the infinite number of liberations and vehicles
> Are included within these great means of realizing the unexcelled
> nature.

FACILITATOR GUIDELINES

INTRODUCTORY TEACHINGS

These introductory teachings serve as the map to guide readers through this book, which has been laid out by Drubwang Tsoknyi Rinpoche. First, we establish the basis, the buddha nature. Next, we are led to admit that our experience is one of confusion. Thereafter we can apply ourselves in the methods, the practices on the path to clear away our confusion.

It is important for students to nurture an openness and a willingness to learn and practice in accordance with this tradition. It is fundamental to emphasize that this book does not attempt to create a new system. On the contrary, it encourages a very established approach presented in an accessible style. The sequential arrangement of teachings in this volume is based on *The Light of Wisdom*, root text by Padmasambhava and commentary by Jamgön Kongtrül the Great, translated by Erik Pema Kunsang (Rangjung Yeshe Publications).

It is good to begin by first reading the root verses of *The Light of Wisdom*, Volume I, and the root verses corresponding to what is quoted in *The Jewel Ornament of Liberation* by Gampopa, chapter 1, translated by Khenpo Gyaltsen Rinpoche (Snow Lion Publications).

CHAPTERS 1 AND 2

We need to develop trust in our own inherent ability to reach enlightenment through our natural possession, our buddha nature. Continue with the *The Jewel Ornament of Liberation*, chapter 1.

CHAPTERS 3 AND 4

This chapter and the next are supports for each other. There are several ways to approach discussion of this material depending on the group or student. One way might be to read and consider them together. Another way is to take each separately and use *The Light of Wisdom*, Volume I, chapter 8, "The Meaning of the Ground," pp. 68–82.

CHAPTER 5

Nonverbal practice is introduced here. Henceforth meditation should precede each discussion session. Students should engage in whichever shamatha or vipashyana meditation practice they feel comfortable with or follow those explained in this chapter.

Shamatha is important because it is a preparation for all the later practices. Shamatha practice, training in being quiet, reduces our negative attitudes. It calms down our busyness and selfish preoccupations and makes us both more open and flexible in our minds and more suitable recipients for the teachings.

CHAPTERS 6 THROUGH 8

The path is unfolded in terms of both view and conduct. We need the correct attitude on how to approach the practices to rid us of our deluded perceptions. There are no levels to skip to get to the more exciting teachings. There is a reason for how the path is arranged and is to be traversed. That is, to keep harmony between view and conduct.

Students should be encouraged to go into depth in their study and comprehension of the teachings. Supporting texts for understanding this piece are *The Words of My Perfect Teacher* by Patrül Rinpoche, part 1, chapter 1, pp. 7–19 (Shambhala Publications), and *Cutting Through Spiritual Materialism* by Chögyam Trungpa, pp. 13–18 (Shambhala Publications).

CHAPTERS 9 AND 10

The Words of My Perfect Teacher, part 1, chapter 6, "How to Follow a Spiritual Friend," pp. 137–66, and *The Light of Wisdom*, Volume I, "How to Follow a Spiritual Guide," pp. 87–94.

Most of us can agree that the ordinary, material reality of our every-day experience lacks magic and meaningful satisfaction. Stepping onto the spiritual path is not entering a fantasy world or traveling down the yellow brick road. Instead it is the genuine way to reconnect with the ex-tremely subtle and sublime. To generate this vividness and access the necessary trust that is the merging point, there is no better method than reading the wonderful life stories of realized beings. Even if we cannot immediately generate devotion or have not met our own teacher, such works offer inspiration that will lead us in the right direction.

An extraordinary experience happens when we come into the pres-ence of a realized master. Orgyen Tobgyal Rinpoche explained this when recounting meeting Tulku Urgyen Rinpoche:

> People were so delighted when they met him. Many foreigners changed their whole perspective on life from only one meeting and felt extraordinarily blessed. Practitioners felt that they received blessings, and even ordinary people still felt that something unusual had happened. Whoever came into his presence never felt tired, even after several hours had passed. That is totally unlike being in the presence of some politicians, when you cannot wait to get away.
>
> Tulku Urgyen Rinpoche's very presence was powerful. Without any concern for personal hardship, he always aimed to do his ut-most to benefit sentient beings. He was also extremely humble and self-effacing—totally in tune with Shantideva's bodhisattva ideal. He treated everyone, whether important or ordinary, with the same affection and attention, teaching everyone equally. In order to bring the highest benefit he always tried to communicate in the listener's own terms. And it was not only in his teaching, but also in all his conversations, that you would find the bodhisattva ideal of ocean-like activity clearly reflected.[40]

Masters who have completely "severed the ties of selfishness and pursue only the welfare of others"[41] are unlike mundane people. Receiv-ing teaching from such individuals generates trust in their words. We skeptical Westerners, unless we can identify an authentic source, tend not to pay attention to or take seriously what is being explained. From the very outset, we need to associate the validity of this profound mate-rial with an extraordinary reality. Once we have some experience with a qualified master, that is not so difficult. However, if we have not met such a being, the precious genuineness needs to be instilled in the stu-dent's mind in a believable and viable manner. As Tulku Urgyen Rinpoche said, "It is not only because I am Buddhist that I believe the Buddha. It is because there have been so many since him who showed very special signs of accomplishment. That is why I feel I can safely believe all his words. It is very important to have trust in the Buddha's teachings if one wishes to apply them. If one tries to apply them without trust they won't help much."[42]

From the practical point of view, because of our dialectical training we need to apply all three unmistaken measures in order to have trust. These are: "the unmistaken quality of the Buddha's words, the unmistaken quality of the statements of noble beings and the enlightened masters, and the unmistaken quality of our own root guru's oral instructions which we put into practice. By combining these unmistaken qualities with our own experience, innumerable people have been able to reach a state totally free from doubt,"[43] and so can we by combining these with our own intelligence and experience.

We can meet qualified teachers these days. Again, I cannot overemphasize the importance of attending seminars and retreats with them. Many wonderful and realized teachers frequently travel all over the world to instruct and practice with fortunate groups. Additionally, there are dedicated students, working with masters, who help to organize these programs. As an example, simply go to the Web sites of the Rigpa fellowship, under the guidance of Sogyal Rinpoche, or the Shambhala Centers, under the guidance of Sakyong Mipham Rinpoche, to get information on these events.

Recommended life stories, listed at the end of this book, include: *Lady of the Lotus-Born, The Life of Marpa the Translator, The Life of Milarepa, The Life of Shabkar, The Lives and Liberation of Princess Mandarava, Lord of the Dance,* and *The Lotus-Born.*

CHAPTER 11

We have now reached the point where students can engage in the following practices collectively or on their own. What has previously been primarily theory can be mingled with practical application. An essential point to accentuate is proper motivation. Motivation is twofold. We are practicing to benefit countless beings and to realize the true nature not only of our minds but of reality as well.

Tsoknyi Rinpoche tells how one of his teachers, Nyoshul Khen Rinpoche, would, quite often and repeatedly, in the middle of an extremely profound teaching, stop and ask his disciples to check their motivation.

Moreover, he prompted them to "readjust" in case there was some incorrect attitude prevailing. Tsoknyi Rinpoche further relates how Khen Rinpoche would simply sit with his students during this readjustment period, sometimes for fifteen or twenty minutes. So, if such a great master trains his gifted students in this way, shouldn't the rest of us examine ourselves at least as carefully? Moreover, Tsoknyi Rinpoche feels that "It is not merely the students who need to check their motivation; it is the teacher as well. Good motivation needs to be connected with compassion; there is no other way."[44] Periodically check and fine-tune, if necessary.

Another application of the wake-up practice is to use the liturgy as a preliminary before each session. This is a convenient method that Kyabje Dilgo Khyentse Rinpoche inspired us to adopt. In this way not only can we supplicate our teacher and rest in a state inseparable from his or her mind; we also have a reminder for engendering the correct attitude preceding each practice session.

CHAPTERS 12 THROUGH 14

These teachings, the Four Dharmas of Gampopa, are by themselves a complete path for enlightenment. The first of these, "How to turn one's mind toward Dharma practice," includes the four mind-changings. At this point, use *The Words of My Perfect Teacher*, pp. 19–131. This book gives the clearest and most accessible material. An additional source is *The Jewel Ornament of Liberation*, pp. 57–66 and 83–121. These teachings continue through the next few chapters.

Tulku Urgyen Rinpoche explains how the four mind-changings and the preliminary practices originated and are to be applied:

> For authentically applying yourself to this path [Vajrayana], all the panditas of India and lamas of Tibet have mentioned that it is indispensable to purify obscurations and gather the accumulations. However, since the Dharma is extremely vast and extensive, it is difficult for one person to practice all its details. So these masters condensed the essence of all the sutras and tantras into four things to reflect upon called "the four mind-changings" and five things to practice, "the preliminaries of the five times 100,000."[45]

Before committing to the preliminaries, we need to become convinced of the necessity of taking on these practices and completing them.

In my own experience, application came about in the following way. I became a Vajrayana student after many years as a Zen practitioner. I liked the simplicity of Zen practice and was quite skeptical of the complications I attributed to Vajrayana practice. My refuge lama was a very plain, highly accomplished master of the Drukpa Kagyü lineage. The style of Drukpa Kagyü suited my Zen sensibilities in that it is very careful, orderly, and exact. You proceed systematically; you do not begin the next practice until you have completed the one you are engaged in. Gegan Khyentse insisted that before proceeding with the extraordinary preliminaries I spend several months on the ordinary preliminaries known as the four mind-changings. He was both skillful and wise, because after contemplating these four mind-changings in detail, I was more than willing to begin the "complicated" ngöndro practice.

There are two ironies in this tale. The first is that it was not until I did the "highest and most secret" Dzogchen practices that I came to understand the profundity of the four mind-changings. And the second is that the simplicity of Zen is embodied in many of the Vajrayana masters with whom I have studied, from Gegan Khyentse to my root teacher Tulku Urgyen Rinpoche. What were complicated were my preconceptions, nothing more.

Students should be encouraged not to externalize the teachings on the sufferings of the six realms. Even if, as beginners, we are skeptical of the existence of places like the hells and hungry ghost realms, we can easily find the tendencies toward these places in our own stream-of-being. Take anger, for example. Observe how we can blaze with the self-righteousness of the Hot Hells. Internally we become preoccupied and consumed with the intensity of that emotion. Haven't we heard people say things like "I was so angry that I saw red"? Then there is the total isolation and defensiveness of the cold, steely anger that separates us from other people, as if in an icy environment—the Cold Hells. Haven't we justified such feelings repeatedly?

It is the same with the propensities for the other realms. Don't we experience greed, selfishness, stupidity, attachment, jealousy, and pride? Don't we abandon the wishes of other people when they interfere in what is best for ourselves? Don't we try to manipulate reality to suit our needs and lose the ability to rejoice in the success of even our friends? Certainly, numerous times we hold ourselves and our own concerns to be paramount and more important than others. Such behavior is a vivid reminder of each of the six realms brought into our present situation. Repeatedly, we relinquish altruism in favor of what is most comfortable for *me*. We need to admit our own proclivity for these experiences. All these realms "exist" due to the deluded perceptions of our unvirtuous minds.

Cutting Through Spiritual Materialism, "The Six Realms," pp. 138–47, and *The Myth of Freedom*, pp. 23–40 (both Shambhala Publications) provide excellent explanations of the states of mind predominant in these realms.

CHAPTERS 15 AND 16

Please refer to the guidelines for chapter 12 on the first of the Four Dharmas above. This Dharma, "How to ensure that one's Dharma practice becomes the path," includes teachings on the preliminary practices of the five times 100,000.

The last two Dharmas are "How to make the path clarify confusion" (teachings on development stage, recitation, and completion stage) and "How to let confusion dawn as wisdom" (teachings on how to gain certainty, realization of the natural state by means of the three great views).

As mentioned in the preface, *The Dzogchen Primer* includes explanations on the first of the Four Dharmas and part of the second. The two subsequent volumes for the study program continue from the second Dharma through to the end of the fourth Dharma.

Continue using *The Words of My Perfect Teacher* and *The Light of Wisdom*, Volume I.

CHAPTER 17

As Tulku Urgyen Rinpoche says,

> Failing to purify the obscurations and gather the accumulations will prevent you from realizing the true meaning of self-existing wakefulness. Therefore, it is essential to first endeavor in the practices that facilitate purifying obscurations and gathering the accumulations. There are also two kinds of accumulations: merit with concepts and nonconceptual wisdom. The accumulation of merit with concepts includes the preliminary practices, the ngöndro, as well as the yidam practice. The nonconceptual accumulation of wisdom is the training in samadhi, the natural state of your self-existing wakefulness."[46]

CHAPTERS 18 AND 19

Continue with *The Words of My Perfect Teacher*, pp. 171–92.

Also include *Cutting Through Spiritual Materialism*, "Surrendering," pp. 23–30.

CHAPTER 20

This piece is good to use as a model for individual and group practices employing whichever preliminary practice text you are familiar with. If the group feels confident, they can include meditation practice within this as noted by the ringing of the bell.

CHAPTER 21

Now we are introducing another major text that can be used consistently with this topic: *The Way of the Bodhisattva* by Shantideva (Shambhala Publications). Additionally, rely on *The Words of My Perfect Teacher*, pp. 195–251, and *The Light of Wisdom*, Volume I, pp. 115–34, as supports for the next three chapters.

CHAPTER 22

Study *Cutting Through Spiritual Materialism*, "The Open Way," pp. 97–104, beginning with: "The whole point is. . . ."

CHAPTERS 23 AND 24

Supplement this with *Cutting Through Spiritual Materialism*, "The Bodhisattva Path," pp. 167–78.

CHAPTERS 25 THROUGH 31

Take *The Light of Wisdom*, Volume I, "The View of Ultimate Bochicitta," pp. 135–46, as a primary source to help clarify and elucidate confusing points.

This last section of the book introduces many new concepts and terms. Engaging in detailed analysis could take many years. What is offered here is an overview. A further condensation can be included in these points: If we begin to examine our commonly accepted ideas about reality and ourselves, will they hold up under intense scrutiny? Can we conclusively establish the true existence of our thoughts, feelings, and perceptions?

Here is the perfect opportunity for the predominantly critical Western attitude to turn on itself and discover what is real and what is not. Encourage the student to question in these ways. All approaches have one primary goal: to integrate the teachings into our present experience in order to fully facilitate personal transformation.

If it all gets a bit too heady, try watching *The Matrix* on DVD or video, or sing Milarepa's song "Wisdom through Meditation" aloud with a pleasing melody.

CHAPTERS 32 AND 33

Conclude with in-depth discussion of *The Light of Wisdom*, Volume I, "The Meditation of Ultimate Bodhichitta and Its Result," pp. 146–55.

NOTES

1. Tulku Urgyen Rinpoche, *Rainbow Painting* (Boudhanath: Yeshe Publications, 1995), p 24.

2. Vajrayana here refers to Mahamudra and Dzogchen. Tulku Urgyen Rinpoche, *As It Is*, Volume II (Boudhanath: Rangjung Yeshe Publications, 2000), p. 235.

3. Sogyal Rinpoche, keynote address, Buddhism in America Conference, May 1998. Published as "The Future of Buddhism," *Rigpa Journal* (January 2000), p. 13.

4. From Chökyi Nyima Rinpoche, *Present Fresh Wakefulness* (Boudhanath: Rangjung Yeshe Publications, 2002).

5. Tulku Urgyen Rinpoche, *As It Is*, Volume II (Boudhanath: Rangjung Yeshe Publications, 2000), pp. 234–35.

6. Tsoknyi Rinpoche, unpublished oral teachings.

7. Sogyal Rinpoche, "The Future of Buddhism."

8. These quotations from *The Jewel Ornament of Liberation* were orally translated by Erik Pema Kunsang.

9. *The Light of Wisdom*, Volume I (Boudhanath: Rangjung Yeshe Publications, 1999), p. 84.

10. *Nangjang* training—literally, "training in refining experience"—is the personal process of resolving the nature of reality and experience by means of the profound teachings of the Great Perfection. An extraordinary example of this method of practice is found in Dudjom Lingpa's *Buddhahood Without Meditation* (Padma Publishing, 1994).

11. The unwholesome habitual tendencies of one's mind are like the rigidity of a piece of wood or the unyielding quality of an uncultivated field. A

"hard virgin field" means wild lands or wild meadows that are hard and difficult to cultivate. [JOKYAB RINPOCHE]
Grain free from the defects of blight, frost, or rot. [JOKYAB RINPOCHE]

12. Padmasambhava here plays on the phrase "eight wordly concerns": concerns are synonymous with *dharmas*, which can also mean Dharma teachings.

13. The "transitory collection" refers to the continuity of the five aggregates—physical forms, sensations, conceptions, formations, and cognitions (consciousnesses).

14. Say your ordinary name at this point.

15. The "body of Mahamudra" refers to the rainbowlike form of one's personal yidam. See Padmasambhava, *Dakini Teachings* (Boudhanath: Rangjung Yeshe Publications), "Vajrayana Mind Training."

16. The "vehicle of mantra" means Vajrayana, while the "vehicle of philosophy" includes both Hinayana and Mahayana.

17. The seven-branch practice of prostrating to the Three Jewels, apologizing for negative actions, making offering, rejoicing in the virtue of others, requesting to turn the Wheel of Dharma, beseeching to not pass into nirvana, and dedicating the merit to the enlightenment of all sentient beings.

18. Liberating the beings in the three lower realms to a state in which they can practice the Dharma. Helping the beings of the three higher realms to cross the ocean of samsara and attain emancipation. Relieving the aspirant bodhisattvas with the attainment of the bhumis.

19. A Hindu system claiming that liberation can be attained by imitating the conduct of animals.

20. The mistaken view that an ego or self-entity is inherently existent within the continuity of the five aggregates.

21. The term "truly high" simply refers to a rebirth in the three higher realms within samsara: humans, demigods, and gods.

22. The three spheres are the concepts of subject, object, and action.

23. This refers to the two main aspects of Dzogchen practice: *Trekchö* of primordial purity and *Tögal* of spontaneous presence. These two practices must be learned through the oral instructions of a Dzogchen master.

24. The *Lama Gongdü* version had combined the teachings on refuge and bodhichitta into one. Here, the last lines read: "These advices on refuge and bodhichitta, known as the foundation of precious gold, are the basis of all Dharma practice. They are in harmony with all practitioners and are special instructions to be treasured by everyone. According to the oral instructions given by Padmakara, the Master of Uddiyana, for the sake of the beings of future generations, I, the Princess of Kharchen, committed them to writing and concealed them as a precious treasure. May they meet with all worthy people in the future. Samaya."

25. An alternate spelling would render this line as: "In this state, the eminent nature," or "the nature of which is beyond compare."

26. To explain this quote, "From this sugata essence there is nothing whatsoever of the faults of the two obscurations to remove, since it is primordially untainted by defects; nor is there, moreover, even the slightest new to add or some new achievement to gain because of being primordially endowed with the basis for freedom through being devoid of extraneous, momentary elements as well as with the qualities of freedom and maturation. Look correctly and truly into the true and unmistaken view, the basis that is not empty of the elements of unexcelled qualities and is free from something to accept or reject, remove or add. And thus, to see the true fruition is the total and unexcelled freedom from the two obscurations." [JOKYAB RINPOCHE]

27. To explain this quote, "I, a bodhisattva, have no such pretense as holding the individual notions of settling in the meditation state of emptiness that is like space or emerging from it during the postmeditation that is like a magical illusion. And why is this? It is because of fully realizing that emptiness is forever the nature of all knowable phenomena." [JOKYAB RINPOCHE]

28. Jamgön Kongtrül here plays on the literal meaning of *shamatha* and *vipashyana*, "calming down and remaining" and "seeing clearly."

29. All the extremely profound sutras state that the complete realization of the twofold egolessness, that is, not seeing any fixation on concreteness, free from extremes and utterly unbiased; that is the true seeing of the suchness of the buddhas. [JOKYAB RINPOCHE]

30. The two obscurations are the obscuration of disturbing emotions and the cognitive obscuration. [JOKYAB RINPOCHE]
    The five eyes are the physical eye, the divine eye, the eye of knowledge, the Dharma eye, and the buddha eye. [JOKYAB RINPOCHE]
    The six superknowledges are the superknowledge of miraculous

power, divine hearing, divine sight, perceiving the minds of others, recollecting former lives, and the exhaustion of defilements. [JOKYAB RINPOCHE]

31. The seven bodhi-factors are: concentration, full discernment of phenomena, mindfulness, diligence, rejoicing, pliancy, and impartiality.

32. To explain this quote, "Having fully turned the three successive Dharma Wheels of the causal teachings of the philosophical vehicles, which apply the causes for a buddhahood that is not a fruition in the present situation, [the Buddha prophesied] that the short path of the resultant Vajra Vehicle, which applies the fruition of buddhahood in the present situation 'will appear twenty-eight years after I have passed into nirvana.' " [JOKYAB RINPOCHE]

33. Generally speaking, the causal vehicles are so called because of being led along or journeying "by means of this," while the resultant vehicles are so called because of being led or journeying "right here." Thus Mantrayana is superior because of embodying both cause and result. [JOKYAB RINPOCHE]

34. The eight collections of consciousnesses are the all-ground, the defiled mental consciousness, the mental cognition, and the cognitions of eye, ear, nose, tongue, and body.

35. The paths of ripening and liberation are two vital parts of Vajrayana practice: the empowerments that ripen one's being with the capacity to realize the four kayas and the liberating oral instructions enabling one to actually apply the insight that was introduced through the empowerments. [CHÖKYI NYIMA RINPOCHE]

36. Development and completion are the two main aspects, the "means and knowledge" in Vajrayana practice. Briefly stated, development means positive mental fabrication, including visualization and mantra recitation, while completion stage means resting in the unfabricated nature of mind.

37. In this statement about the special qualities of objects, time, situation, and mental faculties in Mantrayana, "objects" means to enjoy the five sense pleasures, "time" means to swiftly achieve the fruition, "situation" means to experience everything as purity, and "mental faculties" means the methods that correspond to the person of the highest and other types of capacity. [JOKYAB RINPOCHE]

38. The level of Great Regent refers to the tenth bhumi of the Cloud of Dharma, the level at which the regents of Buddha Shakyamuni abide,

as for instance Avalokiteshvara, Mañjushri, and Vajrapani, and the other of the Eight Close Sons. [TULKU URGYEN RINPOCHE]

The defilement of the tendencies of the three experiences of transference refers to the actual obscuration of the transference of the elements during union, but to define it as just that is too small a scope. It also covers the channels, winds, and essences; body, speech, and mind; the three realms; and the outer, inner, and secret.

The phrase "three experiences of transference" means the three aspects of appearance, increase, and attainment. The initial transference from the *nadi* abodes during union and the final emission of transference from the body are both coarse. The coarse, as well as the subtle and intermediate, all manifest as the obscuration that prevents the meditation state from being unceasing. The three experiences occur no matter what arises, be it virtuous, evil, or neutral. This is the subtle cognitive obscuration mentioned in the teachings of Mantrayana.

The coarse version is the [process of] dying or union. The intermediate is when fainting or falling asleep. The subtle is during a sneeze or a hiccup. The extremely subtle happens unceasingly during any thought occurrence. However, the degree of subtlety between sleep and union can be reversed.

It is generally taught that this subtle defilement of the three aspects of appearance, increase, and attainment is more subtle during union than when falling asleep. The reason for this is that slight breathing still takes place during deep sleep, while it is said that the movement of breath ceases for a moment when the bodhichitta of the union transfers.

The obscuration of transference of the *kunda-like bodhichitta* of union is the manifest obscuration. The obscuration of the tendencies is unmanifest and subtle. The obscuration of union taught in the context of the *Uttara Tantra* refers to dullness, lethargy, and drowsiness, and to agitation, excitement, and thought occurrence that obscure the unified state of dhyana. [JOKYAB RINPOCHE]

39. The path connected to the fourth empowerment is the Great Perfection, including the practices of Trekchö and Tögal. [TULKU URGYEN RINPOCHE]

40. Orgyen Tobgyal Rinpoche, quoted in Tulku Urgyen Rinpoche, *As It Is*, Volume II, p. 28.

41. Ibid., p. 29.

42. Tulku Urgyen Rinpoche, *Repeating the Words of the Buddha* (Boudhanath: Rangjung Yeshe Publications, 1992), p. 39.

43. Ibid., p. 41.

44. Tsoknyi Rinpoche, unpublished oral teachings.

45. Tulku Urgyen Rinpoche, unpublished oral teachings, 1983.

46. Ibid.

GLOSSARY

AKANISHTHA (*'og min*). The "highest"; the realm of Vajradhara, the dharmakaya buddha. Can also refer to the highest abode of gods in the form realms.

ALAYA (*kun gzhi*). The basis of all of samsara and nirvana. *See also* All-ground.

ALL-ENCOMPASSING PURITY. All that appears and exists is actually all-encompassing purity. We really should understand that everything, all world systems and all beings—whatever appears and exists, meaning the "perceived" and the "perceiver"—all takes place within the sphere of the three kayas. Everything originates from the three kayas, takes place within the sphere of the three kayas, and dissolves back again into the sphere of the three kayas.

ALL-GROUND (*kun gzhi*; Skt. *alaya*). Literally, "foundation of all things," the basis of mind and both pure and impure phenomena. This word has different meanings in different contexts and should be understood accordingly. Sometimes it is synonymous with buddha nature or dharmakaya; sometimes it refers to a neutral state of dualistic mind that has not been embraced by innate wakefulness.

AVALOKITESHVARA. The bodhisattva of compassion, an emanation of Buddha Amitabha. One of the eight main bodhisattvas.

BARCHEY KÜNSEL, *Clearing Away the Obstacles*, the external practice. A cycle of teachings revealed by Chokgyur Lingpa together with Jamyang Khyentse Wangpo, consisting of about ten volumes of texts.

BARDO (literally, "intermediate state"). The general teachings outline six bardos. Two of these, the bardo of meditation and the bardo of dreams, occur within the bardo of this life, which is defined as the period following birth until the onset of death. The actual process of passing away is called the bardo of dying. The bardo of dharmata occurs immediately after death, with the cessation of the outer and inner breath. Finally, the consciousness seeking a new rebirth is called the bardo of becoming.

BHIKSHU (*dge slong*). A practitioner who has renounced worldly life and taken the pledge to observe the 253 precepts of a fully ordained monk in order to attain liberation from samsara.

BHUMIS (*sa*). The bodhisattva levels; the ten stages a bodhisattva proceeds through on the quest for complete and perfect enlightenment. These ten stages correspond to the last three of the five paths of Mahayana.

BODHICHITTA (*byang sems, byang chub kyi sems*). "Awakened mind," the aspiration to attain enlightenment for the sake of all beings. In the context of Dzogchen, the innate wakefulness of awakened mind; synonymous with rigpa, awareness.

BODHISATTVA. Someone who has developed bodhichitta, the aspiration to attain enlightenment in order to benefit all sentient beings. A practitioner of the Mahayana path, especially a noble bodhisattva who has attained the first level.

BUDDHA NATURE (*bde gshegs snying po*). Sugatagarbha, the essence of the sugatas; the potential for enlightenment or enlightened nature that is inherently present in each sentient being. For a detailed discussion, see Thrangu Rinpoche, *Buddha Nature* (Rangjung Yeshe Publications).

CAPACITY. *See* Essence, nature, and capacity.

CAUSAL AND RESULTANT VEHICLES. The causal vehicles are the teachings of Hinayana and Mahayana that regard the practices of the path as the causes for attaining the fruition of liberation and enlightenment; the resultant vehicle is the Vajrayana system of taking fruition as the path by regarding buddhahood as inherently present and the path as the act of uncovering the basic state. The great master Longchenpa defined them as follows: "The causal vehicles are so called because of accepting a sequence of cause and effect, asserting that buddhahood is attained by increasing the qualities of the nature of the sugata essence, which is merely present as a seed, through the circumstance of the two accumulations. The resultant vehicles are so called because of asserting that the basis for purification is the [sugata] essence endowed with qualities that are spontaneously present as a natural possession in sentient beings, just as the sun is endowed with rays of light; that the objects of purification are the temporary defilements of the eight collections [of consciousnesses], like the sky being [temporarily] obscured by clouds; and that one realizes the result of purification, the primordially present nature, by means of that which purifies, the paths of ripening and liberation. Besides this, there is no difference [between the two] in sequence or quality." (*The Light of Wisdom*, Volume I (Boudhanath: Rangjung Yeshe Publications, 1999), pp. 154–55.)

CHAKRAVARTIN (*'khor los sgyur ba'i rgyal po*). *See* Universal monarch.

CHANNELS, WINDS, AND ESSENCES (*rtsa rlung thig le*; Skt. *nadi, prana, and bindu*). The constituents of the vajra body. The channels are the 72,000 nadis and the 40 million minor nadis abiding in the body. The winds are the 21,600 pranas circulating within the nadis. Connected with them, the essences, which are the white and red bindus, permeate. These three aspects are the subtle bases for body, speech, and mind.

CHETSÜN NYINGTIG (*lce btsun snying tig*). One of the most important Dzogchen instructions, based on a transmission from Vimalamitra. Jamyang Khyentse had a vision of Chetsün Senge Wangchuk that inspired him to write the precious teaching known as Chetsün Nyingtig. Senge Wangchuk (11th–12th cent.) is among the lineage gurus in the Nyingtig transmission, which he received from his root guru, Dangma Lhüngyal, as well as directly from Vimalamitra. As a result of his high level of realization, his physical body disappeared in rainbow light at the time of death. In a later reincarnation as Jamyang Khyentse Wangpo, he remembered the Dzogchen teachings that Senge Wangchuk had transmitted to the dakini Palgyi Lodrö and wrote them down as the terma Chetsün Nyingtig, the "Heart Essence of Chetsün."

CHOKGYUR LINGPA. (1829–1870). A treasure revealer and contemporary of Jamyang Khyentse Wangpo and Jamgön Kongtrül, regarded as one of the major tertöns in Tibetan history. His termas are widely practiced by both the Kagyü and Nyingma schools. For more details, see *The Life and Teachings of Chokgyur Lingpa* (Rangjung Yeshe Publications). Chokgyur Lingpa means "Sanctuary of Eminence."

COMMON AND SUPREME SIDDHIS. *See* Siddhi.

COMPLETION STAGE. "Completion stage with marks" means yogic practices such as *tummo*. "Completion stage without marks" is the practice of Dzogchen. *See also* Development and completion.

DEVELOPMENT AND COMPLETION. The two main aspects, "means and knowledge," of Vajrayana practice. Briefly stated, development stage means positive mental fabrication. Completion stage means resting in the unfabricated nature of mind.

DEVELOPMENT STAGE. One of the two aspects of Vajrayana practice, the mental creation of pure images in order to purify habitual tendencies. The essence of the development stage is pure perception, or sacred outlook, which means to perceive sights, sounds, and thoughts as deity, mantra, and wisdom. *See also* Pure perception; Development and completion.

DHARMADHATU (*chos kyi dbyings*). The "realm of phenomena"; the suchness in which emptiness and dependent origination are inseparable. The nature of mind and phenomena that lies beyond arising, dwelling, and ceasing.

DHARMAKAYA (*chos sku*). *See* Three kayas.

DHARMATA (*chos nyid*). The innate nature of phenomena and mind.

DORJE DRAKTSAL, the secret practice. "Powerful Vajra Wrath." A wrathful form of Guru Rinpoche.

DORJE LOBPÖN (*rdo rje slob dpon*). Vajra master.

DÜSUM KHYENPA, the first Karmapa (1110–1193). One of the main disciples of Gampopa.

DZOGCHEN. Also known as Great Perfection and Ati Yoga, the highest teachings of the Nyingma school of the Early Translations. In this world the most well known human lineage masters are Garab Dorje, Mañjushrimitra, Shri Singha, Jñanasutra, Vimalamitra, Padmasambhava, and Vairochana. Dzogchen has two chief aspects: the lineage of scriptures and the lineage of teachings. The scriptures are contained in the tantras of the Three Sections of Dzogchen: Mind Section, Space Section, and Instruction Section. The first two were brought to Tibet chiefly by Vairochana, while the Instruction Section was mainly transmitted by Vimalamitra and Padmasambhava. In addition, numerous Dzogchen termas were concealed by these masters and revealed through the following centuries. The lineage of teachings is embodied in the oral instructions one receives personally from a qualified master and holder of the Dzogchen lineage. Dzogchen is the ultimate of all the 84,000 profound and extensive sections of the Dharma, the realization of Buddha Samantabhadra, exactly as it is.

EIGHT WORLDLY CONCERNS. Attachment to gain, pleasure, praise, and fame, and aversion to loss, pain, blame, and bad reputation.

EIGHTEEN CONSTITUENTS (Skt. *dhatu*). The six collections of consciousness, the six senses, and the six sense objects.

ESSENCE. *See* Essence, nature, and capacity.

ESSENCE, NATURE, AND CAPACITY. The three aspects of the sugatagarbha according to the Dzogchen system. Essence (*ngo bo*) is the primordially pure wisdom of emptiness. The nature (*rang bzhin*) is the spontaneously present wisdom of cognizance (*gsal ba*). The capacity (*thugs rje*) is the all-pervasive wisdom of indivisibility. This is, ultimately, the identity of the Three Roots, the Three Jewels, and the three kayas.

ETERNALISM AND NIHILISM. Eternalism is the belief that there is a permanent and causeless creator of everything; in particular, that one's identity or consciousness has a concrete essence that is independent, everlasting, and singular. Nihilism in this context is literally "the view of discontinuance," or the extreme view of nothingness: no rebirth or karmic effects and the nonexistence of a mind after death.

FIRST TURNING OF THE WHEEL OF DHARMA (*chos 'khor dang po*). The teachings focusing on renunciation, karma, and the Four Noble Truths.

FIVE AGGREGATES (Skt. *skandha*). The five aspects that comprise the physical and mental constituents of a sentient being: physical forms, sensations, conceptions, formations, and consciousnesses.

FIVE ELEMENTS. Earth, water, fire, wind, and space.

FIVE FEMALE BUDDHAS. Dhatvishvari, Mamaki, Locana, Pandaravasini, and Samayatara.

FIVE MALE BUDDHAS. Vairochana, Akshobhya, Ratnasambhava, Amitabha, and Amoghasiddhi.

FOUR IMMEASURABLES. Compassion, love, joy, and impartiality. Also called the "four abodes of Brahma" because their cultivation causes rebirth as the king of the gods in the Realm of Form within samsaric existence. When embraced by the attitude of bodhichitta, the wish to attain enlightenment for the welfare of others, their cultivation causes the attainment of unexcelled buddhahood.

FOUR MARAS. The first of the four maras, or demons, is the demon of the Lord of Death, which cuts our life short. Second is the demon of the physical aggregates, which prevents the attainment of the rainbow body. Third is the demon of the disturbing emotions, the three poisons that prevent liberation from samsara. Finally there is the demon of the son of the gods, which is distraction in the meditation state and the tendency to postpone practice. Procrastination is the mara of the son of the gods, which creates obstacles for samadhi. The real demon is our conceptual thinking. When we recognize our mind essence, all demons are defeated; the four maras are vanquished and all obstacles are done away with. The main point is to train in that.

FOUR MEANS OF MAGNETIZING. Being generous, uttering kind words, giving appropriate teachings, and keeping consistency between words and actions. Padmasambhava says in the *Lamrim Yeshe Nyingpo*:

Having ripened your own being, gather followers through generosity,
Delight them with pleasing words, and comfort them by being consistent.
Through giving them counsel to meaningful conduct, establish them
  temporarily and ultimately,
In the full splendor of benefit and well-being.

FOUR MIND-CHANGINGS (*blo ldog rnam bzhi*). (1) The freedoms and riches comprising the precious human body that are so difficult to find; (2) impermanence and death; (3) karma, the law of cause and effect; and(4) the sufferings of samsara. Reflecting on these four topics regarding the facts of life causes one's mind to change and be directed toward Dharma practice.

FOUR NOBLE TRUTHS (*'phags pa'i bden pa bzhi*). The four truths are the truth of suffering, of origin, of cessation, and of the path. The truth of suffering refers to the world and sentient beings. The truth of origin refers to karmic actions and disturbing emotions. The truth of cessation is the state of having relinquished both the karmas and disturbing emotions along with their effects. The truth of the path is the paths and levels of Buddhism, the ultimate solution to suffering. The truth of suffering is like a sickness, the truth of origin is the cause of the sickness, the truth of cessation is like having recovered from the sickness, and the truth of the path is like following a cure for the sickness. These four truths can be understood in increasingly deeper ways as the practitioner progresses through the three vehicles.

FOUR ROOT PRECEPTS. Not taking lives, not taking what is not given, not lying, and not engaging in sexual misconduct.

FOURFOLD SPHERES OF PERCEPTION. Same as the four formless realms. The four unenlightened meditative states of dwelling on the thoughts: Infinite Space, Infinite Consciousness, Nothing Whatsoever, and Neither Presence nor Absence of Conception.

GANACHAKRA (*tshogs kyi 'khor lo*) A feast offering; a practice in which attachment and habitual sense perceptions are transformed and become part of the path. A feast assembly is performed by Vajrayana practitioners to accumulate merit and purify the sacred commitments (*samayas*).

GANDHARVA (*dri za*). (1) A class of sentient beings who live on scents. (2) A type of celestial musician living on the rim of Mount Sumeru. A "city of the gandharvas" (Skt. *gandharva nagara; dri za'i grong khyer*) is an imaginary city in the sky, like a fairy castle in the clouds.

GREAT PERFECTION (*rdzogs pa chen po,* Skt. *mahasandhi*). See Dzogchen.

GUHYAGARBHA TANTRA. The widely renowned Mahayoga tantra of the Early Translations.

KARMA. The unerring law that virtuous actions yield virtuous results, and so forth. Voluntary actions of thought, word, and deed, the effects of which determine the rebirths and experiences of individual sentient beings.

KARMAPA. The great master and chief figure of the Karma Kagyu school.

KAYAS (*sku*). *See* Three kayas.

KLESHA (*nyon mongs pa*). "Disturbing emotion." Usually the five poisons known as desire, anger, delusion, pride, and envy.

KUNZANG TUKTIG (*kun bzang thugs thig*). The "Heart Essence of Samantabhadra." A collection of terma teachings revealed by Chokgyur Lingpa focused on the peaceful and wrathful deities as the development stage and on Trekchö and Tögal as the completion stage.

LONGCHEN RABJAM. A major lineage master and writer of the Nyingma lineage. Longchen Rabjam was an incarnation of Princess Pema Sal, the daughter of King Trisong Deutsen, to whom Guru Rinpoche had entrusted his own lineage of Dzogchen known as Khandro Nyingthig. He is regarded as the single most important writer on Dzogchen teachings. His works include *The Seven Great Treasuries*, *The Three Trilogies*, and his commentaries in the *Nyingthig Yabshi*. A more detailed account of his life and teachings is found in *Buddha Mind* by Tulku Thondup Rinpoche (Snow Lion Publications).

MADHYAMIKA. *See* Middle Way.

MAHAMUDRA. Literally, "great seal." A very direct practice for realizing one's buddha nature. A system of teachings that is the basic view of Vajrayana practice according to the Sarma or "new" schools of Kagyü, Gelug, and Sakya. In particular, the essential view of our natural state is introduced directly and without reliance upon philosophical reasoning.

MANTRIKA (*sngags pa*). A practitioner of Vajrayana.

MAYA (*sgyu ma*). Magical illusion.

MIDDLE WAY (Skt. *madhyamaka*). The highest of the four Buddhist schools of philosophy. The Middle Way means not holding any extreme views, especially those of eternalism or nihilism.

MIND ONLY. Chittamatra. A Mahayana school of India, founded on the *Lankavatara Sutra*. Its main premise is that all phenomena are only mind, i.e., mental perceptions that appear within the all-ground consciousness due to habitual tendencies. Positively, this view relinquishes the fixation on a solid reality. Negatively, there is still clinging to a truly existing "mind" within which everything takes place.

NAROPA. The great mahasiddha of India, chief disciple of Tilopa and the guru of Marpa in the Kagyü lineage. See *The Rain of Wisdom* and *The Life of Marpa* (both Shambhala Publications).

NATURE. *See* Essence, nature, and capacity.

NGÖNDRO (*sngon 'gro*). *See* Preliminary practices.

NIRMANAKAYA (*sprul sku*). *See* Three kayas.

NONCONCEPTUALIZATION OF THE THREE SPHERES. Not retaining concepts of subject, object, and action.

PHONYA (*pho nya*). (1) Messenger, emissary. (2) Spiritual consort in Vajrayana practice.

PRAJÑA AND UPAYA. Prajña (literally, "best knowing") is knowledge or intelligence; in particular, the knowledge of realizing egolessness. Upaya (literally, "skillful means") is the method or technique that brings about realization.

PRAJÑAPARAMITA (*shes rab kyi pha rol tu phyin pa*). "Transcendent knowledge." The Mahayana teachings on insight into emptiness, transcending the fixation of subject, object, and action. Associated with the Second Turning of the Wheel of Dharma. Since Prajñaparamita eliminates the most subtle obscuration, this insight is often called the Mother of All Buddhas.

PRANA (*rlung*). The winds or energy currents of the vajra body. *See also* Channels, winds, and essences.

PRASANGIKA. A branch of the Madhyamika, distinguished by complete reliance of refutation and taking no stands.

PRATIMOKSHA (*so so thar pa*). Individual liberation, the seven sets of precepts for ordained and lay people according to the Vinaya scriptures on Buddhist ethics and discipline.

PRATYEKABUDDHA (*rang rgyal, rang sangs rgyas*). "Solitarily enlightened one." A Hinayana arhat who attains nirvana chiefly through contemplation of the twelve links of dependent origination in reverse order, without needing teachings in that lifetime. A pratyekabuddha lacks the complete realization of a buddha and so cannot benefit limitless sentient beings as a buddha does.

PRELIMINARY PRACTICES (*sngon 'gro*). The general outer preliminaries are the four mind-changings. The special inner preliminaries are the "four times 100,000 practices" of refuge and bodhichitta, Vajrasattva recitation, mandala offering, and guru yoga. See Jamgön Kongtrül, *The Torch of Certainty* (Boston: Shambhala Publications, 1977).

PURE PERCEPTION. The attitude of sacred outlook, or pure perception, is the special quality of Vajrayana. Sacred outlook refers to seeing things as they actually are, not in the ordinary deluded way wherein we think that earth is simply solid matter, water is merely water, wind is wind, and so forth. In actuality, what appear to us as the ordinary experience of the five elements are the five female buddhas; the five aggregates are the five male buddhas, and so forth. Therefore, training oneself in pure perception is not a way of convincing oneself that things are what they are not, but rather is training in seeing things as they truly are.

RAINBOW BODY. At the time of death of a practitioner who has reached the exhaustion of all grasping and fixation through the Dzogchen practice of Tögal, the five gross elements that form the physical body dissolve back into their essences, five-colored light. Sometimes only the hair and the nails are left behind.

RIGPA (*rig pa*). The state of awareness devoid of ignorance and dualistic fixation.

RINCHEN TERDZÖ. The Great Treasury of Precious Termas. A sixty-three-volume collection of the most important revealed termas of Padmasambhava, Vimalamitra, Vairochana, and other of their closest disciples, gathered by Jamgön Kongtrül Lodrö Thaye with the help of Jamyang Khyentse Wangpo.

RIWOCHE. Major Kagyü and Nyingma monastery situated between Central Tibet and Kham.

RUPAKAYA (*gzugs kyi sku*). "Form body." A collective term for both sambhogakaya and nirmanakaya. *See also* Three kayas.

SADHANA (*sgrub thabs*). "Means of accomplishment." Tantric liturgy and procedure for practice, usually emphasizing the development stage. The typical sadhana structure involves a preliminary part including the taking of refuge and arousing bodhichitta, a main part involving visualization of a buddha and recitation of the mantra, and a concluding part with dedication of merit to all sentient beings.

SAMADHI OF SUCHNESS. The first of the "three samadhis" of suchness, of illumination, and of the seed syllable. The samadhi of suchness is to rest in the composure of the innate emptiness of all phenomena, as pointed out by one's root master, or simply to imagine that all things are empty like space. The samadhi of illumination is to let natural compassion manifest like sunlight illuminating the sky, or simply to generate compassion for all the beings who fail to realize the nature of things. The samadhi of the seed syllable is the innate unity of emptiness and compassion manifesting in the form of a syllable that is the seed or source from which the deity and the entire mandala will appear during the practice. These three samadhis are the indispensable framework for the development stage of Vajrayana practice. In his *Lamrim Yeshe Nyingpo*, Padmasambhava says, "The main part begins with the profound and vast samadhis which purify the manner of death, bardo, and rebirth: The great emptiness space of suchness is pure like the sky. Rest evenly in this space of the undivided two truths. Emanate the magic of compassion, an all-illuminating cloud of awareness, filling the space, radiant yet without fixation. The single mudra in the manner of a subtle syllable is the causal seed which produces everything. Keep this changeless wisdom essence, manifest in space, one-pointedly in mind and bring its vivid presence to perfection." For more details, see *The Light of Wisdom*, Volume II, pp. 88–89.

SAMAYA (*dam tshig*). The sacred pledges, precepts, or commitments of Vajrayana practice. Samayas essentially consist of outwardly maintaining harmonious relationships with the vajra master and one's Dharma friends and inwardly not straying from the continuity of the practice.

SAMBHOGAKAYA (longs spyod rdzogs pa'i sku). *See* Three kayas.

SAMPA LHUNDRUB. A supplication to Guru Rinpoche as well as a terma of Chokgyur Lingpa.

SAUTRANTIKA. A Hinayana school of philosophy and the second of the four major Buddhist schools. One of its branches was known for its reliance on the sutras instead of Abhidharma.

SECOND TURNING OF THE WHEEL OF DHARMA (*chos 'khor gnyis pa*). The teachings emphasizing bodhichitta and emptiness, that all phenomena are devoid of a self-entity and true existence.

SHAMATHA (*zhi gnas*). Stillness, literally, "calm abiding" or "remaining in quiescence" after thought activity has subsided. It can also mean the meditative practice of calming the mind in order to rest free from the disturbance of thought. Shamatha with support (*zhi gnas rten bcas*) is the practice of calming the mind while using an object of concentration—material or mental or simply the breath. Shamatha without support (*zhi gnas rten med*) is the act of calming the mind without any particular object, resting undistractedly. This practice serves as a prelude for Mahamudra and Dzogchen and should not be mistaken for "ordinary mind" or the view of Trekchö.

SHRAMANERA (*dge tshul*). Novice, a lesser number of vows taken prior to the full ordination of a monk.

SHRAVAKA (literally, "hearer" or "listener"). Hinayana practitioner of the First Turning of the Wheel of the Dharma on the Four Noble Truths who realizes the suffering inherent in samsara and focuses on understanding that there is no independent self. By conquering disturbing emotions, the shravaka liberates oneself, attaining first the stage of Stream Enterer at the Path of Seeing, followed by the stage of Once-Returner who will be reborn only one more time, and the stage of Nonreturner, who will no longer be reborn into samsara. The final goal is to become an arhat. These four stages are also known as the "four results of spiritual practice."

SIDDHI (*dngos grub*). "Accomplishment." The attainment resulting from Dharma practice, usually referring to the "supreme siddhi" of complete enlightenment. It can also mean the common siddhis, eight mundane accomplishments such as clairvoyance, clairaudience, flying in the sky, invisibility, everlasting youth, or powers of transmutation; the ability to control the body and external world. The most eminent attainments on the path are, however, renunciation, compassion, unshakable faith, and realization of the correct view.

SIX PARAMITAS. The six transcendent actions of generosity, discipline, patience, diligence, concentration, and discriminating knowledge.

SKANDHAS. *See* Five aggregates.

SUGATA (*bde bar gshegs pa*). "Blissfully gone." A synonym for buddha.

SVATANTRIKA (*rang rgyud pa*). Branch of the Madhyamika, distinguished by the use of conventional forms of philosophical reasoning.

TERTÖN (*gter ston*). A revealer of hidden treasures, concealed mainly by Guru Rinpoche and Yeshe Tsogyal.

THIRD TURNING OF THE WHEEL OF DHARMA (*chos 'khor gsum pa*). The last teachings of the Buddha, including the sutras on the definitive meaning placing emphasis on buddha nature, the unity of luminosity and emptiness devoid of constructs.

THREE KAYAS (*sku gsum*). Dharmakaya is the first of the three kayas, which is devoid of constructs, like space; the "body" of enlightened qualities. This should be understood in three different senses, according to ground, path, and fruition. Sambhogakaya means the "body of perfect enjoyment." In the context of the "five kayas of fruition," sambhogakaya is the semimanifest form of the buddhas endowed with the five perfections of perfect teacher, retinue, place, teaching, and time, perceptible only to bodhisattvas on the ten levels. Nirmanakaya means "emanation body" or "form of magical apparition" and is the third of the three kayas. This is the aspect of enlightenment that can be perceived by ordinary beings.

THREE SPHERES. *See* Nonconceptualization of the three spheres.

THREE VAJRAS. Our essence, nature, and capacity are the dharmakaya, sambhogakaya, and nirmanakaya. They are also the three vajras—the vajra Body, Speech, and Mind of all the buddhas—which we are supposed to achieve. This real and authentic state is in itself empty, which is dharmakaya. Its cognizant quality is sambhogakaya. Its unconfined unity is nirmanakaya. This indivisible identity of the three kayas is called the "essence body," svabhavikakaya. When we have cut through karma and obscurations and habitual patterns, then the nature of the three vajras is primordially and spontaneously present already within us. Unless we had these, how could we produce the three vajras? The three vajras are present within the ground as the vajra body, vajra speech, and vajra mind, and these are primordially present in all sentient beings as well.

TILOPA (988–1069). Indian mahasiddha, the guru of Naropa and father of the Kagyü lineage.

TIRTHIKAS (*mu stegs pa*). Non-Buddhist teachers of philosophy adhering to the extreme views of eternalism or nihilism.

TÖGAL (*thod rgal*). "Direct crossing." Dzogchen has two main sections: Trekchö and Tögal. The former emphasizes primordial purity (*ka dag*) and the latter spontaneous presence (*lhun grub*).

TORMA (*gtor ma*). An implement used in tantric ceremonies. Can also refer to a food offering to protectors of the Dharma or unfortunate spirits.

TREASURE. Terma. The transmission through concealed treasures hidden, mainly by Guru Rinpoche and Yeshe Tsogyal, to be discovered at the proper time by a tertön, a treasure revealer, for the benefit of future disciples. It is one of the two chief traditions of the Nyingma school, the other being Kama. It is said that this tradition will continue even long after the Vinaya of the Buddha has disappeared.

TREKCHÖ (*khregs chod*). "Cutting through" the stream of delusion, the thoughts of the three times, by revealing naked awareness devoid of dualistic fixation. To recognize this view through the oral instructions of one's master and to sustain it uninterruptedly throughout all aspects of life is the very essence of Dzogchen practice.

TULKU (*sprul sku*). Nirmanakaya. Can refer to an incarnated bodhisattva who works for the welfare of sentient beings, or to the nirmanakaya manifested by a buddha.

TUMMO (*gtum mo*; Skt. *chandali*). A practice to develop inner heat and bliss to consume obscurations and realize emptiness. One of the Six Doctrines of Naropa.

TWELVE SENSE-BASES. The five senses and the mental faculty, plus the five sense objects and the mental objects.

UNIVERSAL MONARCH (*'khor los sgyur ba'i rgyal po*; Skt. *chakravartin*). One who rules over the four continents of human beings. He bears the thirty-two marks of a great being and is assisted in his rule by the seven precious possessions.

UPASAKA (*dge bsnyen*). A Buddhist layman, bound by the five vows (to avoid killing, stealing, sexual misconduct, lying, and intoxicating liquor). The female lay person is called upasika.

UPAYA. *See* Prajña and upaya.

VAJRADHARA. "Vajra-holder." The dharmakaya buddha of the Sarma schools. Can also refer to one's personal teacher of Vajrayana or to the all-embracing buddha nature.

VAJRAYANA. "Vajra vehicle." The practices of taking the result as the path. Also called Secret Mantra.

VIMALAMITRA. A master in the Dzogchen lineage and the crown ornament of five hundred panditas, who had attained the indestructible form of the rainbow body. He received the transmission of Dzogchen from Shri Singha and Jñanasutra. Vimalamitra is regarded as one of the three main forefathers for establishing the Dzogchen teachings, especially the Instruction Section, in Tibet, in the ninth century.

VINAYA (*'dul ba*). "Discipline." One of the three parts of the Tripitaka. The Buddha's teachings concerning ethics, the discipline and moral conduct that is the foundation for all Dharma practice for both lay and ordained people.

VIPASHYANA (*lhag mthong*). "Clear seeing" or "wider seeing." Usually refers to insight into emptiness. One of the two main aspects of meditation practice, the other being shamatha. Vipashyana at the shravaka level means insight into impermanence, suffering, and egolessness. At the Mahayana level it means the insight into the emptiness of all phenomena, the perceiver as well as the perceived. At the inner Vajrayana level this insight is equal to the thought-free wakefulness that is the direct remedy against basic ignorance, the root cause of samsara.

WHEEL OF DHARMA (*chos kyi 'khor lo*). The cycle of teachings given by the Buddha; three such cycles, known as the Three Turnings of the Wheel of the Dharma, were taught by Shakyamuni Buddha during his lifetime. To turn the Wheel of the Dharma is poetic for giving teachings.

YIDAM PRACTICE. In Vajrayana, the main practice that traditionally follows the preliminaries. It includes the two stages of development and completion and is a perfect stepping-stone for approaching the more subtle practices of Mahamudra and Dzogchen.

YOGACHARA (*rnal 'byor spyod pa*). The Mahayana school of philosophy established by Asanga and linked to the Mind Only school and the Sutras of the Third Turning.

YOGIC EXERCISES. Exercises utilized in, for instance, the Six Doctrines of Naropa.

RECOMMENDED READING

Chang, Garma C.C. *The Hundred Thousand Songs of Milarepa*. Boston: Shambhala Publications, 1999.

Changchub, Gyalwa, and Namkhai Nyingpo. *Lady of the Lotus-Born: The Life and Enlightenment of Yeshe Tsogyal*. Boston: Shambhala Publications, 1999.

Chinese Buddhist Association of the United States. *A Treasury of Mahayana Sutras*. University Park: Pennsylvania State University Press, 1983.

Chödrön, Pema. *Start Where You Are: A Guide to Compassionate Living*. Boston: Shambhala Publications, 1994.

Chökyi Nyima Rinpoche. *Indisputable Truth*. Translated by Erik Pema Kunsang. Boudhanath: Rangjung Yeshe Publications, 1996.

———. *The Union of Mahamudra and Dzogchen*. Translated by Erik Pema Kunsang. Boudhanath: Rangjung Yeshe Publications, 1986.

Gampopa. *The Jewel Ornament of Liberation*. Ithaca, N.Y.: Snow Lion Publications, 1998.

Khunu Rinpoche. *Vast As the Heavens, Deep As the Sea: Verses in Praise of Bodhicitta*. Boston: Wisdom Publications, 1999.

Khyentse, Dilgo. *Enlightened Courage: An Explanation of Atisha's Seven Point Mind Training*. Ithaca, N.Y.: Snow Lion Publications, 1993.

———. *The Excellent Path to Enlightenment*. Ithaca, N.Y.: Snow Lion Publications, 1996.

———. *The Wish-Fulfilling Jewel*. Boston: Shambhala Publications, 1994.

Kongtrül, Jamgön. *The Torch of Certainty*. Boston: Shambhala Publications, 1994.

The Life of Marpa the Translator. Translated by the Nalanda Translation Committee. Boston: Shambhala Publications, 1995.

The Life of Milarepa. Translated by Lobsang Lhalungpa. Boston: Shambhala Publications, 1977.

Lingpa, Samten, Lama Chonam, and Sangye Khandro. *The Lives and Liberation of Princess Mandarava: The Indian Consort of Padmasambhava.* Boston: Wisdom Publications, 1998.

Norbu, Thinley. *Magic Dance: The Display of the Self-Nature of the Five Wisdom Dakinis.* Boston: Shambhala Publications, 1999.

———. *The Small Golden Key: To the Treasure of the Various Essential Necessities of General and Extraordinary Buddhist Dharma.* Boston: Shambhala Publications, 1999.

———. *White Sail: Crossing the Waves of Ocean Mind to the Serene Continent of the Triple Gems.* Boston: Shambhala Publications, 2001.

Orgyen Tobgyal Rinpoche. *The Life and Teachings of Chokgyur Lingpa.* Boudhanath: Rangjung Yeshe Publications, 1990.

Padmasambhava. *Advice from the Lotus-Born.* Translated by Erik Pema Kunsang. Boudhanath: Rangjung Yeshe Publications, 1996.

———. *Dakini Teachings.* Translated by Erik Pema Kunsang. Boudhanath: Rangjung Yeshe Publications, 1999.

Padmasambhava and Jamgön Kongtrül. *The Light of Wisdom,* Volumes I and II. Translated by Erik Pema Kunsang. Boudhanath: Rangjung Yeshe Publications, 1999 and 2000.

Patrül Rinpoche. *The Words of My Perfect Teacher.* Boston: Shambhala Publications, 1998.

Patrül Rinpoche and Dilgo Khyentse Rinpoche. *Heart Treasure of the Enlightened Ones.* Boston: Shambhala Publications, 1993.

The Rain of Wisdom. Translated by the Nalanda Translation Committee. Boston: Shambhala Publications, 1989.

Rangdröl, Shabkar Tsogdruk. *The Life of Shabkar.* Ithaca, N.Y.: Snow Lion Publications, 2001.

Shantideva. *The Way of the Bodhisattva (Bodhicharyavatara).* Translated by the Padmakara Translation Group. Boston: Shambhala Publications, 1997.

Sogyal Rinpoche. *The Tibetan Book of Living and Dying.* San Francisco: HarperSanFrancisco, 1992

Suzuki, Shunryu. *Zen Mind, Beginner's Mind.* New York: Weatherhill, 1970.

Thich Nhat Hanh. *Old Path, White Clouds.* Berkeley: Parallax Press, 1991.

Thondup, Tulku. *Enlightened Living.* Boudhanath: Rangjung Yeshe Publications, 1997.

———. *Masters of Meditation and Miracles.* Boston: Shambhala Publications, 1999.

Thrangu Rinpoche. *Buddha Nature.* Translated by Erik Pema Kunsang. Boudhanath: Rangjung Yeshe Publications, 1988.

———. *Songs of Naropa.* Translated by Erik Pema Kunsang. Boudhanath: Rangjung Yeshe Publications, 1997.

Trungpa, Chögyam. *Cutting Through Spiritual Materialism*. Boston: Shambhala Publications, 1973.

———. *Journey Without Goal*. Boston: Shambhala Publications, 1981.

———. *The Myth of Freedom: And the Way of Meditation*. Boston: Shambhala Publications, 1976.

Tsogyal, Yeshe. *The Lotus-Born: The Life Story of Padmasambhava*. Boston: Shambhala Publications, 1993.

Tsoknyi Rinpoche. *Carefree Dignity*. Translated by Erik Pema Kunsang. Boudhanath: Rangjung Yeshe Publications, 1998.

Tulku, Chagdud. *Lord of the Dance*. Junction City, Calif.: Padma Publishing, 1992.

Tulku, Tarthang. *Lalitavistara*. Berkeley: Dharma Publishing, 1983.

Tulku Urgyen Rinpoche. *As It Is*, Volumes I and II. Translated by Erik Pema Kunsang. Boudhanath: Rangjung Yeshe Publications, 1999 and 2000.

———. *Rainbow Painting*. Translated by Erik Pema Kunsang. Boudhanath: Rangjung Yeshe Publications, 1995.

———. *Repeating the Words of the Buddha*. Translated by Erik Pema Kunsang. Boudhanath: Rangjung Yeshe Publications, 1996.

CONTRIBUTORS

BUDDHA SHAKYAMUNI, literally, "the Sage of the Shakyas," is our historical buddha. He was born in Lumbini near the foothills of the Himalayas in what is now Nepal, attained enlightenment in Bodh Gaya, turned the Wheel of Dharma in Sarnath, and passed away in Kushinagar. For a detailed account of his life, please read *Lalitavistara* (Dharma Publishing).

CHÖGYAM TRUNGPA RINPOCHE was a Buddhist meditation master, scholar, artist, and visionary. He was the founder of Naropa University in Boulder, Colorado, and of Shambhala Training and was the former abbot of the Surmang monasteries in Eastern Tibet. His seventeen years of teaching in the United States and Canada left an indelible mark of authenticity on the practical application of American Buddhism. For his biography, please read *Born in Tibet* (Shambhala Publications). For more information, go to www.shambhala.org

CHÖKYI NYIMA RINPOCHE is the oldest son and a spiritual heir of the widely renowned late Dzogchen master Tulku Urgyen Rinpoche. He is the author of *Indisputable Truth* and *The Union of Mahamudra and Dzogchen* (both Rangjung Yeshe Publications). His Holiness the sixteenth Karmapa recognized Chökyi Nyima as a reincarnate bodhisattva and advised him to turn his efforts toward instructing Western practitioners, transmitting Tibetan Buddhism to the rest of the world. He is the abbot of one of the largest Buddhist monasteries in Nepal, located at the sacred Boudhanath Stupa in Kathmandu, Nepal. For more information, go to www.shedrub.org

DRUBWANG TSOKNYI RINPOCHE was recognized by His Holiness the sixteenth Gyalwang Karmapa as a reincarnation of Drubwang Tsoknyi, a renowned master of the Drukpa Kagyü and Nyingma traditions. Later he was brought up by the great master Khamtrül Rinpoche. Among his other teachers are Dilgo Khyentse Rinpoche, his late father Tulku Urgyen Rinpoche, Adeu Rinpoche of Nangchen, and Nyoshul Khen Rinpoche. Tsoknyi

Rinpoche is the head of the Drukpa Heritage Project to preserve the literature of the Drukpa Kagyü lineage. He is also the abbot of Ngedön Ösel Ling in the Kathmandu Valley of Nepal and author of *Carefree Dignity* (Rangjung Yeshe Publications). For more information, go to www.pundarika.org

DZONGSAR KHYENTSE RINPOCHE was born in Bhutan in 1961 and was recognized as the main incarnation of the Dzongsar Khyentse lineage of Tibetan Buddhism. He has studied with some of the greatest contemporary masters, particularly H.H. Dilgo Khyentse Rinpoche. From a young age he has been active in the preservation of the Buddhist teachings, establishing centers of learning, supporting practitioners, publishing books, and teaching all over the world. Dzongsar Khyentse Rinpoche supervises his traditional seat of Dzongsar Monastery and its retreat centers in eastern Tibet as well as his new colleges in India and Bhutan. He has also established centers in Australia, North America, and the Far East. These are gathered under Siddhartha's Intent (*www.siddharthasintent.org*).

KHENCHEN THRANGU RINPOCHE ranks as one of the foremost masters of the Kagyü lineage. He lives in Kathmandu, Nepal, and teaches in numerous countries around the world. He is the author of *Songs of Naropa* and *King of Samadhi* (both Rangjung Yeshe Publications).

MILAREPA (1040–1123) was one of the most famous yogis and poets in Tibetan religious history. Much of the teachings of the Karma Kagyü schools passed through him. For more details, read *The Life of Milarepa* and *The Hundred Thousand Songs of Milarepa* (both Shambhala Publications).

PADMASAMBHAVA was the miraculous great master who brought Vajrayana to Tibet in the eighth century. He is also referred to as Guru Rinpoche, the precious teacher. For his biography, please read *The Lotus-Born* (Shambhala Publications).

PATRÜL RINPOCHE was a great nonsectarian Tibetan master of the nineteenth century and one of the foremost scholars of his time. He was known not only for his scholarship and learning but also for his example of renunciation and compassion. His most famous works include *The Words of My Perfect Teacher* (Shambhala Publications) and his commentary on *Three Words Striking the Vital Point (Tsigsum Nedeg)*, the epitome of the Dzogchen teachings.

SHANTIDEVA was a seventh-century master at Nalanda monastic university. He is regarded as one of the eighty-four siddhas and was the author of the *Bodhicharyavatara*, published in English as *The Way of the Bodhisattva* (Shambhala Publications).

THINLEY NORBU RINPOCHE is an extraordinary teacher of the Nyingma lineage. His father, Kyabje Dudjom Rinpoche, was a great treasure revealer and scholar. He is the author of *White Sail* and *Magic Dance* (both Shambhala Publications).

TULKU THONDUP RINPOCHE is an exceptional teacher and translator of the Nyingma lineage. He is the author of *Masters of Meditation and Miracles, Enlightened Journey, The Healing Power of Mind, Boundless Healing* (all Shambhala Publications), *Enlightened Living* (Rangjung Yeshe Publications), *The Practice of Dzogchen* (Snow Lion Publications), and *Hidden Teachings of Tibet* (Wisdom Publications), to mention a few.

TULKU URGYEN RINPOCHE was born in eastern Tibet on the tenth day of the fourth Tibetan month in 1920 and passed away in Nepal on February 13, 1996. His Holiness Khakyab Dorje, the fifteenth Gyalwang Karmapa, recognized him as an incarnate. He studied and practiced the teachings of both the Kagyü and Nyingma orders of Tibetan Buddhism.

In the Nyingma tradition, Tulku Urgyen held the complete teachings of the last century's three great masters: Terchen Chokgyur Lingpa, Jamyang Khyentse Wangpo, and Jamgön Kongtrül Lodrö Thaye. He had an especially close transmission for the *Chokling Tersar*, a compilation of all the empowerments, textual authorizations, and oral instructions of Padmasambhava's teachings, which were rediscovered by Terchen Chokgyur Lingpa, his great-grandfather.

Tulku Urgyen established several monasteries and retreat centers in Nepal. The most important ones in the Kathmandu region are at Boudhanath, the site of the Great Stupa; at the Asura Cave, where Padmasambhava manifested the Mahamudra Vidyadhara level; and at the Swayambhunath stupa. He primarily lived at the Nagi Gompa Hermitage above the Kathmandu Valley. He is the father of tulku sons Chökyi Nyima Rinpoche, Tsikey Chokling Rinpoche, Drubwang Tsoknyi Rinpoche, and Yongey Mingyur Rinpoche.

Rinpoche instructed a growing number of Dharma students in essential meditation practice. He was famed for his profound meditative realization and for the concise, lucid, and humorous style with which he imparted the essence of the Buddhist teachings. His method of teaching was "instruction through one's own experience." Using few words, this way of teaching pointed out the nature of mind, revealing a natural simplicity of wakefulness that enabled the student to actually touch the heart of awakened mind.

CREDITS